AMERICAN RAMBLE

AMERICAN RAMBLE

A Walk of Memory and Renewal

Neil King Jr.

ILLUSTRATIONS BY GEORGE HAMILTON

MARINER BOOKS   NEW YORK   BOSTON

HarperCollins books may be purchased for educational, business, or sales promotional use. For information, please email the Special Markets Department at SPsales@harpercollins.com.

FIRST EDITION

Designed by Chloe Foster

Library of Congress Cataloging-in-Publication Data has been applied for.

ISBN 978-0-358-70149-1

23 24 25 26 27 LBC 5 4 3 2 1

For Kevin, my brother,
who saw so much that others missed.

And for Shailagh, my ballast and beacon.

Henceforth I whimper no more, postpone no more, need
    nothing,
Done with indoor complaints, libraries, querulous criticisms,
Strong and content I travel the open road.

—WALT WHITMAN, "SONG OF THE OPEN ROAD"

CONTENTS

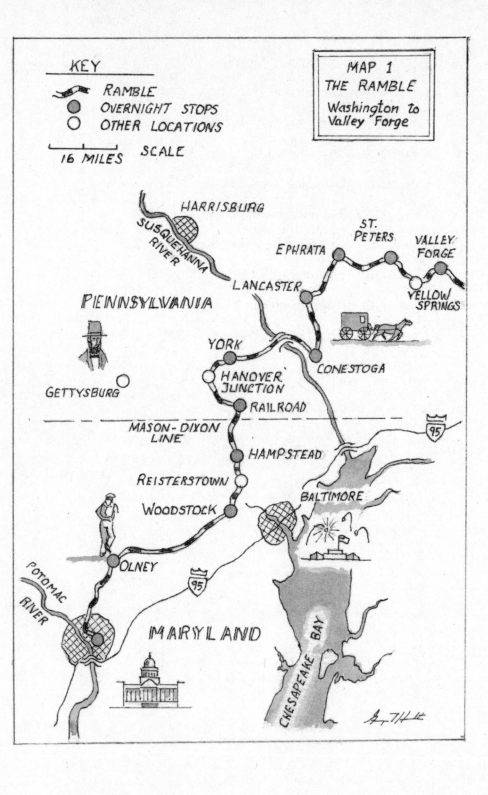

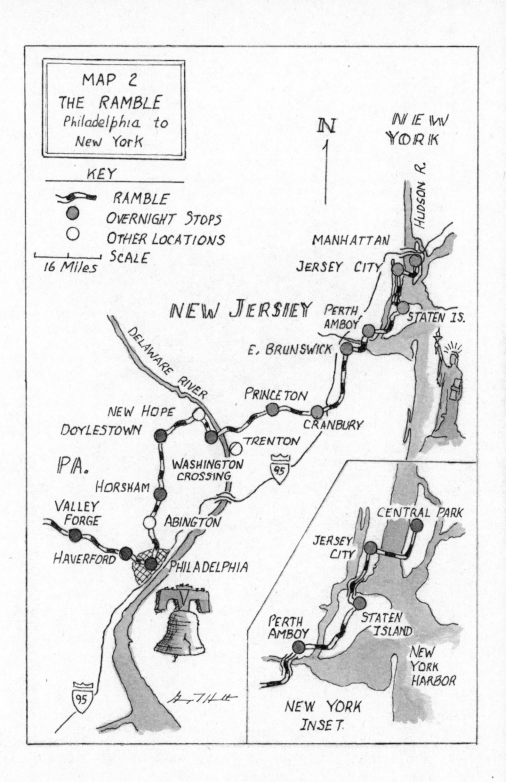

MAP 2
THE RAMBLE
Philadelphia to
New York

KEY

RAMBLE
OVERNIGHT STOPS
OTHER LOCATIONS
SCALE

16 Miles

N

NEW YORK

HUDSON R.

MANHATTAN
JERSEY CITY

NEW JERSEY

PERTH AMBOY

STATEN IS.

E. BRUNSWICK

PRINCETON

DELAWARE RIVER

NEW HOPE
DOYLESTOWN

TRENTON

CRANBURY

95

PA.

WASHINGTON CROSSING

HORSHAM

VALLEY FORGE

ABINGTON

HAVERFORD

PHILADELPHIA

95

CENTRAL PARK

JERSEY CITY

STATEN ISLAND

PERTH AMBOY

NEW YORK HARBOR

NEW YORK INSET.

CHAPTER 1

THE PRE-AMBLE

O ur house stands along a row of white maples nine blocks east of the U.S. Capitol, as it has since Ulysses Grant was president. Tens of thousands of times in our twenty-two years there I have opened the wrought-iron gate between the garden and the sidewalk for trips to work, dog walks, early runs, quick jaunts to the store for a clutch of bananas, or with daughters in hand on a Christmas morning.

This trip was different. On a fresh morning in late March, I stepped past the threshold of our front door, tugged the garden gate closed behind me, and set off to walk to the city of New York. A slow stroll, I liked to say, down a fast lane. An easy walk along a founding swath of the country that most travelers want to put behind them. A congested landscape usually seen as a blur, along a corridor named for a train, the Acela, whose name in turn is a faster form of *accelerate*. *Ad + celerare,* from the Latin: toward something, whatever it is, swiftly; to hasten the occurrence of a thing you want over.

No hastening anything on this trip. I wanted nothing over.

I kissed my wife, Shailagh; said goodbye to my brother Jeff; scratched my Airedale behind the ear; and turned north. I was off to talk to America, to listen to her, to examine her, to wonder over her, at what we all hoped was the end of one of the roughest patches in our history. I wanted to think about what we are, and once were, and still yearned to be. To poke among the graveyards of our past and brush the moss off forgotten things. To chew over this American project and come to some hazy conclusion over whether America was still possible or had seen its best days.

I wanted to dip into the deep pockets of our national memory, to pause with families rooted in place over centuries. To touch the aboriginal images carved in stone and hold in my hands the sacred books that speak to our beginnings. Most of all I just wanted to walk, breathe, feel the legs underneath me, and take in the days as the sun arced overhead.

I had had my own upheavals, too, after a cancer welled up and fogged my future. So I wanted to go measure my own time against the many timekeepers I would pass along the way. The homesteads gone to seed. The tottering barns. The church clock towers. The decaying edges of cities. The valleys carved by a million years of flowing water.

People looked at me askance when told of this lark. They were repelled, I think, by the mere idea of walking this stretch of ground. They saw a stooped figure skulking past the wharves of Baltimore and treading along the shoulder of Interstate 95. They saw a tall man with graying hair tossed in the lee of careening semis and grubbing for Cinnabons at the Molly Pitcher Service Area.

"And for what purpose?" they would ask.

"Purpose?" I said to one baffled inquirer over dinner one evening, a decorator of Georgetown sitting rooms. We were dining at a table for six. It was winter. Snow fell outside. "To walk until I summon forgotten thoughts. To assay the landscape and the state of mind of the citizenry. To measure distance by footfall. To take in a horizon that is impossibly far away, and then put it behind me." Those were roughly my words, anyway.

"Oh, so you hope to clear your head" was her response.

"You could say that."

Truth is, there was no concise encapsulation of the purpose for this walk. One could summon Buddha or Wordsworth or Thoreau's humble paddling on the Concord and Merrimack rivers. One could note that Thoreau never once paused to explain the purpose of his paddle that later became his first gem of a book, *A Week on the Concord and Merrimack Rivers*. All that the Concord River contained—the "occasional logs and stems of trees," the shining pebbles, the floating cranberries—"were objects of singular interest to me," he wrote, "and at last I resolved to launch myself on its bosom and float wither it would bear me."

To which I said, "Precisely."

My intent, like his, was to take a singular interest in all I encountered. To turn my attentions away from the noxious chatter of Washington, the tribal feuding on television and computer screens, and care only for the particularities I found along the way. To shrink my horizons to that of a walking man and to root my views of the world in what I encountered step by step. To honor and respect what I saw.

"Attention," the late poet Mary Oliver wrote, "is the beginning of devotion."

I had obsessed for months over so much that seemed relevant to this walk. The remaining traces of the earliest people, the Algonquin and Lenape and all the others. The first mapping of the land. The flow here and there of the Dutch, the Swedes, the English, Germans, Scots Irish. The fleeing streams of men and women escaping slavery, and later Jim Crow. The battlefields I would pass through and the routes the soldiers took coursing this way and that. The felling of the trees, the tilling of the land and the killing of its wildlife to where barely a bird remained. How brawny men made the steel and laid the tracks for the trains to run. How the native trails turned into cart tracks, stage routes, toll roads, and finally into the highways I would skirt as I made my way north.

My walk was, in reality, its own explanation. You embark on a long solitary stroll in part so as not to explain it. You go to cast aside all such distractions. You go for the fun of it, the promise of pure serendipity, and simply because you can, as though the entire way there you should walk beneath a red banner of freedom, with trumpets tooting, like some footloose believer drawn by the lure of Jerusalem. *Possum ergo faciam*—I can, therefore I will.

Ahead of me now, hours and days and weeks down the road, stood the glistening monuments, the ruins, the river valleys, the proud farms, the abandoned railroad tracks, the battlefields, the grave markers. The malls, distribution warehouses, freeways, iHOPs, Taco Bells.

In medieval times the pilgrims who walked to Rome or Jerusalem would turn a ring or a badge or a necklace into a contact relic by touching it to some holy cloth or the whitened shank of a saint. Some would chip a flake of marble from a shrine or abscond with the fingernail of a prophet. My version of that, which I rubbed between finger and thumb, was a silver tetradrachm from Periclean Athens, a coin with the profile of Athena on one side and an owl on the other, given to me by a friend. A worn piece of silver that had traveled the Mediterranean in 400 B.C., my own pilgrim's badge, was going now on another journey.

———◆———

There was a backstory, as with everything. Years earlier I had joked about walking to New York, back when I was in the full thick of life and the two weeks or so needed for such a journey seemed a laughable indulgence. Exactly how would one walk through a landscape hostile to the pedestrian? I plotted on old maps the routes I might take, the crossings over water, the cutting through woods in darkest New Jersey, and it all seemed as exotic as the Congo did to Stanley. The years slipped by.

Then I suffered a jolt. Cells gone rogue unleashed an enemy

inside, a cancer in my esophagus that I tried to defeat over two long attempts. Specialists in fluorescent rooms infused me with chemicals, week after week for an entire fall. Day after day huge machines whirred and groaned as they radiated my insides. I was brought low to be built back up, went the thinking. A surgeon—she of the deft hands and steady knife—cut away portions of me and remade my insides during ten hours of darkness.

The odds of being around a few years hence gyrated from absurdly low to tolerably decent, then back again when I had a recurrence. The whole of it, beginning the very day of my diagnosis, devoured four years. The experience scrubbed my eyes and gave the days much greater vibrancy. Grief found a way of blending with joy and deepening it. Sorrow, I learned, is the shadow of love, because what is sorrow but the fear and pain of losing what you love?

Simple things—the sight of children playing in a park, wind blowing through trees—assumed an otherworldly radiance and stopped me in my tracks. A slice of lemon cake, a sip of turmeric tea, a dab of spicy hummus on a cracker: familiar foods took on new flavor and exploded in my mouth. The scrambling of the calendar, the whiting out of all presumed years beyond the one at hand, gave me an urgent clarity and rendered me freer than at any point in my life. I felt weightless like a dry sponge ready to absorb. Were there an algorithm to gauge a soul's freedom, I told friends before setting out, mine would come back stamped "fully unburdened."

My aim now was to be as footloose at sixty-one as many of us are at twenty, but minus the angst of figuring out who I was to become. "I can't squander what time I have on pettiness," I scribbled in a notebook amid the worst of it, "unless it is the pettiness of forests and the tedium of rivers and streams." I beat back the recurrence—a flare-up in my lymph nodes and yet another fall of chemo and radiation—and then tiptoed into a meadow broad enough to see no trees on the other side. I was not in the clear but in a wide clearing with the sun pouring down.

As the year began, I wrote a tally of my good fortunes, a practice I highly recommend. If you start small and build out, it can clarify the magnitude of your blessings. You start with elemental things, like: A heart that beats. Eyes that see. Blood that flows. Lungs that breathe unimpeded by gunk. A mental windshield not too splattered with bugs.

Failing to note the absences will cut any proper list of good fortunes in half. The bones that aren't broken, the illnesses or hates you don't have, the aches you don't feel. Like many things that are unswervingly good—oxygen, say, and water—health is likewise transparent and easy to miss when you have it. Then you get to the meaty stuff. A wife you love. A house that isn't falling down.

About a month before my departure, the whirring machine that scanned my insides saw no malignancies or gathering clouds. "See you in six months," my oncologist said with a goodbye wave in early March. Magic words, those. I was ready to go.

———◆———

This walk had first been set for March a year earlier until we all began muttering about a pandemic. A weirdly named virus raged around the globe and began sickening and killing thousands, then hundreds of thousands, then millions worldwide. The virus cast all plans asunder, and worse. For me, in just weeks, it rendered the very act of walking block to block, county to county, foolish and forbidden. No one wanted to see a stranger coming up the drive. When the library that holds the books for the Mystic Order of the Solitary in Ephrata, Pennsylvania, told me the archives were closing and that I could no longer page through the 361-year-old illustrated saga of Christian martyrdoms, the famous *Martyrs Mirror,* I knew the game was up.

In the year in between, the nation's mood grew sour, aggrieved, vindictive. We had an election, the worst in living memory for creating new wounds and worsening old ones. We were fighting over statues, over which of our national dead to honor and which to cast aside. We were fighting over our origins and the stories we tell our children about our past. What we include, and what we leave out. We were fighting even over the origins of the virus and whether to take the shots meant to protect us from it. We were fighting over whether our very election had been honest or not. All that, too, gave added grist to the walk.

My path, roughly sketched in my mind but also on pages torn from an old Rand McNally, carved a shallow arc through the founding territory of our nation, its original heartland. I would cut up through Maryland, Pennsylvania, and New Jersey—along Underground Railroad trails, through woods along the Mason-Dixon Line, over the Susquehanna, past Mennonite and Amish farms, through battlefields and cemeteries, along lanes and stream-beds at Valley Forge and on to Philadelphia.

From there I would duck north to a cave where a hunchbacked Quaker once lived, then to Doylestown where Henry Mercer packed his museum with the forgotten shards of early America. I aimed to cross the Delaware when the shad were running, then cut through a corner of New Jersey, dip into Princeton, and hike to the top of a trash mound with a view of airports, rivers, and islands before entering New York Harbor by boat as Henry Hudson had. My destination for this ramble was The Ramble, where those great Central Park designers Frederick Law Olmsted and Calvert Vaux brilliantly spoofed the parallel streets and avenues of the emerging Manhattan with a wondrous tangle of pathways designed to discombobulate. To take a curved arc to a twisted path, listening to the people and places along the way.

There were, of course, pilgrimages within the greater pilgrimage. Way stations that were their own little Romes and Canterburys.

A dot on the map in northern Maryland called Young Man's Fancy. Some mysteries, if I could find them, along the Mason-Dixon Line. A train depot south of York. Two sacred rocks in the Susquehanna. A seventeenth-century leather holy book at a place called Muddy Creek Farm. A stone farmhouse where the ninth generation of the same family lived. A bone cave, now buried, on the edge of Valley Forge. A prison in Philadelphia that brought Alexis de Tocqueville to America.

All of that felt right. From the first falls of the Potomac to the bedrock schist of New York, around 330 miles. The largest town along the way, other than Philly, would be York, Pennsylvania. Such was the plan, the tracings drawn with a pencil, easily altered and erased if other ideas arose as I went.

Attached to my rucksack was a collapsible fly rod, just in case any rivers tempted. Inside were shorts for hot days and wading in water. A laptop, two notebooks, toiletries, two shirts, a rain jacket, an extra pair of pants, a flask for carrying water. Just the shoes I had on, springy and light and perfect for walking. The barest of essentials.

Infantry men in 1776 tromped off to fight the British with four pounds of gunpowder and sixteen pounds of lead. A single muzzle-loaded long gun weighed eight pounds, easy. On the other hand, the anonymous Russian mystic who wrote *The Way of a Pilgrim*—dear to the heart of J. D. Salinger's Franny Glass—set off with far less: "My worldly goods are a knapsack with some dried bread in it on my back, and in my breast-pocket a Bible. And that is all."

The explorer and author John Muir was of a similar mind. He wandered off into the California woods with what he had in his pockets. The great Adirondack waif of a grizzled wanderer George Washington Sears, aka Nessmuk, managed to stick to under twenty-six pounds in gear when he crisscrossed New England by canoe in the 1870s. And that included "extra clothing, blanket-bag, two days' rations, pocket-axe, rod and knapsack" along with his sturdy watercraft, the *Sairy Gamp,* made of white cedar with elm ribs, which weighed in at just over ten pounds. "Go light; the lighter the better, so that you have the simplest material for health, comfort and enjoyment," he wrote in his invaluable *Woodcraft.* I was still too burdened at eighteen pounds.

There was something joyous all the same in the essential simplicity of that little bundle on my back. An hour before setting out I made a quick inventory of my house, walking room to room and floor to floor, and counted thirty-eight chairs, six beds, four sofas, at least a thousand books, and the better part of a container load of other sundries: lamps, blankets, spoons. I don't know for sure, but I bet John Adams owned, maybe, five pairs of pants when he died in 1826. I owned four times that number. My will, if we still wrote wills as they did in colonial times, would have run to hundreds of pages. "And to my nephew John I bequeath my brass candlesticks."

Like the whole of our species, there was a time I moved much lighter on the earth. I used to crisscross the country hitching rides. I went around the world at twenty-two with little money and a backpack, picking my way job to job. One summer in college, I quit my job as a New York City cab driver, gave up my rented room, and set off for a long summer in Central America aboard a Greyhound bus from New York's Port Authority. Stuffed into a bicycle messenger bag were a tangle of clothes, a pair of cowboy boots, and the selected poems of García Lorca. When the Greyhound clerk asked where I was going, I said, "Give me a one-way ticket to Laredo, please."

———◆———

There's nothing heroic about walking to New York. It is a humdrum feat by any measure, unworthy of mention on the morning news. It is no trail through Appalachia to the peaks of Maine. No

Everest looms along the way to surmount. No Grand Canyon to get across. No Cyclops to gobble me while sailing home from Troy. No Amazon requiring a machete in the belt for vines or snakes. No warlords or highwaymen along the way to loot one's knapsack. The gravest peril was a driver looking at his phone.

Other men and women have followed roughly my same web of roads and paths on similar journeys, hundreds of millions of them, whether by foot or horse or carriage, train or car. George Washington, to name one, traced a route a bit more direct when he departed by carriage from Mount Vernon, fifteen miles downriver from my house, for his inauguration in Lower Manhattan in April 1789. "About ten o'clock I bade adieu to Mount Vernon, to private life, and to domestic felicity; and with a mind oppressed with more anxious and painful sensations than I have words to express, set out for New York," he wrote in his diary. I set out with a lighter mind and better teeth but would encounter Washington's ghost many times as I went north.

"Don't go too early," friends warned. "It will snow on you. It will be too cold."

"You can't go now, not with the virus still raging."

"You had better get your shots first, both of them."

"If you were younger and I was your mother, I would lock you in the closet," said my doctor, who called me Forrest. Through my illness, she had delivered the most resonate advice. "Just walk through it," she said. "No matter what it is, just keep walking and fighting and searching for something else."

Her counsel on the eve of the walk was more prosaic. Stay hydrated, she said. Check yourself nightly for ticks. "And don't get run over."

We know, from our Middle English, that April is the month for such a sally. Chaucer said so in the opening lines of his *Canterbury Tales,* lines that made me thrill with recognition and bend over in joy when I read them while walking weeks later along a suburban

street in Staten Island. "When in April the sweet showers fall . . . /
Then people long to go on pilgrimages." All winter I longed to do
just that, and now my house, wife, and dog were receding behind
me. I waved to a neighbor, who gave a hearty "Godspeed." Another
trotted down his front steps to hand me a raisin bagel for the road.

Spring held back, as though reluctant to declare itself, so by the
time I departed, the forsythia were just preparing to flare. The days
had lengthened. Syringes had deposited into my left shoulder two
chilly doses of liquid freedom. Some establishments were opening
from the long pandemic freeze. People would now walk with their
mask dangling from one ear instead of firmly covering nose and
mouth. Baseball's Opening Day was four days off. All the elements
were in my favor. The moon, propitiously, was in Waxing Gibbous.

I set out that Monday morning, nine days into spring, north
up Ninth Street, eager to see if anything of interest might crop
up along the way. As I turned to wave to Shailagh, the Marine
Corps barracks five blocks away broke out in a recorded rendition
of "The Star-Spangled Banner" through the loudspeakers of the
commandant's mansion, as they did every morning at 8:00 sharp.
It was a brassy version in the style of Sousa, and to those strains I
padded the first blocks of an arcing path over rivers and freeways
and farmlands to where the Hudson spills into that big harbor
with Lady Liberty and her torch. The sun hung warm over my
shoulder. There was birdsong in the trees. I had a skip in my step
and a satchel on my back, and could feel within blocks a little bliss
seeping in.

~~Cheerios~~

~~Eggs~~

~~Cottage Chips~~

~~Big Bags Chips~~

Jacks Salsa

Alouette

~~Eggo Waffles~~

~~Nutty Bars~~

~~Swiss rolls~~

~~Salad Stuff~~

~~French Fried Onions~~

~~Pastry~~ ~~Pie Crust deep dish~~ (2)

~~Muzarella~~

~~Mac + Cheese - 2~~

~~Skinless Sausage~~

~~Lana Broth~~

~~Tuna Fish~~

~~Pk. Jaw~~

~~Worch. Sauce~~

~~Sunflower Seeds~~

Shish Kabobs

~~Bread~~

~~Butter~~

~~Deodorant~~

~~Nu Floral~~

~~Scent~~

~~Coffee Aid~~

CHAPTER 2

TIME AND THE RIVER

There is no single now but a multitude of nows, an infinite number. So philosophers and scientists say. Just as there is no single past, or one continuum that leads from then to now, but an endless multitude of continuums. The Greeks intuited that. Heraclitus with his river you could never step in twice. Aristotle did not believe in absolute time but saw time as a measure of change. In a world without change, there is no time.

I could tell within blocks that my walk would bend time, that for the body in motion time moves more slowly. The walk would make the present more expansive but also open layers of the past to my inspection.

Through the bare limbs you could see the milky marble of the Capitol dome as I turned left up East Capitol Street. The midpoint of that dome divides Washington into unequal quadrants. The bronze eagle feathers on the crest of the Statue of Freedom, 288 feet above the East Front Plaza, mark the axis around which the city turns. My destination for the day was due north of the city; heading west first was one way to get there. After walking the length of the National Mall to stand before Abe Lincoln in his mighty chair, I would head north up Rock Creek. Up that way, first north and then bending northeast, weeks down the road, was New York City.

Crowds had gathered thick on the Capitol's grounds on December 2, 1863, to see the workers lower that head onto the Statue of Freedom and bolt it into place. Others peered through opera glasses from the open windows of the buildings nearby. "Immediately that the head was adjusted, the hoisting of a flag signaled to all below that the statue was complete, and cheer after cheer filled the air from the throats of the large concourse present," said the *Evening Star*.

Often, when out walking and catching sight of that dome and statue, I would think again about how Lincoln had pushed to complete and then ornament that dome in the thick of the war as proof of our persistence and a show of faith in the country's continuance.

Years earlier, the man in charge of approving the precise design for the Statue of Freedom was none other than Jefferson Davis, then secretary of war and the future president of the Confederate States of America. Davis quibbled when the sculptor proposed crowning the figure with a liberty cap, a traditional symbol of freedom derived from freed Roman slaves and popularized during both the French and American revolutions. The history of that cap, Davis wrote, "renders it inappropriate to a people who were born free and should not be enslaved." That firm enforcer of slavery was also, in his own mind, a committed defender of liberty.

As I approached the Capitol, the grounds remained blocked by the detritus of our most recent insurrection. A mob had stormed the building with notions of overturning an election. One man had roamed the halls with a large Confederate flag over his shoulder. Many similar flags had waved from the scaffolding outside, erected there for the inauguration of the new president. I had walked to the Capitol that afternoon to see the riot unfold, just as I had crisscrossed the Mall in the days before to watch as the crowds filtered in from across the country. Today, the high fence put up after the siege still ringed the grounds, but workers had just taken away the much broader perimeter barrier laced with razor wire. A cluster of National Guard troops stood behind the high fence eating donuts in a patch of sunlight. One of them offered a soldierly wave as I walked by.

If some Cassandra had come before me at the start of 2020 and said, "You will cast your vote for president in Nationals Park and will enter that park for the first time all year, because the team will have played no games there before a live audience," I would have said, "Yeah, right." And if she had said, "In the meantime, 550,000 of your fellow Americans will have been felled by a virus you've never heard of, including the parents of many of your closest friends," I would have scoffed and said, "That's ludicrous. No way." And if she had said, "Through the summer your city and many others will be wracked with riots and clouded with tear gas after a policeman kills a Black man in Minneapolis," I would have recoiled in astonishment. And if she had then said, "When you depart on that walk of yours to New York, a year later than first planned, you will have to detour around a Capitol compound completely encircled by seven-foot-high fencing, and manned inside by troops with automatic weapons, after a mob, believing the election had been stolen, ransacks the building at the beginning of the year," I would have blanched and said, "Please, stop. This is all too much."

We absorb the unimaginable with astonishing ease and move on.

I thought of my own time around that dome as I walked down the western slope of the Capitol grounds. How immense and fleeting the Washington years felt, bordering soon on half my life. My wife and I had met as aspiring journalists in Chicago in 1989, just as the Iron Curtain fell. We'd spent a few years in Florida before the drama in Eastern Europe became too strong to resist. Shailagh and I went overseas childless and unmarried in 1992, with the mere suggestion of work on arrival and no more luggage than we could carry aboard a Prague-bound train from Paris. We arrived in

Washington in 1999 as staff writers for the *Wall Street Journal,* married with two young daughters, Lillian and Frances, solid résumés as foreign correspondents who had roved the whole of Europe, and a seagoing containerload of furniture and other household effects.

I figured we might stay in the nation's capital for a decade or so before heading somewhere else. On six bracing Januarys since then, each of them four years apart, I watched presidents on those very Capitol steps raise their right hand and swear to protect the Constitution of the United States. I'd run down and back up that hill hundreds, maybe thousands of times. I'd watched my kids sled on its west-facing slope and had stood at its top to see the national fireworks on innumerable Independence Days. On the morning I strolled by with a pack on my shoulders, we'd been in that one house and called this our neighborhood for three years shy of a quarter of a century. That, like all the recent horrors, was hard to fathom.

"Brisk sunshine" is how the weather folks described my first day out, and that fit the morning well as I cut down the Mall with the sun at my back. Gusts blew brisk from the south, and the sun poured down warm. You could see the cherry trees in full pink flower around the Tidal Basin, like the smudge from an impressionist's brush. Just past the Smithsonian Castle in the middle of the grassy Mall, a thin blanket fluttered over a subway grate and when I got closer, the wind revealed the dark matted hair of a half-naked man sleeping there. I knew he was alive only by the rise and fall of his chest.

At the foot of the Capitol I had stopped to take in Ulysses Grant, placid in his battered field hat atop a Tennessee Thoroughbred, peering over the reflecting pool. The sculptor Henry Merwin

Shrady devoted twenty years of his life to that monument—the bronze lions, the meticulous cavalry and artillery units in the thick of battle—then collapsed and died two weeks before its unveiling on April 27, 1922. A month later, a sea of dignitaries arrived to present the Lincoln Memorial to the nation. In a single spring fifty-seven years after the end of the Civil War, the president and his general assumed their places, one at each end of the National Mall, together keeping an eye on the whole of the city.

If you looked just right, you could see Grant on his horse from the top steps of Abe's Doric mansion. You could see, too, the subtle shift in the color of the stone midway up the Washington Monument, a fault line that spoke to the decades it sat unfinished, when its construction was interrupted by political feuds, war, and indecision. On the morning of every presidential election since 2008 I had come to the top of the Lincoln Memorial steps to sit and watch the sun rise over the Capitol and to say a silent prayer for the country, that it might act wisely and choose the best one. These steps and the man inside are among the most-visited places in all America. Pick any two of us at random and we likely have those steps in common. There may be none holier in all the land.

The memorial is a temple to Lincoln in his huge marble chair, but even more, it is a temple to his words. I went to the north wall, as always, to read what he said at his second inaugural, forty-two days before his death. No president has packed more into each sentence. "Until all the wealth piled by the bondsman's two hundred and fifty years of unrequited toil shall be sunk, and until every drop of blood drawn with the lash shall be paid by another drawn with the sword."

Grant and Lincoln got their marble and bronze remembrances that same spring at a time of seething racial tension in the land. Tens of thousands of Black soldiers had returned a few years before from fighting in Europe, changed beings, more worldly and confident. They had gone across an ocean to defend democracy and wanted it more strongly upon returning home. Jim Crow was in full swing. Lynchings and racial violence soared.

"This country of ours, despite all its better souls have done and dreamed, is yet a shameful land," wrote W. E. B. Du Bois in his trumpet blast of a manifesto, "Returning Soldiers." He wrote those lines in May 1919, during that year's brutal spate of lynchings and mass killings, later called the Red Summer. KKK membership spiked, above all in the North. White rioters torched Tulsa's Greenwood District two years later. At the Lincoln Memorial dedication, a year after that, ushers led a contingent of prominent Black invited guests to a segregated section cordoned off by Marine guards.

From Lincoln's house I turned north and saw swoop before me the shadow of a large bird. For the whole of the walk my most constant aerial companion would be the *Cathartes aura,* as it's called, the "cathartic breeze" of the turkey vulture, with its spreading feathered fingers and black-and-white underwings, America's most common raptor. When walking or fishing, when sitting on the wall of a bridge or standing outside a barn talking, time after time I smiled or laughed to see its shadow pass at my feet. I have always envied those birds their soaring powers, no matter what they eat for supper. They are ghastly up close but regal in flight. Masters of the rising thermal.

I cut northeast to walk along the foot of that glistening black granite wall where the names of all the Americans who died in Vietnam are engraved. You walk and run your fingers along the wall and feel the imprint of all those names and see your fleeting reflection as you go.

I wanted to stand before another seated man, my last before leaving the city. Albert Einstein sat there sprawled with his famous formula in his lap. There a plaque reminded me that our sun is just one of two hundred billion other stars that make up our galaxy. Our sun and all other suns are situated within a vast flattened disk of stars that orbit the galaxy's center. Even traveling at 514,000 miles per hour, it takes our sun at least 220 million years to orbit that center, so it will have barely budged in its rounds during the whole of our lifetimes. Our galaxy, with its center beyond all human reckoning, is but one of billions upon billions of other galaxies, each with its plethora of stars, thousands of which still twinkle though they are long dead. When you look into the sky at night—made as we are of our own form of stardust—you are looking deep into the past. There is no common now.

"No, not all the way up there. That's too dangerous," a mother said. Her young son had grabbed a bronze chunk of Einstein's wild hair and was trying to climb atop his head. The boy groaned as she eased him down and took a picture of him sitting atop the formula in Einstein's enormous lap.

———◆———

It is one of the city's many wonders that you can exit Washington to the north entirely by river, along the winding shores of Rock Creek, and see barely a house the entire way. I descended to the creek from the high span of Wisconsin Avenue and followed the water north toward its source. I was barely an hour from my house and already, in spirit, well out of town.

Rivers derive their power over the human mind by being both a symbol of constancy and a symbol of perpetual change. Carving the land, forever in motion. They are the most fixed and immutable aspect of any topography, but never for a minute what they were before. Keep walking until you get to the river. It is just past the river. After you cross three rivers you will be there, changed for having crossed them.

I sat on a log and ate lunch along a bend in the river just above Boulder Bridge, thinking about how we apportion and allot our time and how nature knows no stickier force than inertia.

Interrupting our rounds to break away, even for a month on a lark like this, can seem like diving off a high cliff. When taking such a plunge, every molecule in your body prefers the calm and tells you not to do it.

As I got up to leave, I stood to watch the river flow and bend around the rocks and thought about how any of us manage to seize our more magical stretches, our extended periods of maximum freedom. Fishermen work seams—seams between slow water and fast, between deep water and shallow, between sunlight and shadow. The eddies around rocks, the bubble lines along banks. That's where the fish are.

Grabbing long moments like this walk is also a matter of playing the seams. It's a matter of timing. All of us have little fissures in our lives that provide us greater than normal moments of freedom. You play the seams when you identify those moments and seize them. That window between high school and college. Immediately after college. Coming out of the army. Moving between houses or states or continents. Changing jobs. After a breakup or divorce. Having your kids move out of the house. Recovering from an illness that realigns your bearings.

Events or moments that cause a break in the regular order and open fissures through which we can slip into a different place. We talk about freedom of choice, but we don't talk enough about how freedom itself *is* a choice. We have enormous powers, powers beyond our day-to-day reckoning, to create our own reality. Americans have it wrong when it comes to what Emerson or others meant when they talked about self-reliance. It wasn't the ability to live deep in the woods and eat what you kill. It was about the faith to rely on your own instincts and live by your own lights. That is the truest form of self-reliance. If only for a moment I had broken the inertial bonds, and as I kept going upriver, every inch of me was glad for the movement.

After my surgery I had sent my pathology reports to a cancer doctor in Chicago I'd never met and pressed him to give me a blunt sense of my odds. What did he care? He was never going to talk to me again. "C'mon, doc, give it to me straight," I said to him over the phone.

"Half of everyone in your condition won't be alive two years from now, and even fewer a year after that," he told me, sparing the spoonful of sugar. "Yours is an aggressive cancer, and once the cancer cells are loose in the highways of the lymphatic system, they are very hard to track down and obliterate."

I pictured ten men on a wall, with five gone after two years, and two more gone a year later, and another a year after that. That phrase alone—"the highways of the lymphatic system"—opened a seam in my mind.

A couple of months later I sat with a financial planner, neat in his office in crisp shirt and tie. Unaware of any doctor's findings, he laid out charts showing how my wife and I would have this much in five years and maybe even more when I died after eighty-five. How nifty it all looked when put into lines sloping this way and that, how you deplete your life account as you build up the financial one.

———◆———

All walks have their inspiration, however long ago. In my early twenties, I spent a month at a Buddhist monastery in the mountains outside Kandy, Sri Lanka, midway through a slow trip around the world. The head monk assigned me a simple hut on a hill with windows overlooking lush valleys. It had a wooden bed inside with a woven mat for sleeping. Outside, running the length of the hut, was a path for pacing while meditating, maybe ten yards long and two yards wide. The head monk advised against long walks as that would be idle sightseeing, the seeking after beauty and dis-traction. The walking path was meant for confined movement, to focus on the motion and not on the ground being crossed.

Over time I succumbed to the lure of the valleys and took long strolls through the rice paddies. The longer I walked, the more taken in I was by the sight of the farmers harvesting rice and the buffalo up to their nostrils in the water. The more those things captivated me, the more I was failing at being a monk. The more I failed at being a monk, the more I wanted to walk through the rice farms.

The whole world beyond beckoned, and I left that little hut and its ten-foot walking path to continue with my travels, casting aside my monkish ambitions.

"I will come back," I told the head monk, but I didn't.

Forty years later, I was on this long walk to see what peace it might bring and what crevasses of understanding it might pry open. It was, even if the good monk might not agree, its own form of meditation.

A dozen miles or more upriver, huffing now and my pack feeling heavier, I emerged into the neighborhoods and watched as the houses got much smaller and the parked cars outside more numerous and more utilitarian. I had left D.C. and was in Mary-land now. There were vans parked along the curbs with multiple ladders on their roofs and pickup trucks with bins in the back. This is where the working people lived who built the patios and the houses and tended to the gardens of the people who lived closer in.

These first few days would be tough, each more than twenty miles with an unfamiliar burden on my back. I had front-loaded the pain, knowing I would get stronger as I went. I kept shifting the straps on my pack and tightening and loosening the belt. My calves complained through the last few miles.

As the shadows lengthened, I left the ticktock of little houses and entered an expanse of roads and big-box stores where the pedestrian became an oddity and afterthought. Sidewalks would emerge and then vanish. Orphan walks, I came to call them. You would have a place to put your feet and then you'd have to find your own way along a grassy shoulder. A few miles south of Olney, Maryland, I came upon a cluster of men on their knees tossing tiny dice and passing around tens and twenties in a Home Depot parking lot. Men for hire who had taken journeys far longer and more arduous than mine to be there. They looked up astonished to see me watching them.

I secured a turkey club wrapped in white paper from a sandwich shop in the old Higgins Tavern, built in 1823 and owned and operated for nearly a century by two women. I stuffed the sandwich in my pack as dinner for the night and kept on for another mile or so, past houses with neat curving yards and shiny cars in the drive, toward the former country estate of Franklin Roosevelt's long-serving interior secretary, Harold Ickes.

———◆———

Ickes bought the house and its 230 acres in 1938, when the country was still at loose ends and before the war jolted the economy back to life. Houses with little gazebos and swing sets in back had since gobbled up every foot of the farm, so that you wondered how the big house could still be there until it emerged suddenly at the top of a cul-de-sac, its six Doric columns reaching two stories high. The sun dipped behind the house as I dragged myself up the front drive, twenty-two miles and ten hours after latching my gate. It was known now as the Olney Inn.

Ickes was a righteous curmudgeon, a stocky man with wire-rimmed glasses. When the Daughters of the American Revolution barred the great Black contralto singer Marian Anderson from performing at Constitution Hall in 1939, Ickes arranged for her to sing on the steps of the Lincoln Memorial. The crowd, seventy-five thousand strong, stretched all the way up the slopes of the Washington Monument. Ickes introduced Anderson in the Midwestern twang of his native Chicago. "In this great auditorium under the sky, all of us are free. Genius, like justice, is blind. Genius draws no color lines."

Sue and Nancy, my hosts, hadn't had a guest for weeks, so my arrival at the inn stirred palpable excitement. COVID stole the Christmas season, the weekend getaways, the weddings. Asked if they had any drink about, Nancy said they had a bottle or two left over from last year and handed me a tall glass of ice and a magnum of warm rosé. I felt like a king sitting alone in Ickes's old parlor eating my club sandwich with pink wine on the rocks. When I stood, my legs and back reminded me of all the miles we had crossed.

My room, just behind me, was where FDR stayed during his many nights there. I imagined him reading in the wing chair with his long cigarette holder. The sink in my bathroom was a little lower, the tub easy to get in and out of. I thought of FDR moving around in his wheelchair. Hefty tomes packed the bookcases in the study, among them multiple bound copies of Ickes's *Secret Diary*. I selected *Volume 2, The Inside Struggle, 1936–1939,* and took my rosé to read beside the darkened fireplace.

I turned to a page that described when Ickes and FDR and a few others had played poker well past midnight exactly where I sat, reading about their game that night. Ickes noted how he served Virgin Island rum cocktails before dinner and then sparkling Burgundy during the meal. "Ruth gave us a very good dinner," he wrote, speaking of the cook. After, Ickes opened a bottle of 152-year-old Scotch whisky—"as well as some 1811 Napoleon brandy." On top of that, FDR drank four bottles of beer.

"It was a lively game and money changed hands pretty rapidly," Ickes noted the next day. Of the liveliness of all that liquor and the game that followed, I had no doubt. I sprawled in FDR's tub until all the achiness leached from my legs.

CHAPTER 3

THE PARABLES

Morning brought tight tendons and joints, a balky back and shoulders, but within a mile the legs limbered, and the soreness ebbed. After the long COVID lull, Sue and Nancy came to see me off beside a breakfast table heaped with eggs and toast and hot coffee for the road. My arrival had suggested better times to come.

As the city's outskirts gave way, the stretch of asphalt I'd walked since the afternoon before—Georgia Avenue, which shoots north from near the White House—narrowed from six lanes to four and then finally to two with scant room for a walker on its shoulder. A city avenue was now a country lane. Here and there you would encounter the gnarled carcass of a deer or a fox and see the rare footprint of a previous human that made you wonder why anyone had come this way before.

What had once been a deer path, an Indian trail, a lane to haul carts by, was now a road strictly for cars. The neighborhoods had entryways with flowerbeds and ornamental trees and carved signs named for groves and villages that never existed. There was Old This and Old That, but the roads were all new and the asphalt still black and shimmery. I went on in mounting excitement for the sight of the first farm, first grain silo, first whiff of manure.

I came into Brookeville, my first intact hamlet, where President James Madison sought a bed for the night in August 1814 as the

British attacked Washington and burned the White House. The president and his retinue arrived by horseback and spent all of one night in a nearby house. My first country cemetery emerged on the edge of town. It was established by Methodists in the 1830s. The morning shadows fell long across the cemetery grass. The earliest markers were illegible under the layers of lichen. We think of stone as enduring and a reliable place to lodge memories, but wind and rain had smeared the names.

You enter a different time when you step into a cemetery. That mix of finality with our attempts at eternity faintly amuses, seeing how the older the place, the clearer it is that finality wins. I smiled at the toppled marker that boasted how the beloved buried there would never be forgotten.

Neat brick and stone houses, better kept than the tombstones, lined the road through town. Brookeville was a Quaker settlement, tidy and prosperous, and you could feel its tidiness still. The blacksmiths, millwrights, tanners, farmers, they all did well. They traded what they grew or made in lieu of money. Alongside the old Brookeville Academy, a forsythia was in early bloom, a flaming yellow that would follow me all the way to New York.

Outside town a man stopped in his pickup and rolled down the window. "Want a ride?" Another man dressed head to foot in reflective yellow nodded as I scurried past his road crew. I came upon my first barn, a red faded structure with an old cow chute coming up one side, long out of use. A stone manor house stood beside it where some eminence once lived, his time now lengthened by a bronze plaque at the entryway:

IN

MEMORY

OF

THOMAS DAVIS

PATRIOT

Poor Tom, whoever he was, died in 1749, years before the French and Indian War and decades before the colonials actively bristled against the British. I was curious as to what sort of patriot Tom was. Ben Franklin used the word "patriot" as early as 1730, but it didn't pop up often in early America until the 1770s. The word doesn't appear in Washington's papers at all until October 1775 and then again on August 1, 1776, when the general issued an order against regional fractiousness and jealousies among the ranks of his army. A patriot, in Washington's eyes, was a soldier who didn't bicker and threaten to return home unless given proper pay.

In the twenty-six miles since the previous morning, I had gone through the inner ring of the well-off town burghers, and then through the outer ring of the itinerant workers, and then through the ring of the office managers and junior account executives. Finally, I was breaking into the open, and into the land of the horse farm people.

The houses of the long-ago rich were welcoming, with long tree-lined lanes leading up to shady porches. You thought you might receive a glass of lemonade there. The houses of the new rich were menacing, with spiked fences and black Suburbans in the drive that looked like they might have gunmen inside. You imagined tripping alarms if you walked their way.

I had left what I decided to call Greater Capitolia, the broad blotch of towns and burgs that revolved around Washington. It was a land inhabited largely by people from anywhere, few of whom work with their hands. People with signs in their yards expressing wholesome thoughts like: LOVE IS LOVE. NO HUMAN IS ILLEGAL. I was going north into a more Southern scape now, toward a line that had long ago divided the slave states from the free ones. I saw the first of several Confederate flags that morning flapping from a high pole in someone's yard. I would be walking through many micro nations along the way to Manhattan, clusters of custom and belonging and attitude that went back, often, to the earliest days, even as the people drifted in and out. A residue that remained like fingerprints. I would try to catch the faint outlines of each as I went.

———◆———

The day brought two parables reminiscent of Chaucer or the Gospels of Luke or Matthew. When you walk, I soon realized, parables happen as they have for walkers since earliest times. One was bright, the other dark.

The first I will call the Parable of the Two Bridges.

I was on the road to Woodstock, Maryland, barely half a day's walk from the outer reaches of Washington, when I came to a bridge over a river with no space for a pedestrian to cross. The highway that had once been Georgia Avenue bent into woods just past the bridge, providing no warning of oncoming cars. There were two lanes, two white stripes, two guard rails, and not an inch for a human to squeeze past the racing cars and trucks.

The pilgrim was not going to risk that, so I went down a narrow lane that happened to shoot off to the left and cut across a small meadow where I tried to cross the river by foot. It was too wide and too deep, and no stones or fallen trees offered any other way over.

Coming back up to the road I saw an older couple approaching, just out for a morning stroll, as jolly and unexpected as could be. It was like the past was walking toward me, so I just stood and waited for it to arrive. They greeted me warmly and without suspicion. The man had a neat, perfectly white beard and wore a flannel shirt and khaki pants with both knees worn through. The woman wore a scarf tied around her hair and a sweater she probably knit herself.

Her faded denim skirt went nearly to the leather sandals on her feet, held tight with little buckles.

"Beautiful morning," the man said. His name was John Herder. His wife's name was Susan. I told them about the bridge, and how I couldn't cross it, and how I was looking for another way over. "This is the way the old highway went," John explained. "Down the road a bit you will come to an old bridge, and that will take you back to the main road."

He then asked where I was going and I said, "To New York via York County and Lancaster County and then across to Philadelphia."

"Lancaster County?" John said. "We used to live in Lancaster County."

I told them I was going to the town of Lancaster and then up to Ephrata because there were things I wanted to see there—a cloister, a copy of the *Martyrs Mirror*—and Susan's eyes widened in astonishment. "We used to live in Ephrata with some plain folk people on a farm there, but we left twenty years ago and haven't been back for years," she said.

Mennonites, Amish, sometimes even Quakers still call themselves plain folk or plain people. They do not believe in ostentation or vanity. Simple clothing. Churches without pomp or no churches at all. Much of America, particularly north of Washington, was settled by people who called themselves plain, including the Puritans and the Methodists.

Susan began describing their friends' farm, where it sat on a short road called Crooked Lane along the banks of the Conestoga River. How they used to live in the house right next door. How they hadn't been in touch with their friends, the Hoovers, for many years, but assumed they were still alive and still doing well. "They are getting on now, as we all are, but I have to imagine they haven't passed," she said.

A thought occurred to me. I said to them, "Look, when I get

to Ephrata, I will find the Hoovers' farm on Crooked Lane and inquire as to how they are, and I will let them know that you are well and fine."

They both brightened at the idea. Susan brimmed with excitement as she gave me their information, which I jotted in my notebook. I took a photo of the two of them looking frankly and earnestly my way, no attempt at a smile. Only later did I notice that John had his finger wedged between the pages of a book, which he must have been reading to her when they saw me on the road.

We said goodbye and they wished me luck. When I got to the other bridge on the little road, vines and trees and other vegetation were slowly devouring it, so the bridge was impassable to cars but was the perfect pathway for a pedestrian. One bridge I couldn't cross led me to a bridge no car could cross. I found that fact, and the whole of the past ten minutes, so marvelous that I laughed out loud.

When I crossed that little bridge over Cattail Creek, I was amazed that by avoiding one bridge and taking another, I became a messenger of good tidings between plain folk who hadn't been in touch for years. If before I had been a pilgrim, now I was a courier, a deliverer of good news. I returned to the main highway a different person in the same shoes.

And then there was the Parable of the Empty Water Bottle, a darker story.

In the middle of the afternoon, feeling faintly biblical now after my morning encounter, I was walking through a neighborhood of new mansions two or three times the size of Mount Vernon or Monticello. I was parched. Stupidly, I had let my water bottle run dry. A big commercial flower nursery down the road had already rebuffed me. A worker had kindly pointed me to the nearby staff watercooler, but then a woman had said gruffly, "May I help you?" And when I had told her I was on a long walk and in need of some water, she had ordered me off the property immediately. They allowed no trespassers, she'd said.

"Then why did you ask if you could help me?" I asked.

"Sir, you need to leave now."

"So, you will water the flowers but not the thirsty stranger?" I relished the role of the scornful prophet, waving to her as I left.

The woman had accused me of trespassing—stern stuff in a country where property rights now stand as sacred. It wasn't always that way. Trespassing wasn't a crime in the country's infancy. Most of the countryside was open range, and the wanderer could pass over whatever land he pleased. All that changed right after the Civil War, as landowners in state after state sought to control the movements of those who had just gained some modicum of freedom. America became a No Trespass nation starting in 1865.

Walking waterless now through a ritzy enclave in the Baltimore exurbia, I saw a young white man in his thirties coming down a long drive from a big house. I was walking through what had been a huge farm two decades before, once owned by a family named Sullivan, until developers chopped Sullivan's farm into parcels bearing houses larger than any when the country was born. The young man had a phone in his hand and earbuds in his ears. I stopped and held up my water bottle and said, "Can I ask you a question?"

He took the earbuds out and said, "If you stay at a distance." I laughed, as I was standing at least fifty feet away. I knew it would be outrageous to ask him outright if he could fill my water bottle, so instead I said, "I am on a long walk and have run out of water. Do you have any idea where I can find some water nearby?"

He thought about it for a moment—truly thought about it—and then began to offer elaborate directions for how I would have to go back the way I'd come, and then turn right and then right again to find a store "that is basically parallel to this road but a couple miles away."

I said that I didn't want to go back the way I'd come and would continue the way I was. When I thanked him and started to leave, he told me to be careful. I stopped and looked back at him. "What do you mean, be careful?"

"This is a family neighborhood and people can be touchy and suspicious of people just walking through like you are on your way to somewhere else. They don't know what your intentions are."

I was agog. I walked back toward him and asked if I could tell him a small story. He said I could.

I told him about how there's a writer right now, a guy named Paul Salopek, who is walking across a large part of the globe on assignment for the *National Geographic*. "A decade-long experiment in slow journalism," he calls it. When he crossed the country of Georgia over forty-two nights, the people there spontaneously invited him into their homes every night on the way. "Like a human baton, I am passed from stranger to stranger across continents," he later wrote. The Georgians offered him food and lodging naturally, without thinking. It's just the way they are.

"That's why this is a screwed-up country," I said to the man in front of his house, and wished him well.

Again, he got me to stop. "Don't get me wrong," he said. "*I* don't see you as any sort of threat. You look like a thoughtful and harmless person to me. That was an interesting story you told. I'm just saying what other people think. How other people are going to see you. And I agree, this is a screwed-up country." It never crossed his mind to take the bottle and walk into his house and fill it himself.

Before I left, he said one last thing that rattled in my brain. "Besides, I used to wear a hoodie around here when I was a teenager," he said. "So I know what it feels like when people look at you strange."

That, in its twisted way, got to the nub of it. When you set foot into the world, you want to be received for who you are. You don't want to be a reflection of the baseless fear and distrust that others harbor. When others see you as a threat, when they put their fear on you, God knows what can happen. You can be shot to death walking back from the store, as Trayvon Martin was, or while out jogging, like Ahmaud Arbery.

I was astonished that this guy saw me as a threat, or at least wanted me to know his neighbors might see me as such. That astonishment was a measure of my freedom. It was a measure of the privilege I felt to walk where I pleased, to stop random strangers, to talk to whomever I wanted without fear of complications. A Black man taking a similar walk would not have shared my astonishment. He would carry with him a presumption that the very complications I didn't fear could, for him, turn deadly at any turn.

I went on with my water bottle still empty. It took me forty-five minutes to get out of that huge subdivision with all the mansions at the end of long drives, and in my naivete I half expected the kid to drive up in his car and apologize and offer a water bottle, but that never happened.

I thought about goodness and what makes a person good. You can be good in the simplest sense but also callous and lacking in the most basic generosity and humanity. Are you then still good? I thought of that Samaritan on the road to Jericho.

Yes, we should judge ourselves and others on how we treat our friends and family. On whether we are good parents or good sons or daughters or good neighbors. But that's the easy part. Above all—and pretty much every holy book says the same thing—we should judge ourselves and others on how we treat strangers. Treating strangers with instantaneous suspicion and distrust, lacking the immediate impulse to fill a person's water bottle, is not a good sign for any society.

These ideas extend to the very roots of Western culture. Ho-mer's *Odyssey* is an epic-length treatise on how to treat the stranger. Odysseus was gone so long he returned home a stranger, rec-ognized only by his dog. The goddess of hospitality, Hestia, was among the highest of Greek deities. A passage in Genesis describes how Abraham "planted an *aishel* in Beer-Sheba, and there he pro-claimed the name of God of the Universe." Interpreted by some to mean an orchard and by others an inn, the *aishel* was a symbol for hospitality, an acronym for the three Hebrew words for feeding, drinking, and lodging. Providing those three is a holy rite.

What do the Georgians have that we have lost? Why are they so ready to open their houses? In this, we Americans are the ex-ception. The Pashtuns of Afghanistan and Pakistan have a code, Pashtunwali, that puts the highest premium on granting hospitality to strangers, without question or remuneration of any kind. *Mel-mastia,* they call it.

When Bruce Chatwin poked through Patagonia in the 1970s, he was routinely put up in farmhouses and barns. So was Patrick Leigh Fermor when he walked from Holland to Constantinople in the 1930s. In village after village in Germany and Austria, Fer-mor recounted in *A Time of Gifts,* mayors would ask the local inn-keeper to give him shelter, supper, and a mug of beer, "all on the parish . . . a survival, perhaps, of some ancient charity to wandering students and pilgrims." When Rory Stewart walked through Iran, Afghanistan, Pakistan, India, and Nepal between 2000 and 2002, he later wrote in *The Places In Between,* "in more than five hun-dred village houses, I was indulged, fed, nursed, and protected by people who were poorer, sicker, and more vulnerable than me."

Before I set off on the walk, people would ask, "Where do you plan to stay along the way?" And I would say, "Farmers will take me in. People will throw open their houses to the wandering pilgrim." I tried to keep a straight face. "Neil, I don't care how charming you are," said one woman I sat beside at a dinner in

Maryland, who lived on a former plantation. "I would grab a gun if I saw you coming up my drive at nine o'clock at night."

There was a time I often crossed the American continent by relying on the kindness of the random driver. Once, outside Lancaster, Pennsylvania, a few days up the road from where I was now, my uncle dropped me off to hitchhike back home to Colorado. It was the late 1970s, deep into the gloaming of the final twilight of the age of hitchhiking. Uncle Jim was beside himself with worry. Everything in his being told him it was sheer stupidity for me to hitchhike home. He offered to buy me a bus ticket, but I declined. He dropped me off, basically in tears, and two days and just six rides later, a kind driver drove out of his way to deposit me in downtown Boulder.

People think hitchhiking ended because hitchhikers became more dangerous. But that wasn't really it. The practice faded because drivers themselves got scared. Or their cars were too clean, too personal to allow entry to a random stranger. Our worlds of trust and fellowship shrank as our private worlds expanded. We had our headphones, our Sony Walkmans, our cassette tapes. Or now our earbuds, our podcasts, our hyperindividualized channels of news or entertainment. Who wants some grubby stranger barging into that?

We have farmed out our hospitality to the hotel and restaurant industries and all transportation to trains, buses, airplanes, taxis, and Uber. We have sanitized and made a business of the whole of it. We're hospitable if we put up friends or make them dinner. But that is not the origin of a bedrock concept as old as man.

I walked until I found water at a Dunkin' Donuts.

———◆———

I was due west of Baltimore now, caught in a snarl of roads where a major highway crossed Interstate 70 in a place called West

Friendship. Laughter helps when navigating areas like this because no thought was ever given to the ambler. You dash across lanes of traffic when a red light holds back the surge of cars and trucks. It is humbling, in the best of ways. No glamour here. You're a wanderer, skittering along the shoulder of a road. You keep company with candy wrappers and roadkill as the cars hiss by, venomous. You know the drivers look at you with pity if they look at you at all.

When I got to a fire station not far from the donut shop, I collapsed in a shady patch of grass tucked behind a stand of pines and drowsed, briefly, propped against my backpack.

Wandering to see and understand was once a thing in America. If you wanted to get a feel for the place, even remotely claim to grasp it, you had to walk it, ride it, take a stage through it, as so many writers and thinkers and even George Washington had done. You had to float its rivers and suffer saddle sores. You had to go from colony to colony or state to state, brave river crossings, risk lice and bedbugs, take notes, knock on doors, sup with people at their tables.

For more than a century the printing presses on both sides of the Atlantic—but loudest of all in England—spat out accounts of grand tours of America. The most sustained burst of these examinations began around 1820 and lasted at least twenty years. Some became famous and still draw readers. Alexis de Tocqueville, of course, sailed over in 1831 to wonder at America's pitfalls and great potential. Charles Dickens made his tour eleven years later and found a country both charming and infuriating.

Most lovable are the lesser known or forgotten wanderers whose scribblings once drew thousands of readers but have since fallen into the general landfill. Writers like Elias Pym Fordham, who came in 1817 and gave the world a two-volume account of his wanderings and later surveyed what became Indianapolis. His book contained chapter headings like "Vices of the western Pennsylvanians" that cry out for attention. Or the acerbic Emanuel Howitt, who came to poke around the United States in 1819 and captured his thoughts in a series of letters to his sister at home in England. Howitt was distressed by the disorder of the young America and wasn't drawn to stay. Or women like Harriet Martineau, whose two-volume *Society in America,* published in 1837, left no stone uninspected. Everything fell under her withering microscope.

These writings joined the riotous debate over what the young America would be, whether it would survive into robust adulthood or fall to a dissolute adolescence. Everywhere these men and women went, they asked: Who are these Americans? What sets them apart? Can a unity be formed from this cacophony of Puritan, Quaker, Catholic, Dutch, German, Scots Irish, African, Indian? How to meld the coastal gentry with the uncouth mountain man, the stolid farmer with the brawling city-dweller, the enslaver with those appalled by that institution? Can something enduringly good be made from this mess?

Washington's struggles with his unruly troops had become, decades later, a national challenge. He had struggled in the early months of the revolt to turn his ragtag group of frontiersmen, farmers, sailors, fishermen, and cobblers—all in different garb, with different weapons, speaking many tongues—into a unified whole. But when he did, however briefly, the country's prospects shifted for the better. That unity has remained elusive ever since.

These writers experienced their own parables, and they weren't always treated kindly. Many found the young America grotesque, a land of jarring contrasts, unlikely to ever gel into a unified whole.

When published, Howitt's letters each began with a summary of its contents. Reads one:

Dreadful roads.—Musquitos.—Rattlesnakes.—Miserable
settlers.—Horse drops through fatigue.—Wretched condition and

prospects of settlers.—No grain but rye to be seen.—Deserted
land.—Obliged to leave a tavern at night, by vermin.

Pretty much to a person these travelers marvel at the cantankerousness that ran through early America, a headstrong bossiness where even boys smoked cigars and thought of themselves as men. Howitt gives a marvelous distillation of the grumbling Americans he'd met along a grim week of walking a hundred miles through western New York in June 1819. Fusty diction aside, it reads as if it could have been written a month ago.

"They murmur," he writes. "There is something amiss they cannot account for: one attributes it to the pride of the cities, whose inhabitants can wear nothing but silks, for which they drain the country of specie; another charges it to the banking system,—and a third, to the war. Some are democrats, some are federalist; but all are kings and nobles,—every man a ruler, and yet nothing pleases. Such is the happiness of this country. Here, at least, it is a dream and a phantom; and the further we seek it the further we are behind."

I walked on from the fire station until I came to a park where a sign beside an empty baseball diamond mysteriously informed me that Uranus is 1.75 billion miles from the sun and has twenty-seven known moons. Farther on, as the sun dipped into the trees, I stopped for a burger at a roadside bar on the banks of the Patapsco River, twenty miles northwest of where that river becomes Baltimore Harbor. When I went on from there and crossed a wide bridge, I still had another two miles to walk uphill through a deepening dusk to get to the basement unit of a stranger's house, rented remotely days before. I let myself in below their deck. I could hear their footsteps overhead, but we never saw one another nor spoke. I arrived weary, worn out in the legs, eager for bed, and not much interested in conversation then anyway.

CHAPTER 4

BOLTS OF BEAUTY

You cut through a neighborhood and a man stands curbside, about to haul his trash bin back to his garage. With no prodding at all he begins to deliver a sermon, one hand propped on the bin. Your walk has a purpose, he says. First to bring harmony to yourself and then to the whole country. You stand there astonished, the lone member of his congregation.

I had set out early and revived, a fine mist on the face, and walked for an hour before stumbling upon Ted, the curbside prophet. There was rain in the forecast on the last day of March and I wondered if I would cross the Hudson and arrive in Manhattan more pleased with the country, or less.

I passed houses set back off the road with the shades drawn. The most squalid of these were also the ones that demanded you stay away, with KEEP OUT and NO TRESPASS signs nailed to trees and fence posts, as though you had any desire to enter. A bicyclist shot past without a nod, which surprised far less than the man in a pickup who lifted his hand from the wheel to give a two-fingered wave—the first acknowledgment from a moving vehicle in three days.

I was shocked to find an old stone mile-marker, four feet high, perched in someone's front yard. It bore the distances to both Washington and Baltimore, carved in an elegant script, except the distances were wrong and the marker's placement made no sense. Around the bend, a farmer had erected a large sign along the road announcing how fed up he was with imports of oats from Canada, orange juice from Brazil, brussels sprouts from Mexico, beef from Argentina, grapes from Spain. A once-mighty tree in his front yard, planted when the farmhouse was new, had been whittled down to a mere stump. Grandfather trees, I came to call those decrepit hulks.

It was in a development called Woodlands on the outskirts of Randallstown, Maryland, when I came upon Ted at the end of his drive. Ted was a Black man in his early fifties with a hefty frame and a warm face and flashing smile. He wore a tight black T-shirt atop baggy gray short pants and a pair of bright blue and gray running shoes.

We greeted one another, and when he asked, I told him where I had come from, right near the U.S. Capitol, and where I was heading. He sized me up with a long look, processed a few facts, and launched into what you might call the Parable of the Tuning Fork. Ted said it was no problem if I used the phone in my pocket to record the words that flowed from him in a steady stream.

"Here is what you are doing. Here is how I see it," Ted said, looking at me as though he had a bead on my deepest intentions. "You've been close to all that in Washington, the chaos at the Capitol, COVID, the whole police/Black Lives Matter thing. You've seen the shootings and beatings, the killing of George Floyd, the protests and violence that came after. All of that. We all are screaming, we are all reaching out, and your walk is to calm the storm, to center yourself to where you can be anchored in a frequency that will bring everybody into one harmonious vibration. Right now, everybody's out of sync, in the wrong frequency. When you tune in a radio, you get the music, or you get the static. So hopefully, your walk will tune you. When you hit the tuning fork, it will give the right vibration that yields healing."

Ted told me he had been down his own path with dark days, depression, chaos, addiction. "At that point, I was out of sync." He said he was writing a book about his journey that he planned to call *From the Pit to the Palace, a State of Mind*. The little house behind him was not the palace. That palace, as the title said, was a state of mind.

He got back to my walk. "Here's the bottom line," he said. "As you heal, somebody else is going to get in tune and pick up on your vibe and heal. Your frequency can get us all in sync. You know, this is the Passover, this is the resurrection, this is the renewing. And so, you're going on this walk, brother, and it's a holy walk, a walk of worship."

Ted had deemed my walk a holy walk, a healing walk, and I trembled at the thought and the responsibility he had heaped on me. I asked if I understood him right: that by putting myself right, I would help the whole country get back in tune.

"That is exactly what I am saying," Ted said.

That's a lot of weight, I said.

"You can carry it," Ted said. "And it will only get lighter as you go."

We both laughed at that and then Ted said, "Oh, and hey, let me duck inside and get you a water bottle."

When he returned, I told Ted the Parable of the Empty Water Bottle, my first telling of that story, and he shook his head. This was evidence of our need for the re-tuning that my walk was meant to accomplish. Ted was making all the pieces fit together. I told him that in leaving my house three days earlier, I had many destinations for the walk, with the ultimate destination being the island of Manhattan in New York City. But one of those destinations had clearly been to talk about all of this in his driveway as he hauled in his trash can.

"It is good you have a destination," Ted said as we parted. "If you weren't heading somewhere, people might wonder."

———◆———

I went on, thinking about everything Ted had said, but also puzzled by the idea of a walk without a destination. It was oddly hard to imagine moving over large distances without an aim, without a somewhere at the end. Your destination might be a thousand miles away, but it pulled like a magnetic force. It was your purpose, your destiny, the thing toward which you were heading. Even nomads go in pursuit of game or water. Their destinations may shift but they always have one, even when they aren't sure where it is.

In my early twenties I set out one evening on a trip around the world that brought me, many months later, to that hut on a hillside in Sri Lanka. I had spent two years at college in Chicago and wanted to break away from the books. I scraped together the little money I had and flew west from there to Los Angeles, later to Honolulu, still later to Auckland, and then on to Sydney. I bummed jobs and rides and lived low to the ground. I crewed on a sailboat for five weeks along Australia's Great Barrier Reef. I hitchhiked from Melbourne across the Nullarbor and all the way across Australia to Perth and made my way from there to Java. I had no route, no set path, but there was a destination: Chicago. To travel around the world means you head in one direction, east or west, until you return to where you began.

I camped around a fire with Aborigines in Australia's Outback. I traveled deep into Sumatra to play chess with a schoolmaster. I took several boats from there to get to Singapore. I trekked the Golden Triangle in Thailand. I spent weeks living in that open-air hut, distracted by the rice farmers and the water buffalo. I took a job at a warehouse in Germany, and later at a vineyard in Bordeaux. The whole of it took sixteen months. Three weeks before Christmas I sidled up to the bar at the Berghoff tavern on West Adams Street in downtown Chicago and announced, "Well, I've done it," to the drowsy lunchtime beer drinkers there. "I have traveled around the world." They raised their steins and bought me a beer.

That beer, you might say, was the destination.

A mile from Ted's I came to a house along the road where a woman named Jane was out in her drive sweeping mulch into a big pile. She was the spitting image of an aging Gilda Radner, if Gilda Radner had been allowed to age, all frizzy hair and frantic energy. "Where ya heading?" she said, leaning on her broom, the second she saw me.

She then gave me detailed descriptions of the sights upcoming and told me to keep an eye out for Soldiers Delight, which would come up on the left, an expansive place that soldiers loved because of its sweeping views of the countryside. She wasn't sure which soldiers exactly. "Just soldiers."

I thanked her and soldiered on. The view from Soldiers Delight when I arrived there didn't impress, but an old sign told me that for a stretch until 1850, one Isaac Tyson Jr. supplied almost all the world's hunger for chrome from mines there. When you think of chrome you think of Cadillacs and bumpers and faucets, but not of that desultory view from the roadside at Soldiers Delight. On I went toward Reisterstown, figuring I might find lunch there.

———◆———

There was a time when men and women put their stamp on the land. They came, bought a parcel, farmed it, put up an inn at a strategic intersection of roads and trails, and gave that place their name. John Reister did that in 1758. He sailed from Rotterdam, arrived in Philadelphia, then came to a place above Baltimore and assembled an acreage where roads went this way and that and called it, with gusto, Reister's Desire.

I wandered into his desire—now renamed Reisterstown—as

dark clouds assembled to the north, and a wet wind blew. That I sought lunch and shelter in his town surely pleased John Reister, who was honored with a bench—which I later sat on—in the Community Cemetery.

I took a stool at the bar of a tavern in John Reister's town and had ordered a beer and a plate of fish tacos when the skies outside opened up and the rain began to fall in torrents in the parking lot, forming instantaneous puddles, and as it did something strange swept over me. I hesitate to describe it, as if we should keep these things to ourselves.

At that moment, with the fish tacos in front of me and the rain pouring down outside, I felt a wave of joy pass through me as intense as any sudden grief. Pass through me in surges, so I had to bury my face in my hands. If the bartender had turned to look at me, he would've thought I was heaving with sorrow, that I had just received news of some terrible event, but it was precisely the opposite. Others were sitting nearby talking, drinking, dipping french fries into ketchup. And I was trembling with an inner laughter that resembled sobs.

We grope for words to describe emotions like this because they're so mysterious. It's like a tree suddenly swaying but with no wind to move it. We jump for joy or fly into a rage or burst into laughter for a reason, usually. There was no cause in this case: a full-body surge of joy at simply being there. The sight of the rain. The taste of the beer. The warmth of the tavern. The compactness of my belongings beside me in my pack. The simplicity of my life at that exact moment. Who knows why? Thoreau touched on this in a letter to a friend: "We are made happy when reason can discover no occasion for it."

The next afternoon—I jump ahead—a slanting snow blew in from the northwest as I walked along the edge of a field, a barn in the distance, cows in a pasture, and the same wave hit me. I doubled over along the roadside. Again, a sudden surge of joy that came on like a sob for no reason, but with every reason. Something was moving inside.

I must assume, and hope, that we all have these moments. That we are all similarly stricken when walking along a road or sitting at a bar. These moments are the reward for being, as though the earth were sending its voltage through us.

Marcel Proust famously had his moment with his spoonful of madeleine dunked into tea. "No sooner had the warm liquid, and the crumbs with it, touched my palate than a shudder ran through my whole body, and I stopped, intent upon the extraordinary changes that were taking place," he wrote in the first volume of *In Search of Lost Time*. "An exquisite pleasure had invaded my senses, but individual, detached, with no suggestion of its origin."

It was "an all-powerful joy," an "unremembered state which brought with it no logical proof of its existence." As Proust's fictionalized self digs, and probes, and sips more madeleine crumbs, memories flood back. Those crumbs have the power to reawaken past days and unearth the dead. The whole of his childhood village of Combray emerges in his cup of tea.

My joy had nothing to do with memory or the past, though I could recount other such surges, and many since my diagnosis. Bolts of beauty, we might call them, sure to become more numerous as I went. I could still feel its glow when I finished that lunch and walked into the rain.

My stride fell just shy of three feet, so it took many thousands of steps to get from there to where I slept that night, just outside of Hampstead, another ten miles straight north along Highway 30. I kept my head down in the rain and watched the drops splatter at my feet as the puddles grew. When some cars hit the pools in the road just right, they tossed splashes of water far enough to douse my pantlegs, but I didn't care. It would all dry out when I got there.

It doesn't take more than a couple of days for the walker to become condescending toward cars. You begin to see them as the deer, raccoon, or fox might, as lethal ghosts on their way to nowhere. You know that a human is driving but lose the feel that someone inside has a single thought for you, the roadside apparition. Two strangers passing on foot may have at least some inkling of a kinship. They might nod, say hello, wish the other a nice day. But there is none of that between the walker and the human in the car going by. They have five seconds, six at the most, to see what they are passing—the horse, the barn, the naked oak, the rain-drenched walker—and then they are gone. I often forgot they carried sentient beings inside.

As I walked, I called my older brother, Kevin, who was at home in San Francisco. "I had a satori over beer and tacos," I told him as the cars hissed by. We liked to joke about the Zen term for sudden flashes of enlightenment and intense thereness. We liked it because it was known as a word for something that couldn't be captured in words.

"Did it come with salsa?" Kevin asked.

"It did," I said. "Muy picante."

Kevin had mulled joining me for a stretch of the walk before a panther sunk its claws into his head. That's how he described the tumor doctors found on the left side of his brain just before Christmas, fifteen months earlier. It threw off his gait and left him waylaid at times halfway through sentences that were hard to finish. One of the best hikers and storytellers I knew now struggled to do either. His cancer, pretty much the worst variety you could get, had shrunk his horizons of both space and time. It had sent tremors of anguish through our mother, who faced the odds of two of her sons being taken back-to-back. The prospect of all that, the sordid drama of it, horrified me and helped to nudge me out my door.

But the beast couldn't touch Kevin's humor or his ability to marvel.

"I'm awaiting my medal," he said. "I just squeaked past my median survival moment. More than half of everyone in my condition are gone by now."

I had recently slipped past a similar invisible marker myself, that milepost where half your theoretical peers should have perished. I congratulated him on his accomplishment and said I missed him. "You'd love this walk," I said. "I'm just entering the outskirts now of a town called Boring."

"Sounds riveting," he said.

I was staying through this stretch of northern Maryland in nightly rental units above garages or in people's basements. The hosts knew I was there but kept their distance, that being the edict of the land. That evening in my little suite attached to the side of a farmhouse outside Hampstead, with the rain splattering my host's deck outside, one cheery voice, dutifully masked, passed a can of soup through a common door and I saw only her eyes. "Have a nice night," she said.

I set the soup on the shelf and walked a mile back into town, the highway slick with twilit rain, to eat a heaping plate of sticky carbonara at an Italian joint on Main Street. I devoured it gluttonously as an older couple one table over glanced at me, perhaps wondering if I hadn't eaten in days. Heading back with a groaning belly, I passed before the old stone houses of the vanished town gentry, each with its stately porch facing the street. These porches were made for sitting, gazing, gossiping, sharing. They formed an important part of the town common.

When I broke out into the newer parts of town, the houses took on yards and fences and lost their porches. These home dwellers wanted privacy, so they put patios or decks on the backs of their houses and turned away from the town common.

"Twentieth-century man has achieved the sense of privacy in his patio, but in so doing has lost part of his public nature which is essential to strong attachments and a deep sense of belonging," the scholar Richard H. Thomas wrote in his seminal 1975 essay "From Porch to Patio."

With the whole of my legs aching, I lay in the tub that night thinking about that weird satori and letting the hot water soak me until it turned cold. Night after night, I absorbed the carnal pleasures of my lodgings as the exotic luxuries they were, beyond the dreams of any soldier or settler or wandering penitent, with abundant hot water and plush beds with multiple pillows. If there were granola bars or packets of instant oatmeal on hand, I ate them, ravenously. I fell into bed exhausted a little after ten and woke usually well before sunlight, with time to write and think about the day before. The first three days, more than sixty miles. Another twenty or so on the fourth day. I would tumble into bed spent and wake replenished. Among all daily miracles, the renewing power of sleep ranked high in its ability to astonish.

CHAPTER 5

WALKING THE LINE

On a brisk morning that chilled the fingers, I set off to walk to a line drawn by a man named Mason and a man named Dixon, an invisible line that cuts through fields and woods, and one I hoped to walk when I got there. Most of the countryside in between was rolling hills and hollows studded with sturdy old farmhouses built by Germans. You could feel the flintiness of each settlement when you passed it, even now, the resolve to replace wood with stone and to add that extra loft to the barn. The clouds were too thick to allow for shadows but by late morning they broke up and let some sun pour through.

Charles Mason and Jeremiah Dixon didn't know it at the time, but they crossed the Atlantic in November 1763 to scrawl their names across the heart of America. Far-flung forces brought them to Philadelphia and thus made them central to the national story.

It started, of all things, with the transit of Venus across the face of the sun two years earlier. Astronomers eager to calculate the sun's distance from Earth sailed to all corners of the globe that year to make precise measurements of how long it took, from their latitude, for Venus to cross the face of the sun. Among the stargazers were the newly formed team of Mason and Dixon, who made their tabulations from an observatory they built on the Cape of Good Hope after a naval battle kept them from getting to Sumatra.

Mason was the son of a baker from Gloucestershire. His father baked bread while the son studied math and applied it to the skies. The meticulous Mason labored over lunar tables to help mariners determine their longitude at sea, among the greatest puzzles of the eighteenth century. Dixon, five years his junior, was "the son of a Quaker colliery owner of Cockfield," as one historian put it. He, too, had a fondness for astronomy and surveying.

Their Venus measurements helped scientists place the sun 95 million miles from Earth, a measurement that fell just one million miles shy of the actual distance. Their good works earned the pair a royal commission to go resolve once and for all a rancorous border dispute between Maryland and Pennsylvania that had festered for a century. We still measured exact lines on Earth at the time by aligning them with the stars, which is why Mason and Dixon came to Philadelphia to sketch that line with two precision telescopes, clocks, lengths of chain, wooden stakes, and stone markers carved with the Calvert and Penn coats of arms. They placed those crownstones, as they were called, every five miles.

Because of Venus tracing a course across the sun, in other words, Mason and Dixon came to draw their line across a molten swath of America.

After they finished laying out their work in 1767, neither Mason nor Dixon was talked about much. Dixon vanished into obscurity and was buried, at forty-five, in an unmarked grave not far from his birthplace. Mason wrote a dejected letter to Benjamin Franklin after the English surveyor washed back into Philadelphia in 1786, having decided to stake his claim in the youngest of new countries. "Sir, I have a family of Wife seven sons and a Daughter all in a very helpless Condition as I have been confined to my Bed with sickness Ever since I came to town which is twelve Days," he wrote.

He died a month later, at fifty-eight. His grave at Christ Church Burial Ground in Philadelphia remained unidentified for 226 years, after which a displaced marker from the Mason–Dixon Line was put there to commemorate his mortal remains. We don't know why Mason abandoned England for the infant America with his unwieldy family, nor why neither his children nor any of the generations after ever sought to give him a proper memorial.

Mason and Dixon sprang back to life in 1820, when an inflamed Congress fought over whether to allow Missouri into the Union as a slave state. The nasty work of codifying where slavery existed and where it didn't revived interest in the line those two men drew. Just shy of a hundred years after they began to draw that line, General Robert E. Lee and other divisions of the Confederate army crossed it on their one unbridled plunge into the North. They were rebuffed at Pickett's Charge and never came back.

As I rambled along Grave Run Road heading north toward that line, the route took a long dip into trees and finally crossed a stream where I passed a man out walking his dog. It is fascinating, when walking, how even small streams announce their presence far in advance as you begin to descend into the valley that the running water carved. I stopped to admire a huge hewn-log house that stood high on stone footings off the road when the man with his wiry-haired dog came up the road breathing steam and said, "That's my house," proud of it and clearly wanting to talk. His name was Shipley. He wore an old REI rain slicker and had a couple of small loops of silver through his right ear.

"Built by Germans," he said. Which Germans, or when, he didn't quite know, "but I have seen the house marked with a little box on a map from 1834."

Shipley told me the house once had two front doors side by side until it was replaced with just one. "One was for the living to go in and out of day after day, and the other was for the dead to go out of just once on their way to being buried."

I later learned that Shipley's story was common folklore, but I kept thinking about those doors and how strange it would be to go in and out of the one all your life with the other door just waiting to receive you.

Late in the morning, with some slivers of sunlight cracking through the clouds, I took a right up a hill along a tiny road I had gone out of my way to find. Young Man's Fancy Drive was to take me to some tiny hamlet I had seen on Google Maps, a place I could find no records of anywhere else, called Young Man's Fancy. The humorous name, the fancy of it, and the lack of any traceable backstory had made a visit here a must.

I had departed Washington in part to walk through Young Man's Fancy.

The road snaked up behind houses and then bent sharply at the top of the hill and seemed to vanish into the back of a barn. A woman stood beside that barn barking instructions to a truck driver delivering a premade log cabin on the back of a flatbed. She squinted at me as the oddity I was, appearing out of nowhere and heading somewhere else.

I shouted, above the growl of the truck: "Where is Young Man's Fancy?"

She cupped a hand around her ear and said, "Come again?"

My voice wasn't great. I barked again: "Young Man's Fancy. Where is it?"

"You're in it," she said. "This is it."

I didn't understand. There was really nothing there other than a long red barn, a muddy track, and a two-story stone farmhouse that looked across forested hills through windows whose trim was painted a dull red.

"Where?" I said.

"Right here. This farm of mine is Young Man's Fancy."

She explained it had been called that since its creation in the early 1800s, but she didn't know why. We live within stories whose origins we don't know. I know roughly when my house was built, but not exactly when, and have no idea whatsoever about who dug the foundation or sunk the first nails. The man I'd met along the road that morning, Shipley, knew his house was built by Germans, but not which Germans. This woman didn't know the roots of the curious name given to her farm. She didn't know the young man, or the precise nature of his fancy.

Up a dirt lane dotted with puddles, up a fancy drive that wasn't fancy, I cut into the cemetery outside St. Paul's Church, which gave the dead a fine view of surrounding farms and forests. I wandered among the headstones and found something odd. The early stones gave great weight to every day. They made a point of noting not just the deceased's dates of birth and death, but their exact number of years, months, and days, in case anyone questioned the importance of each spin of the Earth. Poor Christiana Roth died on April 19, 1881, "Aged 85 yrs, 11 mos & 22 days." Tiny Malinda Walker died August 26, 1870, "Aged 5 mo. & 11 days." As I crouched before those stones, I saw that the practice of counting every day vanished around the time of World War I. Then the dead were simply allotted their bookend dates. I walked on, wondering if those events—the war, the airplanes, the trenches, the mustard gas—had upended the pace of life in a way that made the precise tally of one's months and days less relevant.

———◆———

To get to that church after stepping out into the morning mist, I had walked up Brick Store Road to Upper Beckleysville Road to Falls Road to Grave Run Road to Shaffer Mill Road to Young Man's Fancy Drive to St. Paul's Road, heading in a wavering path that hewed generally north. I turned then onto Gunpowder Road and took a left onto Baker House School Road, which went down into a hollow with a wide horse meadow and white farmhouse—half wooden, half stone—beneath a towering elm, still bare of any leaves.

I was very much in a border region now, not more than a couple of miles from Pennsylvania. Half an hour's walk or so from that line that Mason and Dixon drew that came to divide free America from its enslaved other half.

When you walk the little roads in these parts—roads named for mills, falls, stores, churches, schoolhouses—you see the courage it took to try to escape slavery and the terror involved in scrambling over these hills and through these woods to get to the mythical North. Even if you have nothing in common with those fleeing souls but feet, lungs, and eyes, being on those roads reveals the profound uncertainties they faced. Whether the man or woman in that farmhouse over there was friend or foe. Whether they would feed you or turn you in. Whether that young man on a horse on the ridge would drag you into the woods. Whether that dog yapping behind the house might lunge your way. What was the Underground Railroad but a system of way stations of people known to be good?

And how foreign the idea that once you crossed a certain line, across that patch of meadow or over that fallen limb or that bend in the stream, your status as a human being changed. There was no break whatsoever in the continuum of stream or forest or meadow or hill but only the beginning of a shift—a theoretical shift—in the mentality and the manners and the laws and the attitudes of the people who lived there.

That is what made laws like the 1850 Fugitive Slave Act so grotesque. So worth fighting a war over. It's why that war broke out eleven years later. Because with the passage of that law, even though you had crossed over that line into the land of the free and had gone hundreds of miles north of it, maybe even all the way to Maine, you could still be captured by federal marshals and put in manacles and dragged back to the other side. Even though you were now in the free states, the federal government was now charged with enforcing the laws that enslaved you in the South. The government had declared a section of the country free, but then muddied that declaration and made it moot.

This was a band of the country where that back-and-forth, that tension for flight and for capture, was rawest over more than a century.

The liberal sprawl of Washington and Baltimore were far behind me now. I had entered a patch of the country where, the previous November, more than six out of ten votes had gone for Donald Trump.

A little after noon I slipped through the doors of the Watering Hole Pub in Freeland, Maryland, within a well-hit baseball of the border. The fence on the far side of the dirt parking lot had a sign, three feet high and eight feet wide, offering Milwaukee's Best Premium beer, fifteen to a pack, for $7.80. Next to it hung a Trump sign of the same size, bright blue, offering to Make America Great Again. It surprised me, barely five months after the election and not yet three since the storming of the Capitol, that this was the first such sign I had seen in four days.

The light of day poured into the bar and then vanished as the door swung closed behind me. I picked a stool. Two men sat at the bar scratching out little numbers on keno cards. They glanced at me when I entered and then looked away, waiting to see if their numbers popped up on the screen. They had piles of torn cards in front of them, little remnants of disappointment as they drank their beers.

MASK REQUIRED WHEN STANDING said a sign on the wall. Barb the bartender brought me a Budweiser, and then a cheeseburger in a red plastic basket with fries. I asked for mustard and ketchup, and she asked where I'd come from, and when I told her I had walked over three and a half days from my house near the Capitol in Washington, she looked at me more closely and said: "Do you work at the Capitol? Are you a lawyer or a judge or something?"

Neither, I said. Just a writer out walking. "Huh," Barb said. "Interesting."

I ate every scrap of that burger and every fry. I even said yes to Barb's offer of a second beer. Barb and the guys at the bar talked of small stuff in little bursts as the random numbers flashed and the keno cards stacked up. Who'd been in lately, who hadn't. What the weather looked like with the weekend coming on. Whether they wanted anything to eat. I was glad for the food and drink, but far more so for my unfettered freedom as I reshouldered my pack and went back into the afternoon and kept going north. The wet chilly air, the churning clouds, one man's fancy as to what the next bend might bring: it was all right there, one step out the door, and yet a world apart from the grinding stillness inside. I gave the sky a little punch of joy.

<hr />

In a few minutes the road curved to the right and suddenly I was in York County, in Pennsylvania, heading due east on a road that was the Mason–Dixon Line itself. Steltz Road it was called, and it cut through a cemetery, with some of the dead buried in Pennsylvania and some in Maryland, and I walked the double yellow line like Dorothy with her little dog until an oncoming car shooed me to the shoulder.

When the road bent to the north toward the town of New Freedom, I stood in astonishment at the bend, marveling at how a small dirt lane kept on straight and dipped across a large field, and then cut through the middle of a very old farm. I stood there for a long time looking down the lane to see if there was any sign of life. Then I skirted the edges of the forest along a shorn cornfield and came to the farm by the back way, arriving first at a two-story cattle barn. It was a farm and a place I will long remember.

Probably sixty or so years after Mason and Dixon had done their work, some ambitious and industrious soul had come to this place and built this farm on both sides of the line they drew. I learned later that his name was Krebs, newly arrived from Germany to an area thick with other Germans. There are Krebses scattered all over the area now. This Krebs put two smaller red barns in Maryland, but the three-story stone house he built solidly and with great pride fifteen feet or so to the north, in Pennsylvania.

Not a soul had lived there for years, from what I could tell, but you could feel the determination of those who came first. You could see the craftsmanship and the scale of their ambition. You saw it in the quarried stones meticulously assembled to build the barn. You saw it in the handmade hinges on the many barn doors, each slightly different in size or shape but serving the same purpose. The barn had eight large cow stalls, a jumble now of fallen timbers when I peered inside.

They had built a long balcony that ran nearly the width of the house, facing south, with the eaves shielding it from rain, all supported from within. You could imagine Mr. and Mrs. Krebs standing there when the place was new and shiny. Standing there one spring morning, looking from the free part of the country into the non-free part a few feet away. The crops coming up, the trees in bloom.

You wondered if they ever owned people here, and if not, if they had ever given refuge to anyone scrambling North. My guess was they had done neither as they milked their cows and tilled their fields, like that farmer in the Brueghel painting where Icarus falls unnoticed.

———◆———

It began to snow as I went on, and my phone battery died, taking my directions and coordinates with it. It was the first of April, and the snow came in horizontally on a strong wind and I doubled over in joy beside a pasture. Another bolt of rapture, as mentioned earlier, without clear cause other than the joy of walking through sudden snow in the second week of spring having just found that farmhouse and marveled at its unexpectedness and its beauty. I zipped my coat up and did a little shuffle on the slick road, feeling like the luckiest man alive. It took hours for me to get over that farmhouse.

I realized I was lost, that I was not on the right route and had to find someone who could set me straight. My destination for the day was over one of the surrounding hills, at an old inn with a suite named for a Confederate general, Stonewall Jackson. But my coordinates felt off, and I feared I was heading toward the wrong distant steeple. I came down a small lane and found a burly man of about seventy with a huge white beard—beard but no mustache— working in a barn stuffed with tractors, my first Pennsylvanian.

He introduced himself as Ken Keeny and shook my hand and invited me into the barn to get out of the slanting snow. Ken Keeny wore muddy leather boots and a very weathered Carhartt jacket. He was the spitting image of John Brown, and just like Brown he was brimming with peculiar convictions. I said I was out sniffing around to get a feel for where we Americans were heading, and with that he jumped right in.

"Evil is taking over," he said. "God apportions his love and care to countries that love him in return, and he is withdrawing that love now because we have strayed, and Satan is moving in. It's either one, or the other. God or Satan. We have to choose."

He cited as evidence of our demise not the horrors of slavery, as Brown had, but the fact that people born boys were becoming girls, or vice versa, and that abortions were freely available across the land. As he went on about the decline and destruction of the country, and how we had to protect Israel "because Jews are the chosen people," I kept looking at the decrepit farm structures across the road, all of them an unhealthy mossy green and slowly giving in to the forces of weather and gravity. Ken made it clear he liked Trump, "the most pro-life president in our history," but his favorite president by far, he said, was Abraham Lincoln. "Now that man governed during a time of real turmoil."

"You could call it that," I said.

Ken said he had joined a small upstart evangelical church recently, but I assumed he was of Mennonite stock. He could easily have played the role of an Amish elder in a movie like *Witness*. He mentioned he was an auctioneer, so we diverged from Satan when I asked him to do the auction prattle, which he did with great gusto as bursts of steam shot from his mouth.

"Can I get a ten-dy and a ten-dy and a ten-dy. There we go! Ten right there! Who can give me a fifteen, a fifteen, let me see a fifteen. Fifteen over there! Can I get a twenty, a twenty, a twenty." The shift in topic took us quickly to a different place.

He showed me all the tractors, seven in all including a gorgeous small red one going back to 1931, all of them set for auction that weekend and all owned, he said, by a farmer who had little time left.

"You know," Ken said, "this area of York County spilling over into Lancaster County is the auction capital of the world. We auction everything. Land, produce, hay, trucks, tractors. You name it, we auction it."

I found myself with Ken Keeny talking across what we now call a cultural divide. His world didn't allow for much wiggle room for the vagaries of birth or the built-in predilections that make us all different. Most of his views, if laid out on Facebook or Twitter, would strike me as abhorrent. You might call him a strict determinist. God assigned us our lot in life—our gender, our sexuality—and who were we to question that or stray from it? That wasn't how I saw things.

He knew his views were deliberately antique. They went back "to our best days as a nation," he said, back to before we'd begun to slip in our morals and our standards in the 1960s, as he saw it. He wasn't sure, when I asked, whether his view of God would ever become ascendant in America again. He looked up at the barn ceiling for a second and shook his head. "I don't see how it could."

By his definition, that also meant God would never bring back the love he'd showered on us in our best days. It was as if the whole country was rotting like the barns around us. A decade here or there and they would all topple over.

For all that, Ken wasn't convincing in his dreariness. If you asked about his tractors, his face brightened again, and he leaped back into talking up the 1941 Farmall M sitting beside us. He patted her big rear tire, a magnificent specimen of thick tread suitable for any muddy field. "She's a real beauty, and freshly repainted," he said. "She'll probably fetch three thousand dollars."

We had our differences, Ken and I, but also at that moment we had our common ground: a patch of dry dirt and hay packed with old tractors and sheltered from the swirling snow. I looked at that 1941 Farmall M and wanted it, even without a field to plow. She was a gorgeous piece of machinery.

When the goods needed selling, Ken Keeny was the man to sell them: land, produce, piles of old shovels, crops right out of the field. Restaurants with customers inside. Ken said he'd sold it all. He once auctioned off twenty semitrailers of hay lined up one after the other in a field outside Lancaster. "I'm the one who finds the best price someone is willing to pay, whoever they are, for whatever product I'm trying to sell."

———◆———

Before I left, Ken asked why I wasn't sleeping in the woods or sneaking into old barns like this for the night. "I'll tell you why," I said. "On account of a tick."

"Come again?" Ken said.

I told him how, the previous summer, I had often plucked tiny deer ticks off me after wandering the fields or woods on Maryland's Eastern Shore. One had squirted his venom in me, which I discovered much later was why my voice fell apart all at once at the end of August. Lyme disease had paralyzed my left vocal cord and turned my rumbling baritone into a wheezy whisper.

"That's why I talk a little weird," I said. "And I wasn't too keen on courting more ticks by sleeping in the woods."

That odyssey, too, had brought me to interesting places. I didn't tell Ken all this, but not talking well had its unexpected upsides, I found. People had to crane to hear me, so yarns and jokes and tableside diatribes were all out the window. When you can't talk well you really have to listen. You hear stories that are new to you—from your wife, your daughters, old friends. You listen more closely to the pond frogs at night, to the redwing blackbirds in the reeds, to the crickets that lingered in the trees all the way into early November. You note the night when the last of those crickets sang.

Loss has a strange way of bringing us things in return. My cancer gave me gifts I never expected. I became, for one, deeply attuned to trees. On every trip to the hospital, I would stand in silence before a stately elm in Georgetown and marvel at its grace in all seasons. I watched it go from a crepuscular tangle of arteries and veins in winter to a spring halo of luminescent green. I watched it leaf, strut its full summer green, go golden, shed its leaves, and stand bare again. Its symmetry and strength and quiet flamboyance spoke to me.

You can see intelligent design in an elm but still wonder at the insidious why of the tiny creatures that crawl in the grass.

I went back out into the snow, thin and billowing now, and stood there for a second looking back at Ken Keeny as he wiped his hands with a rag. I asked if he knew why we'd met and had this talk.

"No, why?"

"Because my phone battery died and forced me to find a human to show me the way. And you were that human."

"Glory be to God for that," Ken said as he tucked the rag in his pocket.

As we stood in that barn talking tractors and auctions and deer ticks, I was glad for my time with Ken, no matter how our views diverged. His directions for getting to my terminus for the night, the inn in the tiny hamlet of Railroad along the old rail line that snaked up to York, were rock solid.

"Going down that hill on the other side is likely to strain the legs some," he said, "but when you get to the bottom, take a right at the tracks and follow them straight into town."

I wished him a good auction and went on. Going down that road on the other side did strain the legs. When I got to the bottom, I took a right at the tracks, just as Ken said, and followed them straight into town.

CHAPTER 6

TWO TRACKS TAKEN

Vigilance against ticks wasn't the only lesson I learned during those months on the Eastern Shore. The converted barn where I had stayed sat beside a pond a few miles from a muddy field where momentous things happened a long time ago. I found the field digging through old maps and books, and then I kept going back, week after week, looking for the ghost of the young Frederick Douglass.

That field and all it had to say helped lay the ground for this walk. It drove home how in the remembrance of our past, we too often neglect the primacy of place and fail to honor the patches of earth where fateful events occurred. So much is plowed under, paved over, washed away.

Douglass devoted seven chapters in his three autobiographies to the single year he spent working that soggy patch of soil on the banks of the Chesapeake, on the farm of a ruthless overseer named Edward Covey. His owner had sent him to the Covey farm at sixteen as punishment for teaching others to read. He wanted to tame the youngster, but instead Douglass tamed the man hired to tame him. He had a brawl there, enslaved vs. enslaver, Douglass vs. Covey, that remains an emblematic moment in American history—"the most celebrated fight between a master and a slave in all of antislavery literature," as one historian called it.

When I found the place where all this happened—the setting for some of Douglass's most lyrical and searing prose—I was struck by its drab anonymity. Just a long rectangle of soggy corn stalks girded on one side by the highway and on the other by the eroding shoreline of the bay. Old battlefields often have an aura, even a beauty about them. This was just a blur of plowed land and a flicker of water to the passing motorist. No marker. No pullout spot along the highway. No remnant of his time. How could anything of importance have happened there?

My many visits to that field left me with the conviction that we should go about our days like itinerant archaeologists, kicking at stones and pulling back vines to see what is hidden there. That we should pay close attention to what the land, windblown and eaten away by the rain, tells us of where we have been.

———◆———

My friend Dante Chinni and I talked about this—the washing back and forth of memory and forgetting—as we set out early the next morning from the Jackson House Bed and Breakfast and headed straight up the railroad bed with a sharp wind in our face. A political writer, Dante had come up from Washington to join me for the morning's walk. We'd had a huge breakfast in the inn's little dining room. Outside, it was a few notches below freezing, so the puddles were brittle and crunched beneath our feet. The sky was a sharp blue dotted with clouds.

I mentioned stopping to see Einstein on the way out of Washington, and that got us talking about the nature of time and of gravity and whether time essentially ceases in a space free of gravity. If nothing pulls, if nothing moves or degrades or changes shape or form, of course there is no time. Just an everlasting stillness.

We talked, too, about whether one's joy in being alive can be made more potent the more we grasp the smallness of our time

on Earth and the insignificance of our status as individuals. We
both firmly agreed that the two are closely interconnected. That
the more fully we understand the brevity of our time, the greater
is our aperture for understanding the enormous grandeur of it.
Smallness, I once heard Pope Francis say from his balcony high
above St. Peter's Square, is the true path to salvation.

We are here to be good and to do no harm and to provide
light and warmth to others like the sun and not just leech it like a
moon, we resolved. But beyond all that we are here to bear witness
in the most fundamental way. To marvel and behold. To take it in.
To be present in a way that tilts toward rapture. We are great to the
extent that we contain the world's greatness.

There were good stretches when Dante and I didn't talk. We
ambled along the dirt lane that paralleled the tracks and gawked at
the barns and the proud rail stations, but mainly at the beauty of
Codorus Creek, which snaked north along those tracks for miles
and would take me into York.

We walked the railbed and thought of shovels, crowbars,
sledgehammers, mules in harness, drums of black powder. Sweat-
ing, sun-scorched men moving dirt and blasting rock and laying
the rails. Even the fine craftsmanship of the barns we passed spoke
to the pedestrian of the countless hours spent building them.

Workers broke ground on the tracks we were walking, the Baltimore and Susquehanna Railroad, in 1829—making it one of the
country's oldest. Their ambition was to run it all the way to the
banks of the Susquehanna at Wrightsville. The line made it up to
York, my destination for the night, with a connector to the river
in 1838. It became the Northern Central, then the Pennsylvania
Railroad, then the Penn Central. Then Hurricane Agnes in 1972
washed away bridges and tore up lengths of track, ending it all and
turning what we were on now into a trail for bikes and strollers.

When the Civil War broke out, bands of Southern-sympathizing
Marylanders targeted the Baltimore and Susquehanna, burning

bridges well up toward the Pennsylvania line. The war claimed its first combat fatalities a week after Fort Sumter, soldiers killed in the streets of Baltimore as federal troops tried to get from one train station to the next on the way to protect Washington. The first Union dead were all from Massachusetts. "First blood," people called them.

I had many destinations for this walk—the Ickes manor house, Young Man's Fancy, the line drawn by those two Englishmen—and another one came into view around eleven when we rounded a bend and saw the stately red-and-white Hanover Junction Station with a Stars and Stripes atop a high pole flapping in the breeze. Here the single set of tracks parted just before the station, with a spur to the left veering west toward Hanover and from there to Gettysburg, while the main line went on toward York.

Abraham Lincoln came this way on a gray, wet November 18, 1863. He was on his way to Gettysburg to give a short address—ten sentences in all—as the dead were so freshly buried from those three days of brutal fighting four and a half months earlier.

That morning, off to give that address, he took the track to the left. On an April morning not unlike this one a year and a half later, he came back again, now on the way to his burial in the Oak Ridge Cemetery in Springfield, Illinois. That day, he took the track to the right.

When he came this way in November, his train paused at Hanover Junction to wait for a delegation of governors who didn't show up. A boy who peered in the train window said he saw Lincoln stooped at a table, writing. A photo in the archives of the Library of Congress appears to show Lincoln in a long coat and top hat standing on the platform, but historians have never verified that was him and doubt the president ever stepped from the train here that afternoon. Could it have been another man who looked like Lincoln? He did make brief remarks at the next stop, in Hanover, ending with the line: "Well, you have seen me, and, according to general experience, you have seen less than you expected to see."

The success of the war and Lincoln's presidency hung in the balance that summer. Public opinion had soured in the North. Soldiers fighting to save the Union weren't so sure about fighting to free the slaves. A draft riot in New York that July turned into a bloody white-on-Black race riot, foreshadowing many more to come. Even with the Gettysburg win, Lincoln was heartsick that Union general George Meade let Robert E. Lee and the Confederates limp back into Virginia and didn't seek to end it all right there.

A mighty engine that shimmered in the sun pulled Lincoln's funeral train north on the tracks to the right. In all, a succession of forty-two engines powered that train through its twisting course to Harrisburg, to Philadelphia, through New Jersey to the Hudson. Everyone wanted their engine to pull the hallowed corpse. Sailors took his funeral car across the Hudson to New York on a ferry. At City Hall, men carried his coffin up a circular staircase. Half a million stood outside to view the body. It went like that in city after city. He traveled along the shores of the Great Lakes, to Cleveland, to Cincinnati and Indianapolis, up to Chicago and then finally to Springfield. One hundred and eighty towns and cities over twelve days. Newspapers along the way printed exactly when his train would pass through each small town. Throngs stood along the route hoping to touch the train, maybe even to see the coffin inside.

His wife, Mary, immobile with grief, didn't accompany Lincoln on his last trip. Only his son Willie did, in his own small coffin, en route from Washington's Oak Hill Cemetery to lay beside his father in Oak Ridge. Willie had died in the White House of typhoid fever at twelve, three years earlier, casting his parents into a deep gloom. With some modifications, the route to their final burial mirrored the triumphal trip—in reverse—that Lincoln took to his inauguration four years earlier.

Dante and I paused silently for a while on the steps of the station to honor the place and breathe in a very different morning at the start of another April. A few bikers rode by. We took pictures of one another on the station's platform, as travelers will. We continued up the tracks heading north. Going to Gettysburg myself would have been a couple of days' walk—thirty-one miles due west—and taken me well off my arc to New York. I pondered the detour but decided to stay the course.

Another friend, Aaron Zitner, joined us for lunch at a tavern in Seven Valleys and we clinked our glasses to salute that we were doing the once unthinkable—having lunch together around a small table inside a tavern. Amid the pandemic and all its restrictions, it was the first time either of them had done that in more than a year.

I watched with sympathy as Dante and Aaron got in a car and drove off. They would head south at high speeds, past exits and other abstractions, back to a city of polling numbers and demographic cohorts, while I would continue the other way along a dirt track with a railway and a creek winding beside it. You adapt so quickly to being on foot that it seems like a gift to set out after a lunch with another four hours to go. That is a long drive to New York but a short walk to York. Our time may be short, but we do have great powers to compress and elongate the minutes we have.

My friends had brought news of a great leafing underway in Washington, eighty miles to the south. As I kept going north, my pace had kept me just ahead of the leaf line. The fruit trees had flowered—the pears, the cherries—but none had begun to leaf. The willows were flashing a subtle green, and the maples had sprouted their bright crimson flowers. The full explosion, though, felt days away. I had picked the best possible moment to get on the move.

———◆———

In the months before heading out, I had obsessed over another springtime saunter that I ran across in the letters of Thomas Jefferson. No one talks about this little trip to Vermont in the spring of 1791, but the details of it, the why of it, the profound oddity of it in today's light spoke to the changing nature of whimsy and the attention we once paid to small things.

In May of that year, Thomas Jefferson and James Madison—two middle-aged founders of a nation and both slaveholders, lest we forget—set out to inspect the north country and examine a nasty infestation of Hessian flies that was decimating wheat crops. They did it because Philadelphia was confining and stuffy, and because Jefferson had a headache, and Madison felt dyspeptic. They had never been that way before and wanted to see something new.

"I think to avail myself of the present interval of quiet to get rid of a headache which is very troublesome by giving more exercise to the body and less to the mind," Jefferson said in a letter to President Washington, informing him of the trip. He was serving then as Washington's secretary of state; Madison was a Virginia congressman.

Jefferson, at forty-eight, was cash broke. To pay for the jaunt, he mooched money from Madison, who appeared perfectly glad to accompany his friend and serve as the trip's financier. Their precise route didn't concern him. He was fine going any old way. "Health recreation and curiosity being my objects, I can never be out of my way," he wrote to Jefferson on the eve of their trip.

Jefferson departed Philadelphia on May 17 in high spirits heading to his New York rendezvous with Madison. He would travel by coach, horse, ferry, and some by foot. He chronicled the basic facts in his book of accountings: "Set out from Philadelphia." Paid the ferryman twenty-three cents to cross the Delaware. And then came the most important moment of the day: "Heard the first Whip-poor-will."

Jefferson, as we know, had a flowing pen that put the final flourishes to the Declaration of Independence, but on this trip north his entries read like Dada. Of their travels on May 28, he noted: "Still water. Polypod. Saratoga. Ground oak. Fort Edward. The small red squirrel."

Everywhere he went he had an eye for the woods, the trees, the peculiarities of flora and fauna. His was the typical slow-paced and meticulous observation backed by an incipient sense of wonder and discovery. Sailing up Lake Champlain, he remarked on what was missing. "It is to be noted that we have seen no poplar, dogwood, nor redbud since we have passed the highlands, nor any fruit trees but apples and here and there a cherry tree. We have seen no persimmons in any place since crossing the Hudson."

Jefferson kept precise tables on the distances traveled and the quality of the roads and bridges along the way, ranking them as "good, midling, bad." They took detours to see waterfalls. They visited battlefields barely fourteen years old then, like Ticonderoga and Bennington. That part of New York and Vermont—the latter admitted just months earlier as the fourteenth state, and the first to ban slavery outright—was terra incognita to most Americans, and the Virginians looked upon it with the eyes of discoverers.

The whole trip north to Lake Champlain and back to New York cost the two men $153.51, according to Jefferson's minute accounting. On June 16, over breakfast in New York, they settled accounts, or nearly so. When he went on his own for Philadelphia, Jefferson still owed Madison $25.94.

It was all well worth it, though. The journey "has rid me of my head-ach, having scarcely had anything of it during my journey," Jefferson wrote to Washington soon after his return. Madison had suffered from terrible bouts of indigestion before the trip. But "Madison's health is very visibly mended," Jefferson said.

The two future presidents had sought recreation: to be refreshed, renewed, revived. Their monthlong ramble had done just that. They hadn't sat indoors, stooped at desks, fretting over the perfidy of the Federalists or cursing the name of Hamilton. They had shaken out their limbs and aired their lungs. They had noted the whip-poor-wills and the lack of persimmons and were the better for it.

———◆———

The rail line as I pushed on north crossed Codorus Creek on an old wooden trestle. You could see the creek shimmer between the weathered railroad ties. I stood and watched it flow around the bend and tried to spot, beside that fallen tree or behind that rock, the undulating shadow of a trout. It was strange, when I thought of it, how a dire diagnosis at the end of a summer four years earlier had reignited my desire to be around rivers. Rivers I'd never heard of not far from my house. Rivers in California and Montana and Wyoming. Rivers in the far south of Patagonia. How that diagnosis and all that followed—rather like Jefferson's headaches and Madison's dyspepsia—had sent me into the woods and put me on this path.

I went along briskly counting my strides, proud of my speed, and laughed at the humor of walking an old rail line, as railroads did more than any force in human history to obliterate the pedestrian. For centuries we have measured human progress by our transcendence over the walker's pace, unaltered since the first bipeds roamed the earth. The horse, the chariot, the chaise, the carriage, the stagecoach, the locomotive, the automobile, the faster train, the airplane, the rocket ship.

The first big leap—going on horseback—wasn't that momentous. Horses go far faster over shorter distances and can haul more weight and can sweep Mongol hordes across the steppes in a mighty wave. But horses don't greatly outpace a human over the course of a day. They had altered the pace of daily life but hadn't upended it.

Trains did that. They brought immediate enchantment and wonder but also dislocation and fear. A passenger aboard one of the earliest steam-driven trains, England's Liverpool & Manchester *Rocket* in 1830, compared the experience to a bird in flight. "When I closed my eyes this sensation of flying was quite delightful, and strange beyond description," the actress Fanny Kemble wrote to a friend.

The *Rocket* could clock thirty miles in an hour, well more than horse or human could comfortably cross in a day. By 1850, trains could top fifty miles an hour. The best stagecoach on the best road barely managed one-fifth of that.

But trains also brought disenchantment and a sense of disembodiment. It's no wonder the arrival of trains overlapped the time when Emerson and Thoreau and their ilk began to dream of transcendence and clamored for the woods. A train rumbled daily within miles of Walden Pond. The Romantics in England had preceded them there.

How slow the world had been before, how measured and open to tranquil musings. "The rapidity of our steamboats and railroad cars deprive us of a great many interesting sights and agreeable reflections, and prevent us from becoming particularly acquainted with any part of our country," wrote the English writer Theodore Dwight in his book *Things As They Are,* chronicling his journeys around America in 1834. "The improved vehicles undoubtedly have their advantages; but while I acknowledge this evident fact, I am not forgetful of those belonging to the old and slower modes."

The Train Age wasn't a decade old, and we were already mourning what was lost.

The same rail line that had once brought coal, iron, guns, machines, and whisky south, and cotton, corn, tobacco, molasses, and bolts of linen north, brought me into York on a late Friday afternoon. Close to a hundred miles in five days. I caught a whiff of creosote and burnt rubber. The tracks cut alongside a high stack of discarded cars and trucks, each bearing the scars of some past collision that had turned them into refuse. Factories and distribution warehouses sprang up. The once elegant and sinuous Codorus Creek, which had flickered for miles through the trees, reemerged now as a gaping concrete culvert designed to channel water.

I walked out of farmland America into what it would become. I was in York with plans to pause there for the day and take in one town through the eyes of three very different personalities.

CHAPTER 7

THE MEMORY BOOM

Jim McClure comes to breakfast like a general to war. He packs a battle plan, maps, charts, briefing papers. He has a revised PowerPoint nineteen slides long. He stands to shake my hand when I arrive at the Prince Street Café, then jumps right in. I barely have time to order coffee.

Jim came recommended as York's ultimate memory keeper, one of those people who knows what every parking lot held before the wrecking ball came. He's a rusty-haired former newspaper editor with a bushy mustache, half Pennsylvania Dutch, half Scots Irish. Raised in Kentucky, he came to York in 1989 to edit one of the town's two newspapers, an outsider turned insider who remains a bit of both. All his writings on York history, every cranny of it, would fill a shelf. You couldn't find a better guide.

Once an outpost on the wild frontier, York has many claims to distinction. It's the original home to York Peppermint Patties. York Barbells and its playboy owner Bob Hoffman put York on the bodybuilding map. Half of all the world's Harleys were once made here. The city was a major force in manufacturing munitions and other gear for the Allied war effort in World War II. A rump Congress adopted the Articles of Confederation in the courthouse in the main square, which now has neither a courthouse nor a square.

That act led the town to boast of being the country's first capital when it is, in reality, the fourth.

Jim could talk about all of this, but it wasn't top of mind. Hunched over his coffee, he cut to the quick on York's peculiar psyche as a proud but troubled hinge between North and South. "York was the largest city in the North that the Confederates took, and York willingly surrendered to those forces," he says in a hushed voice. The café is crowded. Billy Joel croons overhead. Jim doesn't want to impugn York too audibly.

The town fathers, he explains, sent a delegation out to welcome Confederate general Jubal Early and his troops and to escort them into town. The place was awash that late June afternoon in all the goods the rebels so badly needed. "Other towns surrendered grudgingly," Jim says. "York was different. We went out to greet the Confederates."

Jim looks out the window to where Early's men marched up Market Street on June 28, 1863. I hear the thud of boots and see a blur of muddy gray. "Right there, they lowered the American flag."

These moments, to the knowing, are alive all the time. Phantoms dart about town, as they do in any town with any depth of history. Jim knows all the phantoms, good and bad, as though on a first-name basis. He lives among them and is a prime force in summoning them back to life. Hauling up the dead. Rekindling the stories. Drawing the vital connections between then and now.

General Early requisitioned tens of thousands of shoes, hats, and socks from York, as well as $28,000 in cash he says was "furnished by the town authorities." He left York otherwise unmolested and wrote a departing note to tell York's citizenry why: "I trust the treatment you have met with at the hands of my soldiers will open your eyes to the monstrous iniquity of the war waged by your government upon the people of the Confederate States, and that you will make an effort to shake off the revolting tyranny under which it is apparent to all you are yourselves groaning."

To hear Jim tell it, the stain of that capitulation a century and a half ago still lingers. Or did until the city began to deal more plainly with the fullness of its past. The city had long celebrated its colonial roots and its role in the founding of the nation. It had long touted its contributions to the efforts during World War II. "But it took us a long time, a very long time, to get around to remembering and really thinking about the Civil War," Jim says.

York is in the midst of a memory boom now. It is shaking off its long amnesia and is digging up and chronicling and remembering and depicting and translating into art and murals every imaginable aspect of its past, good and bad, comfortable and uncomfortable. This is not a fit of nostalgia for some golden time. Quite the opposite. It is an active and aggressive confronting of the past, both the paved-over scars but also the unheralded heroes and forgotten giants. Some national version of this, I thought, would be so good for the national psyche.

Jim briefs me on the basics. When Mason and Dixon drew their line, York County's southern border constituted almost a third of it. No county had a wider exposure across the slavery divide. Nearby counties to the south, particularly in Virginia, had some of the region's highest concentrations of slave ownership. Major spurs of the Underground Railroad ran right through York. The county traded with and looked to the South. It voted against Lincoln in 1860. Even more so in 1864. In 2020, among all counties in the state, York gave Trump his biggest raw-vote margin, with nearly twenty thousand more than he got in 2016. Old patterns hold.

The reawakening of York's memory happened in spurts. The preservationist phase began nearly half a century ago, when the city elders realized that at the corner of Market Street and North Pershing Avenue stood an ice cream and soda shop that was, beneath its tacky façade, a one-of-a-kind half-timber building whose design flowed straight from medieval Germany.

Known as the Golden Plough Tavern, it was by many years

the oldest structure in the city, built in 1741 but forgotten and neglected until more than two centuries later. It was, for that matter, one of the oldest colonial-era structures west of the Susquehanna. Beside it stood the General Horatio Gates House, built twenty-four years later, also forgotten and also—like the Golden Plough—lovingly brought back to its original form.

Both had seen a multitude of dramas, exhumed and talked about now, and tussled over like family legends. It was there in the Gates house, in an upper room I wandered through the night before, that the twenty-year-old Marie-Joseph Paul Yves Roch Gilbert du Motier de La Fayette—the Marquis de Lafayette—rose to give a famous toast one night in early 1778, during General Washington's winter of discontent.

Years before Washington journeyed north to his inauguration, he was back on his heels in a squalid camp to the east of here, in a place called Valley Forge. He and his Continental Army had suffered a string of losses the fall before. The British had shoved him across the Delaware and taken Philadelphia, pushing Congress to scurry across the Susquehanna and reconnoiter here in tiny York. Rumblings of opposition to Washington's leadership had begun to stir among some generals and others, who gathered that night for dinner in the Gates house.

Lafayette claims he quieted the murmurings of doubt with a well-timed raising of his glass. "I arose from my chair and referred to the numerous toasts that had already been offered in the interests of the American government and the prosecution of the war," he wrote decades later in a posthumously published memoir. "Then I reminded all present that there was one toast that had not yet been drunk. I then proposed the health of the commander-in-chief at Valley Forge. After I had done this, I saw the faces of the banqueters redden with shame."

A bronze statue of the strapping Lafayette, cup raised impishly aloft, stands now outside the Gates house. He wore a COVID mask when I walked by him the night before. Some question, of course, whether that toast ever happened, but Jim McClure thinks it did.

Jim takes me out to walk through all the absences and to point out what used to be. The magnificent school that used to be right here, now a parking lot. The ornate hotel that used to be over there, also a parking lot. In the 1960s and '70s, preservation and destruction had traveled hand in hand, with the destructive forces usually just a little bit swifter. "There was a parking lot panic," Jim says. "The suburbs were booming. The town thought it had to fight back with places to park."

Cars have goosed our amnesia in so many ways.

This human thread of past passions and conflicts, of migrations and striving and conflict, of love, longing, and the urge to get ahead, ran through every block. Thousands of freed or escaped Blacks streamed into York over the decades before and after the Civil War. In the 1920s and '30s, many came north from a single county—South Carolina's Bamberg County, all part of the Great Migration.

Block after block, Jim walks me through a narrated tour of a multiday explosion of racial violence in 1969 that had both sides opening fire on the other from sidewalks and house windows. Dozens were injured. A white cop, Henry Schaad, and a young Black woman, Lillie Belle Allen, were shot and killed. Not until thirty-two years later did the county bring charges. Three men were convicted in the killing of Schaad, and nine in the killing of Allen.

Afterward, Jim says I must go meet with another of the town's great memory keepers.

———◆———

Samantha Dorm is in her fifties, a grant consultant to law enforcement, the fourth generation of her family to live in York. She meets me among the gravestones at Lebanon Cemetery, where I find her standing in a red knit overcoat on a hillside with a view of a nearby Motel 6, an interchange of Interstate 83, and the spires of the city to the south. Before I know it, she's down on one knee, pulling the thick turf back from the bronze marker of a child buried at our feet, after a few months of life, in 1954.

"The earth is working all the time to gobble up these little markers," Samantha says. "It's a constant battle keeping them uncovered."

Lebanon Cemetery is where York's deceased Black residents, including many of Samantha's own grandmothers, aunts, and cousins, went to be buried for more than a century beginning in 1872. Before Lebanon, they were either interred in tiny plots beside country churches or tossed in the town's Potter's Field.

Samantha and some friends started tidying up the place in 2019. Before that, she would come every year or so to lay flowers beside the graves of two of her grandparents. As she and her friends tidied, they began noticing things. Headstones that had sunk into the earth. Plots that lacked markers. As they noticed things and started poking around and probing the soil and asking questions, they noticed still more things, and the cemetery began to devour entire days and weeks of their lives.

They inventoried every headstone and then went month by month through online obituaries and found that at least a thousand people were buried at Lebanon who had no markers noting their existence. Samantha and her team bought metal detectors, swept the ground, and found metal markers and even tombstones that had sunk two and three feet underground. They unearthed those memorials, and hence the lives and stories, of veterans who had fought in every war including the one between the States. Relatives came to stand beside those markers. Some of them wept. They reunited, in some cases, with people they hadn't known existed.

Samantha and her workmates began to look at some of the more imposing gravestones and ask, "Wait, so who is this person? Why was he or she given such an elaborate marker? Why is this couple buried here, near this couple? Why are these graves clustered so close together?" Many of the deceased were among the first generation to have come of age after the Civil War, the very Blacks that so many whites had worried might never do well, if left to their own devices.

What Samantha found when she did the research were not just unknown connections and family ties among the dead, but a whole generation of eminent Black York citizens whose lives and accomplishments had been largely forgotten. Abolitionists. Underground Railroad conductors. Preachers and orators. Businessmen. Police officers. The first woman ever ordained as an elder in the AME Zion Church, Mary J. Small. Military veterans who had done brave things in battle. The man who, as a boy, had laid a wreath of roses on Lincoln's casket when his funeral train arrived in York on that long trip to Illinois.

"Suddenly I realized," she says, "that we were standing among kings and queens. We're standing among them right now, all of these great and accomplished people."

She began, amid all this, to stumble upon threads of her own family story. A great-grandmother buried here she knew nothing about, even though Samantha was ten when she died and had played on the same street as a little girl where that great-grandmother lived. A great-aunt and -uncle whom no one had ever mentioned. She discovered branches of her family that created whole lines of cousins she wasn't aware of. In 2019, when she first came to do some tidying here, she knew of a handful of direct relatives buried at Lebanon Cemetery. She now knows of well over a hundred relatives buried in that ground.

"This place is filled with my family," she says. "They are everywhere."

I ask her how all this forgetting could have happened. How could a whole community in York have let so many stories slip away? She's not quite sure she has an explanation. "I can tell you whose kid went to prison but not whose kid graduated from college," she says. "We just don't celebrate accomplishment like we should."

I ask if there are other Lebanon cemeteries across the country, with similar stories being devoured by the grass, and she lets out a loud sigh. "There are thousands of them. In the South, in the North. Everywhere. So much forgotten history that needs to be brought back."

Late in the day, I go to see Michael Helfrich, the mayor of York, in his eighteenth-century stone hobbit house along the banks of Codorus Creek. A Johnson Controls factory rises on the far side of the creek, and across from that, the Dentsply factory, a maker of false teeth. You pass a block of scrappy row houses, then a basketball court with the nets missing, and suddenly across a stretch of grass beside a chain-link fence sits the mayor's house, as if it just landed there all by itself from 260 years ago.

The mayor throws open the door and says, "Welcome, welcome." His blondish hair is slicked back to a tight ponytail and he's excited, not so much because of me but because he just found a mysterious scrap of parchment tucked within a two-volume history of York from 1907. The parchment is at least twice as old as the book and covered in an elaborate German script.

The mayor of York lives for moments like this. "It's a powwow. Very unusual. Quite an amazing find." When I reach to touch it, he swats my hand aside. "Very brittle," he cautions.

By powwow, he means the German folk magic and faith healing passed down for generations among the Pennsylvania Dutch. They sailed over as starchy Lutherans or Mennonites who shunned the incense of the Papists, but that doesn't mean they scrapped the old forest magic or left behind the works on alchemy and magical spells by Albertus Magnus, the German mystic and doctor who died in 1280.

The word "powwow" they borrowed from the Algonquins, but the origins of its myriad cures go back to the early mists of the European Middle Ages. Some of its inspirations sprang straight from the Bible, like the incantation for proper bloodletting, fetched from Ezekiel 16:6. "And when I passed by you and saw you struggling in your own blood, I said to you in your blood, 'Live!' Yes, I said to you in your blood, 'Live!'"

The mayor apologizes for his German as he begins to translate from the scrap of parchment. "This says, 'A Break to Heal.' It basically instructs how you drill a hole in an apple tree and then you put something inside it—I'm not sure what that word means—and then you recite certain names, and it will heal a broken bone, probably for both humans and animals. It's a spell, like a mix of Christianity and witchcraft."

If America has fifteen thousand mayors from sea to sea, I doubt another is quite like Michael Helfrich. He joined the communal and nature-revering Rainbow Family as a seeker of peace and love in the 1980s, and dropped acid among Oregon's towering redwoods. He lived for years in a van. He spent a dozen years as chief steward of the Lower Susquehanna, working to protect that mighty gorge. When he bought his house twelve years ago for $60,000, he was a lean Spartan who lived with nothing in a tiny apartment. "I had some tie-dye and some crystals." Now almost everything he owns is from the eighteenth century, even his bed.

The full regalia of a minuteman hangs from a peg by his front door. On a small bench beneath it rests a Revolutionary War canteen, knife, powder horn, hatchet, and handful of lead slugs, all ready to go at a moment's notice. In a nearby drawer, he has a copy of the *Pennsylvania Gazette* announcing the just-drafted Articles of Confederation, as if hot off the press. He has a 1792 edition of Thomas Paine's *Common Sense* and is paging through it right now, seeking a salient passage.

Michael Helfrich, it must be said, is passionate about Thomas Paine. Paine is why he leaped to buy the Cookes House, erected by one Johannes Guckes (who later changed his name to Cookes) as a mill house in 1761. Mike bought the house because he's convinced, having studied every scrap of the public record closely, that Paine wrote early drafts of at least part of *American Crisis No. 6* there in the late spring of 1778, just after the French sided with the rebels and the English were looking to pull out of Philadelphia.

You know the opening fanfare of Paine's first *Crisis,* published just days before Washington crossed the Delaware that frosty Christmas of 1776: "THESE are the times that try men's souls. The summer soldier and the sunshine patriot will, in this crisis, shrink from the service of his country . . ." and so on. *No. 6,* written a year and a half later and possibly right here beside Mike's fireplace, begins on a more partisan note: "THERE is a dignity in the warm passions of a Whig, which is never to be found in the cold malice of a Tory."

Paine is Mike's North Star. "This is pretty much everything ever written about Thomas Paine," he says, sweeping his hand along an entire shelf of books, many of them printed when Paine was still alive. Mike reveres Paine—and Jefferson and Franklin, too—but loathes Washington and Adams, who he sees as sellouts. The Jay Treaty, the Alien and Sedition Acts, they gall him to this day. "I mean, c'mon."

"Paine was one of the world's greatest fighters for human dignity, the truest champion of human meritocracy," the mayor says.

If he were to make America great again, I ask, what moment would we have to go back to? Mike doesn't miss a beat. "Our greatest moment was in 1781." Mind you, that's when the British

surrendered at Yorktown but eight years before Washington became president. We weren't really even a country yet. "As soon as
you defeat your enemy you turn back to your differences."

We go outside to sit by his fire pit. Deep in its wide trough
the Codorus spills over a small waterfall behind us and the mayor
lights a cigarette. An osprey hovers, looking for prey. Things turn
philosophical. Mike says he is a "psychedelic Christian Buddhist"
and then gives his two-line synopsis for our purpose on Earth.
"We are all God's mirrors. We are here so that God can enjoy his
existence through us." I nodded when he said that. It echoed what
Dante and I had talked about the day before, that we're on Earth
to bear witness to the wonders of the place. I had come to that
conviction myself over the past few years.

I mention how Jim talked about York's surrender to the Confederates, and the mayor bristles. It's a long-festering sore. "We
had no choice," he says. "We saved our factories and mills, which
helped the Union forces for the next two years. That surrender was
a long-term win."

Does his obsession with Paine and such make him a better
mayor? I ask. "No more so than the acid I dropped years ago," he
says, flicking his cigarette in the fire pit.

Later he clarifies that response, saying his knowledge of all York's
discord over so many centuries has better equipped him to soothe
current tensions and wrestle with the city's many challenges.

The mayor lives on the outer edge of town. Often at night in
the nearby neighborhoods, he hears gunshots. Twelve people were
murdered the previous year in York, a town of forty-six thousand.
The poverty rate among Blacks hovers stubbornly around 20 percent and still higher for Hispanics, little improved in decades. The
town's finances are crap. The mayor is working to sell the waste-
water treatment plant to clear up York's debt woes. More than
Thomas Paine or all that happened after 1781, these are the things
that try a mayor's soul.

Paine's own earthly fate, we must add, wasn't good. His 1791 *Rights of Man* was a global bestseller. Things began to slide after that. He became embroiled in the French Revolution, was tossed in a cell at the Luxembourg Prison, and barely escaped with his head. He published a bitter *Letter to George Washington* in 1796, accusing his onetime hero of treachery, ineptness, and more. When he died, in New York, in 1809, six people attended his burial. A one-paragraph obituary ran in various papers, stuck among the marriage notices and the shipping news. "I am unacquainted with his age," it read, "but he had lived long, done some good, and much harm." An English admirer ten years later secretly dug up Paine's remains and spirited them to England to be properly honored. Except they never were. The admirer died. The bones got lost. Legend has it that some were turned into buttons.

Historians since have been far kinder to his memory. "In a fundamental sense," wrote one, "we are today all Paine's children."

I shivered walking back to my little rented room that night along the yawning Codorus Creek. Not because of any chill but from a sense that ghosts were scampering about town.

A couple of months earlier, after I'd published an essay about that field where Frederick Douglass had his famous brawl, the owner of the land nailed NO TRESPASSING signs to all the fence posts along the road, to keep away the curious.

Here in York, the opposite was happening. Fences were coming down and the memories freed.

CHAPTER 8

THUNDERBIRD, WALKING MAN

On a bright Easter morning, I left the city of York along a road that would take me to another walking man, a far older one with huge hands and feet, carved into an enormous gray rock many hours east. On a day of rebirth and reawakening, early in the month of flowering, I was off to stand on a sacred rock in the middle of the Susquehanna, my first big river on the way.

Easter tells a story of death and resurrection all in three days, aptly set in the month that brings the dead back to life. I got to thinking about April, Chaucer's month for pilgrimaging, and the joy of walking through it. No month brings more commotion, more drama and volatility. Shakespeare was born in April and lavished it with love. "O, how this spring of love resembleth / The uncertain glory of an April day / Which now shows all the beauty of the sun / And by and by a cloud takes all away." The curmudgeonly T. S. Eliot saw deeper contradictions. The cruelest month, he called it, "breeding lilacs out of the dead land, mixing memory and desire, stirring dull roots with spring rain."

Birds were out but hardly a soul wandered anywhere as I passed a church whose steps spilled down to the street. A mother stood there with a tall, overstuffed suitcase on little wheels. She had two daughters, the younger of which had just started to walk and carried a stuffed animal in her arms. Her older sister was less than four. The sidelong, guarded way those two girls looked at me stuck in my head for blocks until I turned back, ashamed. They had clearly spent the night outside, and maybe many nights before that. I offered the mother a bag of two muffins and a banana that a café owner had given to me the afternoon before. She looked at me skeptically, a little shocked, but took the $20 bill I also offered. She had a dark star tattooed beside her left eye. She took the cash and then slowly reached for the bag. Her daughters immediately stuffed their hands inside and pulled out the muffins, which they began to devour. That little family haunted my morning.

Ten minutes later I passed an old woman standing on her stoop in a nightgown with a cane. She wished me a happy Easter and said her husband had died thirty-eight days before from COVID, as though she'd been counting each day. "He had a bad heart condition and then he got pneumonia with the COVID and that took him down," she said, her eyes still moist. She had to be eighty.

A walker comes along, a complete stranger, and she tells the passerby of her worst pains.

She refused to believe I was walking to Wrightsville and from there to New York. "No, you're not," she said with a knock of her cane on brick. I swore I was. She narrowed her eyes and almost with a whisper, just to test me, she asked, "Do you *really* think you'll make it?" I said I thought I would.

"But do you know where you will sleep every night? Do you at least know that?" She was a tiny bit distraught. I assured her I did know where I would sleep night to night. "That's good. You should always know where you will sleep. God bless you."

I took her blessing and went on. Ted, four days before, when informing me that I was on a holy walk, told me I should always have a destination. This woman on the edge of York said I should always know where I would sleep. It may be gallant to hit the open road, they seemed to be saying, but c'mon, let's go about it with a little common sense.

———◆———

Leaving a good-size town like York is slightly different from leaving a city like Washington. The development patterns aren't the same, just as different types of trees have different rings when you cut them. You walk out of York past the old chockablock worker housing along the main street heading out of town, the town houses where the cobblers and bricklayers once lived set one next to the other. That gives way to the slightly spaced well-to-do houses with their neat lawns and porches, most still inhabited by people with the occasional flag flying that tells you something of the tribe inside.

After that, you come to the still larger old manor houses with bigger yards and porticos where a carriage might once have stood. These had been turned into the workplaces of chiropractors and undertakers and tax accountants and drug treatment counselors. They attempt to preserve a certain sedate classiness with their upkeep and their signage, knowing there is some tradition to uphold.

Then those houses peter out into what was once countryside but is now a dreary expanse of the familiar outlets providing donuts, sandwiches, gasoline, coffee, burritos, quick lubes, new tires, all provided by corporate America for the fleeting needs of the people. Those then cede the onetime pastures to the goliaths, the gray and white boxes, the stores that attempt to contain everything within their walls. Not just Bed, not just Bath, but also Beyond. The land of Walmart, Kmart, Target. You can feel small as a walker passing these structures, or you can feel proud, and tall, like an aboriginal passing a tent encampment of invaders who will soon be gone.

It wasn't until I put behind me a collection of houses about six miles out that I broke into something still resembling countryside and suddenly smelled hay and alfalfa and cow manure and took a deep breath and lengthened my stride. I was back in farm country again. Billowy clouds cast shadows like dark islands on the plowed fields and every now and then I passed a stone house that had once catered to the carriage trade or served warm ale.

As the miles slipped by, I kept looking for some sign of a big river ahead, the arrival of a horizon that would speak to a vast valley. But surprisingly, for all its girth and power, the Susquehanna hasn't carved much of a trough in the land. You don't see the river until suddenly you do, coming over a rise on the edge of Wrightsville. All at once, there it is, a wide swath of greenish water lit by the midday sun. Two bridges cut across it with the footings in between them of three older bridges taken by fire, wind, and the hand of man.

Two cannons stood off to the side of the road beneath a high flag flapping in the wind. This neighborhood of brick apartment buildings marked the true high-water mark of the Confederacy, that moment in the early evening of Sunday, June 28, 1863, when the rebel forces thrilled for an hour or so, thinking their thrust north into the Union might end well, might break a path toward Harrisburg or Philadelphia. Might turn the tide of the war.

A thousand or so Union soldiers, some of them Black, squared off on this hillside from hastily dug trenches. The more numerous and battle-hardened rebel forces under General John Brown Gordon soon had the Union troops on the run. Desperate to keep the Confederates from crossing the river, they retreated to the covered bridge and then doused it with petroleum and set it ablaze. The bridge was a wonder of effort and design. It ran for more than a mile over twenty-seven stone piers, with a track for horses and carts and another for trains, the longest such bridge in the world.

The blaze raged so bright it could be seen in the night sky from both York and Lancaster.

The *Philadelphia Inquirer*'s man on the spot gaped at what he saw. "Some of the arches remained stationary even when their timbers were all in flame, seeming like a fiery skeleton bridge whose reflection was pictured in the water beneath. The moon was bright, and the blue clouds afforded the best contrast possible to the red glare of the conflagration."

Torching that bridge was an enormous but essential sacrifice. The Confederates scrapped all hopes of advancing deeper into the Union. Five days later, Robert E. Lee lost at Gettysburg and fled back into Virginia.

———◆———

I walked down to the riverbank and drank it in. I sat along the edge and put my hands and then my feet in the cold water and gave out a loud whoop, just to hear it echo against the nearby bridge. I had come to an ancient demarcation, a great barrier beyond which once stretched the American frontier. As late as the early 1700s, the maps at this water's edge ran out of things to say and things to show. Beyond here, from the direction where I had just come, it was all just rumors and mist for the Europeans then swarming the coast.

The river we call the Susquehanna carries water down this rough course for 444 miles over falls and around rocky islands to what we now call the Chesapeake, into what we now call the Atlantic, draining the storms and snowmelt of 27,000 square miles of tiny streams and creeks and rivers. She is the fifth-oldest river in the world, more than 300 million years old and ten times older than the Nile, and the longest river on the East Coast. We should thrill whenever we cross her, whether by train, car—or soon, for the first time for me, by foot.

No lake, no tall mountain or rock spire gives the traveler a firmer sense of place than a large flowing body of water. In the centuries before bridges, rivers like this were a pause point, a place to re-supply and re-pack, talk to the ferry man, your fellow travelers, and find your way across. Rivers like this won instant respect not just for their water but for the challenges—and often the horrors—they posed in crossing them. In long-ago times, in the winter, travelers would often cross with long ladders to keep from being swept away if they broke through the ice.

All old maps start with rivers and coastlines for a reason. They are the original tracings, fluctuating over time but of greater duration even than the mountains but not of the rocks over which they pass. The most sacred places are where water meets stone.

When the cartographers published their early maps of the New World in the seventeenth century, the known facts petered out quickly past the waterside hamlets where the Europeans settled. There were the towns and would-be cities clustered along the Hudson, the Delaware, the Chesapeake, the Potomac, all with names we recognize still—in English, Dutch, French, various native tongues. But the hinterlands were the stuff of mythology—bears standing tall, leaping panthers, bristling porcupines—among concocted hills and mountains.

If any settlements there had names, they were the names given by the native people, names brought downriver by pelt traders and soldiers. Names that have largely vanished from our lexicon. A palimpsest of unpronounceable words whose meanings have been not so much lost as physically erased, along with the people—known as the Susquehannock—who once inhabited them.

Augustine Herrman was among the most remarkable of wandering map drawers to first come this way. He traveled up the Susquehanna in the 1660s and put names to places like no one before him. Herrman both explored and charted the land, while most other cartographers made their maps at desks in London or

Lisbon from the hearsay and measurements of others. It takes a peculiar sort of genius to see the contours of the land as though from on high while sailing in a boat.

Around 1640, Herrman washed ashore on the island that would become Manhattan. He was an utter rarity then as a traveler from inner Europe, thought to be the first Bohemian to arrive in America, and he became one of the continent's first great traders of tobacco. As neither Dutch nor English, he served as a transnational emissary between the Dutch in Manhattan and the English in both Boston and Maryland. It was the latter relationship, with the Calverts in Maryland, that sent him prowling up the Susquehanna.

Not since John Smith in 1608 sailed up the Chesapeake and poked his nose up the Susquehanna to create his first magnificent chart had anyone attempted to chart this wide watery swath of Maryland and Virginia. Herrman devoted ten years to the task, an unheard-of commitment to detail at the time. The result was a meticulous map in four panels, and like all good maps then, a marvel to behold. He presented it to his sponsors in Maryland with the grandiose title: *Virginia and Maryland as it is Planted and Inhabited this present Year 1670 Surveyed and Exactly Drawne by the Only Labour & Endeavor of Augustine Herrman.*

Herrman dotted the shoreline of the bay, running left to right, with all the places we know now. St. Mary's. St. Michaels. Oxford. Baltimore. The Gunpowder River. Where Washington, D.C., stands today, he noted one detail: Turkey Buzzard's Point, an unremarkable nub of land that still goes by that name near the old Coast Guard headquarters and a short walk from where the Nationals play baseball. I have been to Buzzard's Point often on long runs and seen buzzards swoop above that point, as they should.

But the minute you row past Palmer's Island at the head of the Chesapeake and begin to go upriver, you enter another world. Up that way, up toward where I sat now, Herrman diligently concocted spellings for the Susquehannock villages he found and heard about along the riverbanks: Ocktoraro. Cansonanengh. Unondouweras. Kefkoe. Ocquandery. Skawaghkaha.

Try pronouncing any of those names. Only the first has left the faintest whisper of its existence along this whole stretch of the river. I knew if I went asking around these parts, those syllables would ring few bells. They were gone like the echo of my weak voice off the bridge.

I sat now near the very outer edge of Herrman's map, where he had drawn eight tiny longhouses surrounded by a stockade of spiked timbers beneath the words "The present Sassquahana Indian fort." That once legendary but long-vanished fort, a sort of New World Kubla Khan, stood a stone's throw from where the water now washed around my feet. Within fifty years of Herrman completing that map, the people who had inhabited those unpronounceable villages and built that fort were largely gone. Felled in battles with the Europeans or other tribes, taken by disease, or vanished to seek a new form of solitude farther west.

———◆———

I crossed the river on the old Columbia-Wrightsville bridge, built of graceful concrete arches in 1930, faster than we do any such thing now. The river flowed beneath the span and swirled in great eddies around its footings. April is shad season, and I knew from friends that they were coming up the Potomac now to spawn, as they have every spring up most Atlantic-feeding rivers since the beginning of time.

The shad for millennia had fed humans, osprey, eagles, and bears up the entire length of this river. Even in the 1880s, settlers were finding the remains of old nets left by the long-vanished tribes. But shad by the millions stopped coming up the Susquehanna in 1840, when the first dams were built to supply water for the first canals to haul the first shipments of cargo up and down the river. The trains were coming, and also their brief competitors, the canals.

We forget, from our depleted vantage, what an Eden we found upon arrival on this continent. An official investigation in 1882 of what had been lost just on the upper reaches of the Susquehanna breaks the heart, even now. The shad came so large and in such vast numbers that their arrival raised the level of the river as they passed. Gilbert Fowler, born in 1792, wrote eighty-nine years later that the arrival of the shad every April when he was young could be seen from a quarter of a mile away. "They came in such immense numbers and so compact as to cause or produce a wave or rising of the water in the middle of the river extending from shore to shore," he wrote to a special committee.

Fowler had a vision that never came true. "I still hope to live long enough to see all the obstructions removed from one end of the noble Susquehanna River to the other, and that the old stream may yet furnish cheap food to two millions of people along its banks, and that I may stand again on the shore at the old Webb fishery and witness another haul of ten thousand shad."

Looking upriver, I could see the old stone piers of the torched Civil War bridge, and the bridges that came after, since blown away by floods or torn down and sold for scrap. We build, we tear down. We remember, we forget.

It took nearly half an hour to get across the bridge, and when I did, right on time, up drove a white Econoline van with a banged-up 1963 dinghy on a trailer. "Howdy," said the driver when I threw open the side door and tossed my pack inside.

Of all the reasons I had left my house the previous Monday, a big one was to meet Paul Nevin. He was himself a destination.

———◆———

For months, I had been in touch with Paul, which in itself is no easy feat. Paul isn't a phone or email person. I had heard talk of him as another of the great memory keepers along my path, and had sent entreaties, which drew silence. Finally, I heard back, and Paul said by all means he would take me out on the river if the water flow was right.

Paul has obsessed for most of his sixty-four years over a group of large, scattered stones just downriver of the hulking Safe Harbor hydroelectric dam. We were heading there now, his boat rattling behind us as Paul told his story. It was my first time in a moving vehicle since departing my house. But I had no choice. We needed the boat he was hauling.

Paul grew up along the river and knew well of the native people who once lived there. On a museum visit as a kid, he'd seen photos of rock carvings in the river from a thousand years or so ago. Accepted wisdom assumed the carvings were gone: worn away, submerged beneath the dam, or broken up by scavengers long ago. They'd been studied and photographed and catalogued since the Civil War, then brushed aside since the Depression.

Those images he saw as a kid lodged in Paul's brain. In 1982, when he was twenty-eight, he bought an old aluminum Grumman canoe and paddled into the rocky expanse below the dam. He'd devoured all past writings on the Susquehanna petroglyphs. In his bag he carried a tattered copy of the seminal work on the subject: Donald Cadzow's *Petroglyphs in the Susquehanna River Near Safe Harbor, Pennsylvania,* published in 1934. A scuffed copy of the same slim monograph was in my pack, too. I had found it online and brought it along, squeezed into a Ziploc beside Eliot's *Four Quartets.*

"Man throughout the ages has ever shown a desire to perpetuate his history," Cadzow wrote to open his study. "Most permanent but least intelligible of his records are the petroglyphs or rock inscriptions near his ancient habitations."

"I do not know much about gods," Eliot wrote in *Four Quartets,* "but I think that the river is a strong brown god—sullen, untamed and intractable."

When he paddled out that day, Paul just wanted to get a feel for where the rock art had been. To glean what might have drawn an ancient people to devote such effort to carving symbols and images there. Would he feel some of the magic they must have felt? As he paddled around the sloping edge of the largest rock there that summer afternoon, he suddenly saw a crude image of an animal—was it a deer? an elk?—carved just above the waterline.

"Thus began my exploration," he wrote years later of that moment—an exploration that has lasted up to now, four decades later.

It took multiple tugs to fire up the five-horsepower outboard, but when he finally succeeded, Paul could hardly contain his glee. You could still see the boy in him despite the gray hair and wire-rimmed glasses. It was a brilliant, breezy Easter afternoon and he hadn't been to see the carvings since the autumnal equinox, way back in September. "That's far too long," Paul said.

As we shimmied upriver over light chop, Big Indian Rock rose from the water like a huge gray turtle with an entire denuded tree atop its shell, left there after some recent storm. Formed of a mica schist hundreds of millions of years ago and smoothed by the river, the rock was warm to our bare feet when we stepped from the boat.

"This is the first rock the sun touches in the morning, and the last it touches when it goes," Paul said. "This river has been flowing around it for hundreds of millions of years."

You could see some of the carvings, set off in the stone by shallow shadows. But they were furtive, not easily made out. Paul had a way to bring them to life. He filled a bucket with river water and soaked a large sponge. My heart began to race as we went to the head of the rock, where various forms flickered on its surface. Paul told me to prepare myself. Then he crouched and with several swoops of his wet sponge made vivid before my eyes in black and gray a group of spectacular thunderbirds, their wings extended, dripping little feathers. The water turned the rock black but left the carved form gray, so the details leaped out as though just days old.

Protectors of humans, bringers of rain and thus of life, thunderbirds rule supreme in native mythologies and are among the most ubiquitous of stone-carved images across the whole of the Americas. Paul looked up with the sponge in his hand and smiled. I could see he was in concert with the carvers.

Paul roamed the rock, and as osprey and turkey buzzards circled overhead, I saw spring to life, in black and gray, large serpents and bears. Human figures with what looked like the horns of a demon jutting from their heads: medicine men, Paul said. Turtles and still more thunderbirds. I saw the carved tracks of moose and birds and bison.

We got back in the boat and motored farther upriver to Little Indian Rock, smaller but even richer in its offerings, the best concentration of rock art, Paul said, east of the Mississippi. There, Paul crouched and ran his sponge over a snake four feet long. He revealed a large crescent moon and still more thunderbirds.

"This will speak to you," he said. Then he bent and passed his sponge across the figure of a man walking. The walking man had huge hands with fingers extended, as though he could hold or touch anything he wanted. A wavy path ran beneath his oversize feet, taking him somewhere. Vague shapes hovered behind him and over his head. A tingle shot through me when I looked at that figure, as though the carver—or maybe the walking man himself— had just whispered something in my ear.

Paul went then to kneel beside a spectacular circle carved into the schist. "Within this circle we have a bird track, a deer track, an infant human footprint, a snake. We have all the moving creatures within one circle."

We stood and listened to the water gurgle as it rushed around the rock, heading to the bay and to the ocean. Our shadows splashed long across the stone. Just as there are hidden passageways in native mythology that give entry to the underworld, I had slipped through some magical door—the latched gate in front of my own house—and found myself here at this sacred place, toes gripping the warm rock as many other toes had for thousands of years. I shut my eyes to feel the sun and gave thanks for the whole of it.

The first European to document these carvings stood on this rock in September 1863, two months after the battle of Gettysburg. Professor T. C. Porter studied the carvings in detail and concluded they were no mere "offspring of idle fancy." He wrote to his colleagues at the American Philosophical Society that these carvings were, instead, "the product of design toward some end of high importance in the eyes of the sculptors."

Many times, on the first dawn of each season, Paul has come to this rock to see how one or another of the large serpents carved in the schist a millennium or so ago point to that morning's rising sun. "Seeing that, just being here, it gives me hope—or maybe assurance is the right word—that this cycle we're all a part of will continue."

On this Easter afternoon, Paul Nevin had brought me to his church.

The continuance Paul spoke of was everywhere to see. In the carvings. In the osprey overhead and the water gurgling around the rock. In me, the walking man, drawn from afar to take it in.

CHAPTER 9

DOUGHFACE, MEET CLUBFOOT

From the Susquehanna I walked to where I would sleep that night in a small, rented cabin with a side porch and a rocking chair. I walked up through rolling farmland parallel to the Conestoga River, the sun hanging low and golden. If the York County side had been rough-hewn and irregular, everything to the east of the big river, in Lancaster County, spoke to my having arrived in a different place. The orderly spacing of the farms. The quiet ostentation of barns and silos built big, with high ambition. The well-kept look of the land, lovingly manicured by plow since the first settlers arrived in the late 1600s. A poor man's rich country, some called it, as welcoming a place for farming as anywhere on the eastern seaboard.

The beauty of the whole of it—the low sun, the silos like exclamation points studding the hills—made me let out a holler and do a little dance. I threw a stick into a field. I skipped a rock across the road.

I passed an old highway marker telling me that the area had once housed various villages of the Conestoga Indians, "in origin largely the survivors of the defeated ancient Susquehannas or Minquas of Iroquoian stock." The people, in other words, who had lived in all those vanished villages on the earliest European maps. William Penn in 1701 had visited and "made treaties with them."

That Treaty of Friendship was designed to last "as long as the Sun should shine, or the Waters run in the Rivers." The Conestogas were a dwindling band living peacefully among the white farmers, trading baskets and brooms for things they needed.

The marker then dryly noted one of the state's worst atrocities: "The tribe was exterminated by the Paxton Boys in 1763."

At daybreak that December morning, fifty-seven Scots Irish horsemen from a settlement to the west called Paxtang came riding from the edge of the frontier into the Conestoga village. They rode in with rifles, hatchets, scalping knives. Their ostensible purpose was to exact revenge for a series of tit-for-tat skirmishes between Indians and white settlers far to the west and north, part of a war then raging known as Pontiac's Rebellion—among the first of many American race wars to come, you could say.

They caught the few residents still asleep, killed six of them and torched their wooden houses. When the survivors fled to Lancaster for protection, the horsemen gave chase and slaughtered and scalped the remaining fourteen people, eight of them children.

The killings were a political act to tell the pacifist Quaker government in Philadelphia that there would be no more coddling of the Indians, no matter who they were or what they had done. The murders stirred deep outrage in some quarters but swiftly won support among large swaths of the citizenry—other frontiersmen, largely, and the burgeoning working class of Philadelphia. Calling themselves the Paxton Boys, the vigilante mob had swelled to several hundred when it marched on Philadelphia the next month, vowing to attack Indians being harbored there.

The killings sparked a pamphlet war as proponents for and against issued broadsides by the dozens. Benjamin Franklin stepped in with what scholars consider his most impassioned polemic, *A Narrative of the Late Massacres in Lancaster County*. He devoted nearly a third of it to relating the millennia-old tradition of hospitality and protection of the stranger, a tradition found in all cultures.

"See, in the mangled Corpses of the last Remains of the Tribe, how effectually we have afforded it to them!" Whites, he wrote, were now indiscriminately killing Indians simply because of the color of their skin, irrespective of past conduct. They had become the Other. "The Spirit of killing all Indians, Friends and Foes, has spread amazingly thro' the whole Country," Franklin wrote to a friend.

The Paxton mob was turned back just outside the city and the worst of the furor died down. But Quaker pacifism and Franklin's charitable view of the native tribes did not win the war. The Pennsylvania assembly swung that summer against the Quakers and embraced many of the settler's views, including their demand for cash payments for the scalps of slain Indians. The colony built on Brotherly Love turned overtly hostile toward the native population. "William Penn's Indian policy had been admired for its justice and humanity by all the philosophers and statesmen of the world," wrote the Quaker historian Sydney George Fisher in 1920. "Now his grandson, Governor of the province, in the last days of the family's control, was offering bounties for women's scalps."

Despite the initial outrage and wide knowledge as to who the perpetrators were, no arrests were ever made for the Conestoga killings. We are aware of these scattered stories here and there, but the totality of the continent-wide policy of extermination, a policy that culminated with the Wounded Knee Massacre in December 1890, should still have the power to astonish.

In these same environs where I walked now, picking up my pace to get off the road before night fell, German farmers invented the first of the famous Conestoga wagons with their wide curved beds and canvas covers. Those workhorses of the booming colonies, with their teams of oxen and mules, soon choked the former Indian trails and carried goods and settlers south into the Shenandoah Valley and west to where the Ohio drained.

En route to Lancaster from Philadelphia in 1826, the Boston

mayor and future Harvard president Josiah Quincy described passing through "a most beautiful tract of country, where good fences and huge stone barns proved the excellence of the farming. The road seemed actually lined with Conestoga wagons, each drawn by six stalwart horses and laden with farm produce."

I got a carton of chicken fried rice from a Chinese takeout place and then a huge cold can of beer from the Wawa next door before I hiked the last mile uphill to where I would sleep for the night, in a cabin smack up against the road. I sat outside in a rocking chair and ate my Easter supper in huge spoonfuls straight from the carton, washing it down with the beer. As I crawled into bed, I thought of the woman I had met that morning, the grieving widow in her nightgown, and how relieved she'd been that I knew where I would sleep, in a bed, warm, dry, and free of ticks. I was on the far outer edge of Lancaster now, roughly a third of the way to New York.

On my way into town after coffee the next morning, I wound through a neighborhood of twisting streets and fine homes to talk with a man vying to replace President James Buchanan. With his black cane, gray wavy hair combed back, round open face, and crisp flannel shirt with two pens protruding from the breast pocket, Leroy Hopkins opened the front door of his house and welcomed me in. He looked as though he were all of America's uncle. "Please, please, sit down," he said with a wave of his hand.

Leroy Hopkins, at seventy-nine, came widely recommended as an area sage: a professor of German at nearby Millersville University, steeped in regional history, a perennial board member on all sorts of civic matters, a prominent leader of the Black community. At heart, a blend of everything the place had to offer. And with debate swirling over the tarnished memory of Lancaster's native son—the doughface president who helped usher in the Civil War—Leroy's name was on a list of possible replacements for the soon-to-be renamed James Buchanan Elementary School in Lancaster.

I asked him about that. He wasn't glib. "Buchanan's intervention in the *Dred Scott* decision alone should disqualify him as an example for today's young," Leroy said, mentioning a famous moment at the start of Buchanan's presidency when the Supreme Court ruled that the Constitution did not grant any rights and privileges to people of African descent, whether free or enslaved. Even being in a free state gave them no right to freedom.

Leroy knew a lot about his past. It may be fair to say he knew pretty much everything that is knowable about his past. He could fluidly tell stories about his fourth great-grandfather, Cupid Paca, a free Black man born in 1777 and almost certainly—Leroy asserted—the unacknowledged son of William Paca, Maryland's third governor.

"Cupid was a shoemaker, a stonemason, and a land speculator. I have a copy of a transaction he made in 1822, when he bought fifty acres of land and paid $700 cash." He described how you would drive to the land, the turns necessary to get there, and exactly what it looked like upon arrival. On it went, in precise detail. "I am fifty-four percent African and the rest German, Welsh, Scottish, Swiss, Irish, the whole stew," Leroy said. "I know of 604 fourth cousins, and surely there are many more."

I told Leroy about my findings at the Lebanon Cemetery in York, and his eyes brightened at the mention of the place. He had relatives buried there, he said, but had never gone that way. "I don't drive," he said. "Never have."

I told him I would come back one day and take him there, by car. "I would enjoy that," he said, "very much."

Reshouldering my pack after an hour in his living room, I told Leroy that if he had a few drops of Lenape in him, too, he would perfectly embody the place where he lived—or perhaps the whole of the country—that we are all a vast stew of bloodstreams, most of them lost to time. He waved that aside with a laugh. "There are many like me. You just have to know where to look."

Leroy's mention of Buchanan's *Dred Scott* intervention got me thinking, walking north through streets lined with neat little houses now, about a dinner conversation two nights earlier with Mike Helfrich, the mayor of York. Mike had turned to me with a crispy brussels sprout speared on the tines of his fork and asked if I was familiar with a certain James Buchanan speech. You may as well stop right there, I said. No one had ever asked me that, because no one I know had ever read a James Buchanan speech, or ever asked if I had.

Mike explained that he hadn't either, but he'd found a fragment of a Buchanan speech from an old newspaper stuck to the back of a daguerreotype he had unearthed among all his stuff. This sort of thing happened a lot to Mayor Helfrich. "And when I read that fragment and saw he'd made mention of the *Amistad,* I had to track down the full speech, and then when I read the speech, I was astonished by what Buchanan said." The *Amistad* was a Spanish slave ship taken over by African captives off the coast of Cuba in 1839 and later seized by U.S. authorities. That armed revolt for freedom later won the support of the U.S. Supreme Court and made the *Amistad* famous.

I found the Buchanan speech Mike had mentioned online that night and read it for myself. It was Buchanan's farewell letter to Congress, December 3, 1860. It was quite a doozy. Buchanan knew the country was spinning apart and would soon be at war. South Carolina would become the first state to secede seventeen days later. Two and a half months after that, Lincoln would become president. Five weeks later, rebels would open fire on Fort Sumter.

What was the cause of this coming strife, which Buchanan so deeply wanted to avoid? What would light the fuse that would make the entire country finally explode in violence? The president was adamant about where the blame belonged: "The incessant and violent agitation of the slavery question throughout the North for the last quarter of a century has at length produced its malign influence on the slaves and inspired them with vague notions of freedom," he wrote.

Those dastardly slaves were clamoring for freedom. But that wasn't the worst of it, said the president.

As a result of that agitation, Buchanan wrote, "many a matron throughout the South retires at night in dread of what may befall herself and children before the morning. Should this apprehension of domestic danger, whether real or imaginary, extend and intensify itself until it shall pervade the masses of the Southern people, then disunion will become inevitable."

The cause of the coming war, said the president of the United States, was "this apprehension of domestic danger, whether real or imaginary." The night Mayor Helfrich mentioned the speech, I read that part of it over and over. Benjamin Franklin, almost a century earlier, in 1763, had agonized over how a white killing spree against Indians had "spread amazingly thro' the whole Country." Now, in 1860, Buchanan lamented that the fear among whites of violence at the hands of freedom-seeking Blacks, whether real or not, was so potent as to tear the country apart and make war inevitable.

White fear, in both cases, lay at the heart of the country's longest spates of violence and bloodshed.

———◆———

I walked on into Lancaster, Buchanan's hometown and the place where twenty thousand people showed up for his funeral, thinking again about goodness and what makes any of us good. James Buchanan was a jolly fellow who gave to needy widows. He was assiduously middling and conservative to a fault. Congressman, senator, secretary of state, ambassador to Russia and then to Great Britain, he was a man of sterling credentials. He revered the Constitution like a religious icon. In the boardinghouses of Washington his fellows found him witty. Said one scribe after his death: "His large, double-horse carriage used to halt at many a door, and he never departed but his gracious deportment was praised before the sound of the wheels died away."

And he was, for all that, morally vacuous. He loathed agitators above all, especially abolitionists, whom he saw as arsonists attempting to torch the Union. He was no fan of slavery, but he despised as nation-wreckers those who sought to abolish it. Today he is dismissed as among the worst of all presidents, a dullard and a moral coward who helped usher in the Civil War.

But we should own our Buchanans at least as much as we do our Franklins and Lincolns and Roosevelts. He is no less illustrative of our national psyche. We should acknowledge that our Buchanans represent our nature—who we were and are—at least as well as our nobler leaders. Even today, there is likely more James Buchanan in most of us than there is pure Abraham Lincoln. His "apprehension of domestic danger" still pervades the land.

James Buchanan, though, has plummeted out of fashion in Lancaster. The town, I found that fine spring afternoon, is at last officially tiring of the man and casting him aside as it heaps acclaim on Buchanan's antithesis, the fiery Thaddeus Stevens, scourge of slaveholders, avowed enemy of the Confederacy, and archrival to James Buchanan.

I walked up King Street through Lancaster's central square to say hello to Tom Baldrige, the brother of a friend of mine and the longtime head of the Lancaster Chamber of Commerce. Tom welcomed me and threw open the door to his office and proudly waved his arms, like a theater emcee, to show off the large, scowling portrait of Stevens that hung on his wall. "My hero," Tom said.

Stevens was a mere congressman during the Civil War, but as chairman of the powerful Ways and Means Committee, no man exerted more leverage, or used it more effectively. If Lincoln and other white Americans in 1860 were gradualists, at best, Stevens was an outright revolutionary, representative of a tiny slice of the population then who wanted slavery ended immediately, and by any means necessary.

Buchanan and Stevens were born a year apart and both died in the summer of 1868. They both worked as lawyers in Lancaster with offices nearby. Neither man ever married. They shared the same barber, the same physician, the same streets and shade-dappled parks, the same carriage and train rides to Washington. They once or twice had dinner together. One is our yin, the other our yang.

Without Buchanan, the country would be little different. He coddled the South and forestalled war for his four years in the White House. Then he retired to his high brick Federalist house on the edge of town to receive guests and work on his memoirs—the first ever presidential account of a president's time in office—as the nation imploded.

Without Stevens, we would be a far different and lesser nation. Throughout the war he led Lincoln to places—emancipation, Blacks serving in the military—where Lincoln was reluctant or slow to go. After the war he led the charge to revamp the Constitution and to move aggressively on Reconstruction. He was one of the founders of the country's second founding.

As Buchanan's star plunges in his own hometown, Stevens's is fast rising. I felt that I had wandered into one American burg, the crisp and proper town of Lancaster, just as the tectonic plates were shifting, as they were in so many parts of the country. A wrenching give-and-take over what counts as true honor and courage in our past and what does not.

Tom Baldrige and I went to have lunch in the backyard of Wheatland, Buchanan's estate. We sat in the sun around a table with Tom Ryan and Robin Sarratt, who together run Lancaster's historical society, called Lancaster History, and happen to be married. History brought them together, and the rest is history, is their running joke. A snappy couple in their fifties, they had loaded the table with sandwiches and snacks. Starlings flitted and warbled in the trees.

The state of the two men's houses tells much of the story, Tom Ryan said. "Wheatland was always lovingly looked after. The Junior League and some of the highfalutin folks bought it in the 1930s and said, 'We're going to preserve and protect this.' Stevens's house became a drug den and was nearly bulldozed a couple of decades ago."

Back then, Robin said, "no one was paying attention to Stevens's legacy."

Tom Ryan amended that. "Not no one. The African American community knew who Stevens was, knew how important he was, and never forgot. Whites knew of Stevens but had no interest in holding him up as an example. Instead," he said, gesturing toward the house, "they held this guy up."

We got around to the topic of goodness again and how blind we can be to its true nature. How our views shift from generation to generation even if goodness itself, like some Platonic form, remains eternal and unchanging. Buchanan was, by the standards of his time, an honorable man. Prudent, cautious, a stickler for the Constitution. He was also a casual and unflinching racist, and in that way, too, a man of his times.

Stevens was very much not a man of his times, or the times after that, or even really the times after those times. He may not even be a man for these times, were he still around. For nearly a century after his death, he was widely cast as cruel and vindictive, a sourpuss, a petty tyrant. The director D. W. Griffith patterned the dictatorial and power-hungry Austin Stoneman after Stevens in his incendiary 1915 silent film *The Birth of a Nation,* the first movie ever screened in the White House. Fifty-one years later, in his *Profiles in Courage,* none other than John F. Kennedy heaped praise on the courage of three slave-holding senators but called Stevens "the crippled, fanatical personification of the extremes of the Radical Republican movement." Lancaster has come around to appreciating the depths of Stevens's conviction and courage, but to John Kennedy in 1956, he was a mere firebrand "with a mouth like the thin edge of an ax."

———————

"Shall we?" We had finished lunch, and Robin indicated it was time to go see where Buchanan had spent his domestic hours living in bachelorhood in the company of his doting niece, Harriet Lane. Robin swung open the back door, which exhaled a cool stuffiness. Wheatland had allowed in no tours since COVID fell a year before, depriving its ghosts of a year's entertainment. They were pleased to receive us. We went from a lunch of sandwiches, chips, and bubbly water straight into a world of gilt and lace and lugubrious portraiture.

The dining room was set with starched napkins and pink-rimmed china. The plastic, make-believe wine in the goblets was eternal and would never evaporate. In the front parlor, Old Buck himself peered at us from above the mantel with an arched brow and slightly tousled gray hair, his cheeks framed by a high collar and white bow tie. We looked to be rough contemporaries, James and I, if measured by our months on Earth.

"Do you want to see the bed where he died?" Robin was excited in asking the question. "Absolutely," I said.

We went through the study first and stood beside the desk where he wrote his dry but determined self-defense, *Mr. Buchanan's*

Administration on the Eve of the Rebellion. In it, he is the sage and far-seeing one who watches in horror as the storm clouds build. The prime movers, again, are those agitators in the North who simply can't let slavery die its own slow death. Their actions create an equivalent extremism in the South, and both dig their trenches deeper, until war is unavoidable. Buchanan supported Lincoln during the war, but he never forgave the abolitionists. The cotton states, he said, writing here on this leather-topped desk, "were the assailed party, and had been far more sinned against than sinning."

Please, take me to his bedroom.

The bed where Buchanan died was a proud four-poster, not large but high off the floor, its patterned quilt taut and its two pillows plump and free of creases. There was the tin tub where he could sit or stand to bathe with water from a pitcher, and the "necessary chair" to crap in if the outhouse felt too far. I smiled at the earthiness of all this but didn't feel stirred to great emotion. No momentousness hung in the air. It was all so common.

We were heading next to where Stevens had lived in the center of town, but first my hosts took me into a library at the museum just up the hill to show me some things they had pulled from the archives. Stevens lost all his hair in his thirties, so there was his wig. He was born with a clubfoot, so there was his specially designed leather boot.

Scholars have sought to uncover the origin of Stevens's fierce hatred for slavery and for all forms of unfairness or oppression. Most have settled on three factors: that he grew up in Vermont, the first radical antislavery state; that his parents were Baptists, and thus well acquainted with persecution; and that he was born with a disability and knew that peculiar hardship from an early age.

Robin handed me his leather boot, which looked more like a petrified clenched fist and felt stiff and heavy in my hands. "I think you can't underestimate the importance of this. It greatly deepened his compassion," she said.

Stevens lived and worked in a brick Federalist town house on Queen Street, blocks from Lancaster's main square. That was his residence when the Confederates stormed into Pennsylvania and made a beeline for his Caledonia ironworks in Gettysburg. General Jubal Early explained the drive to destroy Stevens's property by saying the Confederacy had no worse enemy in the U.S. Congress than Representative Thaddeus Stevens.

He wasn't wrong. Stevens made sure the war effort was properly funded. He goaded Lincoln to move ahead on emancipation, and finally to support the Thirteenth Amendment, officially codifying slavery's end in the U.S. Constitution. After the war, he fought more aggressively than anyone to assure fair treatment of freed Blacks, though many of his bolder quests—for land redistribution, for instance—failed to win support. He sought reparations for slavery the minute it ended, a call that still echoes today but should have happened then in its fullest form. He was, Frederick Douglass wrote, "more potent in Congress and in the country than even the president and cabinet combined."

His house became many things in succession after his death: boardinghouse, barbershop, restaurant, garage, drug den. It was abandoned for years and finally slated for demolition twenty years ago to accommodate a convention center. It was hollowed out when we walked through it, a mere shell of plaster walls and brick façade. "Watch your step," Tom said. Lancaster History was turning the house into a museum honoring Stevens and his longtime Black partner, Lydia Hamilton Smith.

"We have some of his effects," Robin said, "but in many ways we'll be starting this museum from scratch."

———◆———

When President Buchanan died in June 1868, the papers were unimpressed. The news in most places fell well shy of the front page. It was as if the "Old Public Functionary" had ceased to exist soon after he left the White House seven years before. There was a sense of relief, of bitterness and derision. His peculiar drab cordiality had ushered the nation into war. The *New York Herald* noted sarcastically that he was such a predictable conversationalist that he asked all visitors to the White House the same questions. "Have you been long in Washington? Have you seen the Smithsonian Institution?" He wore for his burial, I noticed in reading the old newspaper stories, the same high collar and white bow tie as in the portrait above the mantel.

When Stevens died in his lodging in Washington two months later, it was as if a sitting president had perished. Some newspapers put him on a par with Lincoln for stature. "A great man has left us," mourned the Philadelphia *Evening Telegraph*—a man who did "more to support the fabric of policy pursued by the United States in the past six years than any other man, living or dead." Many Southern papers expressed a begrudging awe at his memory. "The name of Thaddeus Stevens no longer designates one of the most important actors in a political drama of unsurpassed interest," wrote the *New Orleans Crescent*. "He is not now a political leader or a political opponent; he belongs to history, and that will judge him."

His body lay in state in the Capitol Rotunda as thousands streamed in, many of them Black. They kept the Capitol open all night to accommodate the crowds. Protecting his casket were twenty-five members of the Butler Zouaves, a local Black militia, armed with long rifles. Only two other men had received the honor of a Rotunda viewing, Abraham Lincoln and Senator Henry Clay.

The yellow daffodils beside his grave were in full flower when we came into the Shreiner-Concord Cemetery to see where he was buried. You must smile at a man so brilliant as to put even his death to good use. He had picked a small—and very rare—

mixed-race cemetery near the town center, within feet of a small potter's field, after turning down other possible sites. It was all very deliberate, designed to make a point right down to the end. Day after day, Stevens delivers his final speech.

I REPOSE IN THIS QUIET AND SECLUDED SPOT
NOT FROM ANY NATURAL PREFERENCE FOR
*   SOLITUDE,*
BUT FINDING OTHER CEMETERIES LIMITED AS
*   TO RACE,*
BY CHARTER RULES,
I HAVE CHOSEN THIS THAT I MIGHT ILLUSTRATE
IN MY DEATH
THE PRINCIPLES WHICH I ADVOCATED
THROUGH A LONG LIFE:
EQUALITY OF MAN BEFORE HIS CREATOR

CHAPTER 10

RENEWING YOUR MIND

S he was standing with her knees slightly bent in a patch of grass
and sunlight behind a brick schoolhouse. She was focused on
something in the distance and wore a long floral dress that extended to her ankles. She was in her early teens and had a white
head-covering over a bun of her hair curled neatly in back. I was
walking up the road when I saw her, and then caught sight of a
leather mitt on her left hand, and then heard the solid whack of a
baseball bat. The way she drifted back and so effortlessly fielded
a hard-hit fly ball and hurled it back the other way—that, and all
the rest of it, everything, made me stop in amazement.

I knew then that I had stepped through the wardrobe into a
magical land. For eight days I had been walking. For eight days I
had gone north, and then bent my way east, and had crossed a large
river. It was a Tuesday in early April in the middle of the afternoon,
and an air of enchantment was taking hold.

But let me go back to the morning of that same day. It is a day
that must be told in full.

I left Lancaster that morning on Butter Lane and skirted the
graceful bends of the Conestoga River. By leaving town you depart the world of shops and bustle and reflective glass and slip
into a land of wood, water, horses, and leather. This was the heart
of Amish and Mennonite farm country on a spring morning

impervious to improvement. The red and white maples, the elms, the willows, and the red oaks were all putting out their tiny flowers or turning to infant leaf. Across the fields and around the neat, white houses one could see the palest, most subtle shades of green.

Where Mondale Road crossed over a branch of the Conestoga River, I saw through a fence a tiny grass lane that jumped the river atop an arching stone bridge. I went to step among the river stones to look at it more closely. That bridge was the simplest work of art, and even more so because the lane had nowhere to go once it got to the other side. The water flowing beneath sent shimmering reflections upon the stone arch.

From there over the main branch of the Conestoga I walked through and over my first Amish covered bridge, an elegant red structure with thick curving supports running along either side and two rectangular openings for the buggy riders to see the river as they crossed.

The author of this bridge was a prolific bridge builder named Captain Elias McMellen, who erected many of the area's most celebrated spans in the years after the Civil War. This one he built in 1867 using an arching truss design invented by Theodore Burr, cousin to Aaron Burr. Locals since then have called the span Pinetown Bushong's Mill Bridge, Pinetown Covered Bridge, Nolte's Point Mill Bridge, and Bushong's Mill Bridge, but it was never known for the man who built it, McMellen's Bridge. That would have been immodest. Its official name now, I read, is the Big Conestoga #6 Bridge. Hurricane Agnes roughed it up in 1972, but the area's Amish farmers put it right again soon after.

In crossing the Pinetown bridge, I felt as if I had parted a thick velvet curtain and stepped into a pocket of America as stubbornly resistant to change as any on the continent. A nook of the country with a direct lineage to a stew of religious and social spasms in Europe five hundred years earlier. The Reformation had many faces, but the people known first as the Swiss Brethren were particularly resolute in their embrace of simplicity and their rejection of earthly attachments.

Only willing adults, the Brethren believed, should be baptized into Christianity. You were to turn away from civic affairs, disavow all violence and aggression, and swear no oaths to king or country. This set of practices got them tortured, branded, garroted, drowned, dismembered, burned at the stake. Martyrdom for the persecuted and brave silence while being drowned or burned became its own art form, drawing still more adherents. Their ranks spread across Northern Europe starting in the sixteenth century.

These people became known as the Anabaptists, but differing practices created subgroups, namely the Amish and the Mennonites, and thereafter dozens of splintering factions have spread across the globe, each adhering to differing levels of purity. Their fields and barns soon sprawled across the whole of southeastern Pennsylvania because William Penn invited them there. His was a "Holy Experiment," a colony formed explicitly to take in the religious castoffs of Europe, a community of persecuted minorities meant to live in peace with the native population. The first of the Mennonites arrived in 1683. The first Amish came not long after.

America is what it is in part because a vast swath of its earliest middle ground, the space between North and South, was settled by a pacifist, otherworldly plain folk. Not just the Amish and the Mennonites but also the Quakers, the Pietists, the Dunkers, and others. They tempered the passions of an unruly nation and strengthened the weave of its moral fabric. Most of our earliest experiments have dissolved or died away, little utopian societies whose grounds you can visit for a fee. The plain folk of Pennsylvania—or Ohio, Indiana, Iowa, Wisconsin, North Dakota—live on. Their simple stubbornness, when you see it as a person walking down a road, is worthy of awe.

The plain folk are modest and plain in dress—usually avoiding prints, bright colors, laces, fancy buttons—because the Bible tells them to eschew fineries and adorn their spirits instead. They pin their practices to passages in Scripture and see themselves as inhabiting a separate kingdom, of the world but also a step outside of it. Those that shun cars, electricity, or computers do so because they see those technologies as promoting vanity and self-indulgence and eroding social cohesion. Of course, not everyone likes these restrictions: many flee when they come of age or convert to other practices. But the whole of it endures, and prospers, despite the outside pressures.

◆

Everywhere I went, nearly every lane I walked down, it was laundry day. Sheets, towels, shirts, dresses, trousers, overalls with suspenders hung in the breeze from wires that ran taut through pulleys between house and barn. Their array of colors—great splotches of white, blue, burgundy—made me wish I were Monet with a palette of oils in hand.

I took in this display of wind-tossed cloth as I went along Butter Lane to Mondale Road to Stormstown Road to Quarry Road to Center Square Road to Brethren Church Road to West Farmersville Road. On I went to Cats Back Road to Cider Mill Road to Pierce Willis Road to Crooked Lane to Metzler Lane to Miley Road. At one house I stood transfixed by the billowing of men's shirts on one end, all starched and white, and the lethargic swaying on the other of the same men's heavier black canvas pants.

When I came down Center Square Road, an Amish mother and her very young daughter were working in the front garden near the road. When they saw me, the mother took her daughter's hand, dropped her hoe, and very deliberately walked toward the house. The mother was startled by my sudden appearance but once she was safely away, she politely turned and waved to me. The daughter did the same. They were cordial, but you could see the trace of fear in their eyes.

The first small Amish buggy went by a minute later with a high-stepping horse prancing theatrically, and the young man inside with a straw hat also waved. Men were out plowing, sons mainly, driving large teams of horses or mules to turn the moist soil for that spring's planting. Even if they were three hundred yards away, they would wave or tip their hat on seeing me. We occupied different universes, different centuries in many ways, but we shared the same patch of earth, me on the road, them in the field, and we waved to acknowledge that basic bond.

Outside the Farmersville Butcher Shop, a yellow cinder block structure tucked off the road beside a barn, a young woman in a long, pink-striped apron nodded as I came up the drive. Trays of tiny vegetable seedlings sat on a bench in the shade. As I stepped through the door, the butcher's son emerged from the back room wiping his knife on a bloody apron. Then his dad came out, and we got to talking. They were the Zimmerman family, of Old Order Mennonite stock. Their shop had lights, refrigeration, all that. But no to-go orders, they said.

"We have all the fixings for sandwiches, but we don't make any," the son said when I asked about getting some lunch. "Where you heading?" the dad asked, and I said I had come from Washington, D.C., and was on my way to the Muddy Creek Farm Library to talk to Amos Hoover and look through an old copy of the *Martyrs Mirror*. And then from there eventually to New York.

"Amos up there, he's an historical. He knows about all the old stuff," said the dad, who was also named Amos. I think that made me an historical, too, but I let that pass.

I told them that later that day I would be delivering a message brought all the way from Maryland for the Hoovers, who lived on Crooked Lane, and Amos said he knew the family, of course, and he began giving me exact directions to the Hoover farm. When I came down off the hill where the farm library is, he said, I'd pass through a covered bridge and keep on straight till the road bends by a white schoolhouse, and that was the start of Crooked Lane. "They're down at the far end of that road along the creek," he said. "Can't miss it."

The son had thought some more about my lunch. "I can cut you off some slices of bologna if you'd like," he said. He pulled a round slab of their own concoction from the fridge and cut off two thick slices, dark and spotted with little nibs of fat, and tucked a hunk of farmer's cheese in between, and put that breadless sandwich in a fold of wax paper. "On the house," he said. It made for a glorious lunch as I walked down the road.

A few minutes later I passed a house where a young woman named Linda Weaver stood in the yard with her two children, Miranda and Caleb. Caleb was gripping onto the fence by the cow pasture, dressed in diapers and cooing at the cows. Miranda held three drooping dandelions in her hand. Her mother said they were the first dandelions picked that spring.

I had stopped to say hello to the family and Linda hadn't flinched. She spoke in a timid but unselfconscious way and without guile. She wore a plaid dress that went to her ankles and, over it, what looked like a dark apron flecked with flour. Her dark hair, pulled into a bun, was tucked behind the white head-covering that nearly all the women in the area wore.

She and her husband had just bought the house a few years before, she said. They were fixing it up and all was going well. If anything, the pandemic had been good to them. Her husband worked at the produce place up the street and because people were shopping differently, deliveries were up. I told her a little about my walk and the things I had seen that day and the bologna sandwich the Zimmerman son had handed me. She listened closely and asked where I would spend that night, and when I thought I would get to New York, and whether any family might join me for part of the way. As she talked, both of her kids gathered around her legs and partly hid behind her dress.

I tried to recall having had a conversation so straightforward and lacking in pretense. We were strangers. I was surely an oddity coming down the road. But she'd looked me straight in the eye and shown no suspicion or hesitation or guardedness in talking to me. It was simple plainness and modesty in action.

"I hope you enjoy your walk," she said as I left. "Especially on a day so beautiful."

———————

It was just up the road that I saw the girl with the baseball mitt standing behind the Farmersville Mennonite School. Saw her and heard the whack of the bat and watched her field that fly ball. I went off the road and walked toward her to see it all more closely.

Have you ever had to squint at something because it was that incongruous or that beautiful or otherworldly? In the yard behind the school were two overlapping diamonds where maybe twenty-five boys and girls were playing two very competitive games of softball. It was early afternoon on a gorgeous spring day. They had just had lunch and were playing two games of intense softball at the same time, and I wandered into the outfield right behind the school and took it in.

The balls were hit hard, thrown hard, fielded fast. If you got a single, you tried for a double. This was full-out sandlot softball, no frills about it. On both mounds pitching were two girls wearing different flowery dresses, and they pitched fast, underarm style, and few batters needed more than one pitch before smacking the ball into play. All these kids had known each other since they were babies, so when one stepped up to the plate, everyone knew exactly how to adjust. No sabermetrics here.

Several times the same girl in left field would go deep into the parking lot, past me, and I'd say, "So this kid can hit?" and she would nod her head and get in a crouch and jam her right fist into her glove. The way the young women sprinted in their flowing dresses to catch fly balls on the run was both startling and beautiful.

When the bell rang, all the kids grabbed their little lunch coolers and came running across the field toward me, led by their teacher, a lean, enthusiastic fellow with a broad smile who introduced himself as Neal Weaver. Neal had a baseball glove wedged under his arm and carried his own little lunch cooler.

The minute he heard me describe what had brought me there, Neal said, "Kids, let's all gather around. Let's hear what Mr. King has to say." No fear here, either: his immediate response to my being there was to turn the moment into a lesson for the eighth and ninth graders clustered around me on the lawn.

Recess had ended, but for ten minutes I talked to these kids. They looked on intently and laughed when something I said tickled them—like how good the girls were at softball and how stupid I now thought cars were.

All the girls stood in a cluster to one side, maybe twenty of them, and all the boys in another, just six or so, a few steps away. I remarked how beautiful the land was there, and the farms, and how amazed I was by their softball game, and by the row of bikes over there by the fence, none of them locked.

I mentioned how the country was now consumed in a big debate—as it had been for centuries, really—over our past and future and over what set of people were living right and which weren't. And I said: "With this big battle in mind, I've been thinking all day that you all might just be doing it right."

And then when they all laughed, I asked, "So do you think you're doing it right?"

"That is a great question," said Mr. Weaver. The kids all squirmed and smiled and a few of them laughed, but none felt like jumping in on whether they, the Mennonites, were doing it right compared to all the other experiments in social organization from there all the way to the coast of California.

One of the girls with flushed cheeks and blond hair stood in front wearing a white dress emblazoned with red roses. I could see her name written on a strip of tape across her lunch cooler. She had laughed the loudest at my jokes and had blurted out a couple of comments. "I can see that Miss Hoover is the class spokeswoman," I said at one point, and again, her laugh topped all the others.

Neal explained that the school was a private religious school, staffed entirely by Mennonites, and that he taught math, history, reading, and vocabulary—"and anything else that needs teaching."

Miss Hoover then stepped forward and said, "Mr. Weaver, why don't we sing for Mr. King?"

A roar of approval went up, so Neal Weaver looked at me and said, "Do you have the time for a couple of hymns?" All the time in the world, I said.

The kids flooded into the low-slung, redbrick schoolhouse, went to their desks, and got their hymnals. I was stunned just watching the orderliness of how they all moved, without fuss or jostling, as though they had been drilled on how to enter the school, the classroom, and then how to descend downstairs to the choir room, which seconded as a small basketball court. They all took their places on the three risers, each where they had been many times before, and opened their hymnals. Mr. Weaver stood before them and blew a tuning whistle.

I couldn't believe anything I had just witnessed in the past twenty minutes. Not the softball, not the mighty sluggers in the floral dresses, not our discussion in the sunshine, and above all not that these twenty-five kids were now glancing at me, beaming, preparing to sing.

———◆———

They stood on the cusp of adulthood on a spotless afternoon in early spring. Sunlight poured through the window. You could hear the birds trilling outside. These kids had just eaten lunch outdoors on the grass and played a full-throttled game of softball. Mr. Weaver gave the prompt with both hands, and they began to sing, not of now, not of the sunlight or the birds, but of later. Not of life, but of death and the afterlife.

"Someday, my heart will pulse no more," they sang. "I'll slip away to Heaven's shore. / This earthly life will fade away / into a never-ending day. / Someday I'll find a better place. / Someday I'll run the final race. / My weary feet will cease to roam. / Someday I'm coming home."

They sang another hymn in a lilting three-part harmony, a song of the lifting of grief and a land beyond of rich delight. It was another song of another world, a world "beyond this mortal frame of time . . . beyond these lonesome hills we climb." They sang without the slightest whiff of obligation or duty or because Mr. Weaver had said they should. They were doing it for joy, and to thank me for being there, for having wandered onto their playground and for taking pleasure in what they did.

It may have been the fullest offering of thanks I have ever received. Those voices, how they mixed and soared and played off one another—the girls on one side, the boys on the other, the full light of the afternoon spilling in over their heads—it was all miraculous and beautiful. The simple purity of it, mixed with the lyrics of death and longing for a better place, twisted a part of me. I won't lie. I cried when they sang those songs.

At the end of the second hymn, when the voices faded and they closed their hymnals and looked over at me, smiling, I couldn't find the words. I choked out my thanks and did a little bow and they laughed and filed back upstairs.

As the kids returned to their classroom, I tidied up with the sleeves of my shirt and asked Neal Weaver about the hymns. He said both were written by a cousin of his, Darlene Zimmerman—the first, to mourn the death of her grandfather, and the other, the death of her grandmother. I then asked about the singers and what keeps them here as they grow up and for Neal to explain the simple tenets of the Mennonite faith.

Some will wander but those who feel at home in the traditions they uphold will stay. "And that is most of them by far." As for the faith, he said, it is all about nonresistance and nonconformity, he said. "The nonresistance is pretty much self-explanatory. We don't fight in wars. We don't engage in lawsuits. The nonconformity is more complicated. Most of these kids have some form of internet, but it is limited in scope. We seek to protect ourselves from forces on the outside that could harm us."

I said it was counterintuitive to build a system of nonconformity around social rules and regulations that one then had to conform to. He nodded and said, "Yes, it is a hard concept to understand," and then he quoted a passage from Romans that underpins their thinking: "Be not conformed to this world but be transformed by the renewing of your mind."

When he first uttered that line, mentioning it came from a letter by St. Paul, it floated over my head but hung there, half heard. A minute later I stopped him and asked him to repeat it. When he did, I felt a burst of clarity come over me. It felt charged, like a gentle surge of electricity. I reworked it slightly and said it back to him: "Do not let the world form you. Do not conform to it. Instead, transform yourself through a renewing of your mind."

That's it, he said.

Out of nowhere, Neal had handed me a new frame through

which to see the entire walk. A few words plucked from a letter written two millennia ago had distilled so much of my thinking over the previous week. How we have the powers to slip from the world's restraints and refashion our thinking, refresh our eyes, strip away the clutter and the noise. To renew our minds.

We went upstairs to the hallway outside his classroom and agreed to keep in touch. I poked my head in the classroom and again thanked the kids, who were diligently working at their desks even without their teacher. They smiled and waved, abuzz but already shifting their focus to the task at hand.

Down the corridor, when I bent to fill my water bottle from the drinking fountain, I could hear Neal Weaver address the class after all that hoopla of the wandering stranger who came out of nowhere to tell his story and to hear them sing. And this is what Neal Weaver said: "Now, as you know, we're working on vocabulary, so if you all turn your reading books to page seventeen, we can get started."

The purity of it all, from that cleanly fielded fly ball to Neal's simple statement as he resumed teaching, left me astonished as I went up the road. Setting out one morning on a long walk was my own little act of nonconformity, a pushing back against set patterns and assumptions. A simple act that had set in motion a deeper renewal.

CHAPTER 11

A MARTYRS MIRROR

H ere it is," Amos Hoover said as he handed me the book, hefty as a paving stone. Fifteen inches thick, it was bound in cowhide gone glossy and dark with age, the ornate imprints on its cover nearly worn away by the rubbing of hands. It had two brass latches and leather straps to hook it closed. "No book other than the Bible is more central to Anabaptist identity," Amos said. Many newlyweds still receive a copy on their wedding day.

A Dutch printer and binder had created this particular volume in 1685, the year Bach and Handel were born and New York became a colony. Its title, in Dutch of course, was as bulky as the book itself: *The Bloody Theater or Martyrs Mirror of the Defenseless Christians who baptized only upon confession of faith, and who suffered and died for the testimony of Jesus, their Saviour, from the time of Christ to the year A.D. 1660.*

When I first heard of the *Martyrs Mirror* while doing research for the walk, its mere existence felt utterly exotic and yet foundational to an early portion of our nation's beginnings. Thousands of the earliest settlers had sailed across the Atlantic lugging along this lavishly illustrated compendium of Christian persecutions. Its simple message: your beliefs are worth defending to the point of death. This anthology of woe was the largest single volume ever published in early America, and tens of thousands of copies remain tucked on shelves in farmhouses across America, in Dutch, German, and English. This book partly explained why the kids at the school barely a mile down the road had sung to me two happy hymns about their yearning for the afterlife.

When I heard thirteen months earlier that a virus had closed the libraries and archives in this part of Lancaster County, preventing me from examining this book, I knew I had to push my walk into another season or another year.

I now held in my hands one of the prime destinations for my walk.

I had left the Farmersville Mennonite School thirty minutes earlier and turned left on Cats Back Road to hike to the top of a high saddle of land with a sweeping view of fields, barns, a curving creek, a red covered bridge, and the town of Ephrata in the hazy distance. You could hear the hum of the freeway that cut in between. The low-slung Muddy Creek Farm Library stood on that rise, and Amos Hoover came out of its front door to greet me in a black straw fedora, the headwear for his branch of Old Order Mennonites.

Amos wore black jeans held up with black suspenders over a faded blue button-down shirt. He was impressed by my walk but wanted me to know that at a spry eighty-nine, he logged five miles a day along the same roads. He used to be a farmer but now he's an archivist, a librarian, "an historical," as the butcher down the road had called him. He founded and now runs the library that hugs that ridge of land.

Amos took me inside his memory palace.

The Muddy Creek Farm Library has books—hundreds of copies of the *Martyrs Mirror,* even more massive family Bibles—but its resemblance to other libraries ends there. This library is a community pool, centuries deep, some of it digital, some bound in leather and printed on parchment, whose chief interpreter is very much the brain of Amos Hoover.

His assistant, Jonathan Martin, sat hunched at an old computer that buzzed atop a desk. The machine, in no way tied to the internet, contained reams of genealogical data tracing nearly every family in the area back to their earliest roots. "Just like dogs, we, too, have pedigree charts," Jonathan said with a laugh.

Amos looked over Jonathan's shoulder and picked off a few names. "That man there, I have part of his diary. I know where he is listed in what family Bibles, where he's buried, where he used to live, who he's related to." On he went like that with name after name.

On the wall hung a large, framed diagram that showed a vast semicircle of tiny names in boxes fanning outward from a central root. This was Amos's own family tree. The roots—Generation 1— were his children. He and his wife were the trunk. From there the tree fanned out ten generations wide, with room for 1,020 direct ancestors stretching back to the late 1600s, half of whom represented the tenth generation alone.

Go back far enough, the chart suggested, and we are all related to everyone who ever was. Those of us alive today represent roughly the five hundredth generation since humans began to farm, so Amos's chart was but the tiniest slice of a very long story. The number of your ancestors grows exponentially as the actual population of humans on Earth shrinks. It's a hard concept to get your head around, even when presented in such physical form. Dig just three or four generations back into anyone's family and what you find gets dizzying in its complexity very fast.

The copy of the *Martyrs Mirror* that Amos set before me predated all but a dozen of the eldest ancestors listed on his family chart. The twisted history of this book rivals any in America. As Anabaptist converts were drowned or burned or beheaded starting in the mid-1500s, others wrote of these travails in letters, court records, diaries, and above all, yes, as hymns. A vast corpus grew into a spasm of martyrologies published across northern Europe, and most of all in the Netherlands.

A minister from the Dutch city of Dordrecht named Thieleman van Braght assembled the largest compendium of martyrdom tales, including many that went back to early Christendom, and published them in the expanded and exquisitely illustrated edition in 1685, which sat before me now. Nearly half the book consists of a detailed history intended to show that the Anabaptist outlook—of adult baptisms and turning the other cheek—flowed from practices going all the way back to Christ. The martyrs, van Braght was eager to show, were all earnest believers and the furthest thing from firebrands. His *Martyrs Mirror* ever since has been the ne plus ultra of martyrologies.

To hear Amos tell it, the book became a form of armor for the Mennonites who flocked to North America. Its translation into German and its first publication in Pennsylvania—at the cloister of the Mystic Order of the Solitary up the road, where I would be that night—came in response to an outbreak of hostilities between white settlers and the native tribes in the 1740s, what historians today call King George's War, a preamble to the French and Indian War.

Elders wanted the book put in a tongue they could read to instill discipline and gird the young against any temptation to take up arms and fight alongside the English. Van Braght himself had warned in his preamble that modern temptations to conform would prove even more intense than during the decades of the worst persecution.

One of the thousands of stories in van Braght's book tells of a young mother, Maeyken Wens, arrested on heresy charges and burned at the stake in Antwerp's main square in October 1573. Her death was a spectacle, a form of entertainment, but to prevent her bearing witness the authorities affixed a metal clamp on her tongue to keep her from singing. Amos helped me find the engraving illustrating Maeyken Wens's death in the book in front of me. It depicts not the flames but her two sons digging through the ashes afterward to find the tongue screw.

The story of Maeyken Wens and the tongue screw are spoken of still, more than four centuries later. "Maeyken Wens is a reminder," one Mennonite scholar wrote a decade ago, "that stories from the past that come to shape a tradition are never preserved by accident, even as the past is transformed by the very process of remembering."

That line could apply to the whole of our history.

As Amos talked, describing his own long entanglements with the *Martyrs Mirror,* I paged through the book before me, printed a century before the United States became a country and then hauled across the Atlantic in the luggage of some immigrant who had fled the Dutch lands. It smelled musty and important. Its pages, covered in a Gothic Dutch, were yellowed at the edges but still white and crisp inside.

"Ministers still cite these stories and preach that we are a martyr people," Amos said as I turned from carnage to carnage. A group of men in floppy hats and rolled-up sleeves were chopping off the arms and legs of a man writhing on the ground. One assailant held a knife in his teeth as smoke billowed into the sky. On another page, a group of nobles looked on approvingly as flames engulfed a crowd of men and women, each tied to a high stake of wood. Every sixth or seventh page, another antique horror.

"Most of these are too gruesome to put on the wall," Amos said.

The nonconformity that the Anabaptists so prized had led to these deaths just as these deaths, preserved in the pages of this omnipresent book, still steeled their conviction to remain apart.

Amos began to talk about the little fissures that now define the many subgroups of Anabaptists even within the confines of greater Farmersville. The big tenets bind them together just as differences of custom—or what they call *Ordnung*—set them apart. Much of it had to do with how they did or did not conform to the world.

"There are five groups here that drive horse and buggies," Amos said. "But when we talk of *the* horse and buggy group, we are talking about the Wenger group or the Groffdale Conference. They are the largest group, the most conservative and the most German. Then we have the Stauffer group. Their clothing and buggies are more austere. I can see one of those buggies coming from a quarter of a mile away. They use only steel rims on their wheels and have no windows on the sides."

As he went on with the full taxonomy, I thought of Darwin wandering the Galapagos and marveling at the different types of finches and tortoise he found. They had come as a single species and evolved, and broken into subspecies, and still other subspecies, but all within the same rarified ecosystem in a universe far apart from that freeway I could hear buzzing on the other side of the hill.

We went into the archives where the oldest volumes were stored in a climate-controlled room. I carried the book, as solid as a cinder block. I had walked eight days to hold that book in my hands. It, too, was part of our continuum, like the hinges on the barn along the Mason-Dixon line, or the carvings of thunderbirds on the rocks midstream in the Susquehanna. I handed it to Amos, who slipped it back on the shelf.

———◆———

I had miles to go still, so I thanked Amos Hoover and told him I was off to deliver a message to another Hoover family down on Crooked Lane. How a week earlier in Maryland I had met a couple who knew them, and now that I was here, I had to go pass along their regards. Amos looked at me a little wide-eyed and said he knew those Hoovers and attended the same church but shared no family ties that he knew of. They would be the fourth set of Hoovers I met that day, none of them direct kin.

From the rise Amos pointed me to the Hoover farm, just off to the west, and with his finger he traced in the air how I would walk down that road there and cross the Conestoga over that covered bridge and then keep straight past that schoolhouse. Can you see it, there, where the road bends? Can you see there where the pavement gives way to dirt? You will keep down that way and find their farm beside that smudge of a red barn just before all those trees.

I set off like a herald down the hill for Crooked Lane.

Down Cats Back Road I went exulting at what the day had brought. How with the arching stone bridge and the laundry out to dry and the maples just flowering and the bologna slices from Zimmerman's butcher shop and the hard-hit softball and the floral dresses and the two hymns they sang for me and the letter of St. Paul to the Romans and my hour spent gazing into the *Martyrs Mirror*—how you just don't have many days as rich as this. I marveled that the sun still had two hours left in the sky and then waved apologetically to the cars stopped at either end of the Bitzer's Mill Covered Bridge as I took the whole of its single lane to run through that bridge over the Conestoga River.

As I ran across the span I could smell the warm oak and the double Burr arched trusses of the oldest bridge in Lancaster County, built in 1846, the year when the whole of the West blew open, the U.S. went to war with Mexico, the Mormons streamed toward Utah, and the Donner party froze in the Sierras. This bridge, too, had had other names: Martin's Mill Bridge, Eberly's Cider Mill Bridge, Fiantz's Mill Bridge, and was officially known now as Big Conestoga #2 Bridge.

Crooked Lane starts at a bend in Peach Road where there's a gnarled old white maple tree and a faded white schoolhouse that says, below the peak of its roof, "Conestoga View Built in 1954." I kept on just as Amos told me, and buggies went by—one a Stauffer, the other an Old Order Groffdale Conference, from what I knew now, newfangled Darwin that I was. The young men holding the reins would tip their hat and smile with mouths full of teeth that needed help. They went by close, with me right there on the shoulder. It was warm with a slight breeze, and you could hear the high pitch of tires on the freeway to the right toward Ephrata. The buggies were coequals with the cars on the country roads, but the freeway and all it represented—the speed, the convenience, the far away—resided in another universe.

I went on, thinking of this concept of nonconformity and renewal. Even now, well on in life, I felt the need to push back on the confines of what comes too easily. How the prepackaged clutter of our culture blurs the mind and spirit. We should all seek to simplify. That is the modesty I embrace. But there is also a nonconformity that becomes a shunning of the world, and that holds no appeal for me. The same Maeyken Wens who was burned at the stake in Antwerp wrote to her son beforehand and said: "Hear the instruction of your mother: hate everything that is loved by the world and your sensuality, and love God's commandment." My sensuality on a day like this told me to love much that was loved by the world, and to keep on down that road.

———◆———

The Hoover homestead stood at the end of a long straight gravel drive that then crooked in the middle of their farm, thus putting the crook in Crooked Lane. I could see two tall silos on the left and below them a large red barn. Off to the right below trees that had yet to leaf was a farmhouse, white, nicely kept. Two hundred yards straight across from me as I walked, I could see a man plowing up the earth on a faded old tractor with metal wheels. As he went, he left in his wake great mounds of wet soil ready for the planting. The road took its bend into the farm, and I could smell but not see the horses and cows. Across a grassy slope and past two enormous sycamore trees, the Conestoga River spilled over a small waterfall into a frothy pool the color of dark ale.

I was here looking at this river now because of that bridge the week before that was too narrow to carry me over that other stream. Such is how one thing leads to the other, how turns of chance take you delicately by the hand.

No one was about, and a big dog lay sleeping by the front door, so I decided to go see the man on the plow and hear what he had to say. I dropped my pack on the yard and walked out to the field. He had to have seen me, a tall man coming toward him from another world. But he kept plowing this way and that until we intersected halfway across the field, and I stood there, and he just squinted at me, unbelieving, put the tractor in idle, and climbed down from the high metal seat. I could see fat earthworms twisting in the soil he had just plowed. I could see the tangled threads of old roots. He wore muddy jeans held up by suspenders over a dusty flannel shirt. On his head he had the same black straw fedora that Amos had worn outside the library, also covered in dust.

"Help ya?" he said.

I said I was looking for David Hoover and he looked at me like I might be a bill collector. My tick-depleted voice didn't compete well with the rumble of his idling tractor.

"And why would that be?"

He bent toward me as I told him the story of the Herders, and how we'd met on a tiny lane in Maryland because I didn't want to cross a dangerous bridge, and how I had promised I'd bring their good tidings while on my way to New York City. And he scrunched up his face and said, "Okay, now I got it."

The Herders had mentioned that the Hoovers had a son named Lamar, so I said, "I assume you're Lamar." And he said he was.

Lamar took his hat off and wiped the sweat off his forehead

with the sleeve of his shirt and thanked me for coming by and said he'd be glad to pass along my regards to his folks. I told him that wouldn't do. I really did want to see his folks myself and had walked a long way to do so. He got my point.

"Okay, just go on back up there and look around. The dog won't hurt you. My dad is probably doing chores somewhere." Then he asked: "Where are you putting up at night?" I told him I'd be sleeping in Ephrata that night, and he nodded. For a fleeting second, I thought I might have been invited to spend the night in their barn.

Back at the house the dog rolled on her back to get her belly scratched as I knocked on the door, again and again. No answer. Finally, from across the drive, an old man came out of the barn. His was a craggier, more furrowed look of disbelief, but he was otherwise the spitting image of Lamar twenty-five years or so further down the pike.

"Help ya?" he said.

I told him the story, that I was there as a messenger, and he laughed with a strange toothy laugh that had a cackle in it, and said, "Well, hear that." Lamar had come up from the field and the three of us talked, and David said he was glad to hear the Herders were good, but he didn't care to see the picture I had taken of them. Photos on people's pocket phones weren't his thing, and I didn't blame him.

A couple of times, when the silence fell, you could hear the birds or the water burping from a spigot into a big basin near the house. A pump, powered by the river, was drawing water from the well and spewing it into that basin. That in its own right seemed miraculous.

"Those are the flood lines," Lamar said, when he saw me looking at the small tin markers nailed into a tall sycamore down by the river. The highest one, at least twelve feet off the ground, was for

Agnes in 1972. "Good thing our house and barns are on this rise, or we'd a been swamped," he said.

They owned eighty-eight acres, seven of which had frontage on the snaking Conestoga. Stacked with waterfront tract houses with twin garages and cathedral ceilings, the land would fetch five or six million, easy. But development like that was restricted, and they had no intention of selling and even less desire for a payout. That sort of thinking was the remotest thing from their minds.

"We'll farm it as long as we can make it," David said.

We looked out over the land under a fading sun and then Lamar said, "What about your occupation?" Reporter, writer, I said. "I like to write stories." Father and son looked at each other and laughed. They didn't know what to make of that occupation.

We talked about COVID, and they said yes, it had disrupted things and they had to wear masks at the drugstore but not at church. It was fading now. Would they be seeking out the vaccine? "Nah, don't figure," David said. You could hear heavy remnants of German in his voice.

When I asked if I might take a quick photo of them, Lamar said, "Well, we don't really care for that, but you can if you do it on the sneak." They both stood by the barn, exposing their sides to the lens but glancing my way like bashful schoolgirls. That's what they called doing it on the sneak.

"You enjoy yourself now," David said. "Let the Herders know we're well if you see them."

Father and son were still in disbelief that I'd walked that whole way. "Foot walkin' express," the father said. As I thanked them for their time and went up to the house to get some water from their well spout, they both vanished into the barn. My mission was complete. I continued up Crooked Lane to where it spilled onto East

Metzler Road and then I wound my way to the town of Ephrata for the night, half the way walking on air.

Ephrata is named for the biblical town of Ephrath, also known in Genesis as Bethlehem, so it felt right to bunk at an inn where the floors creaked and the pipes rattled when the hot water came through. A newspaperman more than a century earlier described the place as "a dingy, straggling, unpaved town," but it felt like a prim place now, tucked among hills with a wide Main Street.

A friend, Jeff McGuiness, drove up from outside Washington, and we went to an old steakhouse where Abraham Lincoln peered from the walls in room after room. As we sliced our steaks and sipped our wine, a young Abe stared from a frame over my shoulder, earnest and clear-eyed, his hair neatly combed, his face not yet creased. I felt I had earned the right, with all the miles walked, to the steak's charred fat dunked into a pool of vinegary sauce.

The day had contained so much I nearly forgot I'd come to Ephrata to walk the grounds of its abandoned cloister, where the Mystic Order of the Solitary wrote hymns and published early editions of the *Martyrs Mirror* and slept on wooden beds for much of the nineteenth century. For a year I had kept an eye on the cloister and communicated with its staff. Its closure in the early days of COVID led me to nix the walk for a year.

Twilight was ceding to the darkness of a Tuesday evening when we arrived on the cloister's grounds. Electric lanterns perched high on poles gave off a yellow glow. A cat dashed behind one of the tall, barnlike houses. These oak-planked buildings, plain and imposing and ghostly in the evening light, trace back directly to the architecture of medieval Germany.

A group of German mystic Pietists, led by an ascetic seeker named Conrad Beissel, arrived here on the edge of the American wilderness in 1732. Beissel's core followers were celibate; their strict prayer schedule called for breaking up their sleep for nightly worship. America's first clock tower stood here, complete with a bell to regulate the monastic rounds. Scholars describe the cloister as the first successful experiment in European utopian life in the Americas.

Still, by early in the next century, all the monks were gone. They had pushed back against the world with their own peculiar nonconformity. They spurned sex, slept on wooden benches, and woke in the wee hours to watch for the coming of Christ. It didn't hold. The outside world won.

As I wandered the cloister's grounds, I could see flickering through the bare trees the brighter fires of the victors' camps. A Sunoco Service Station basked in a neon glare beside Memory Lane Automotive. Near the highway on-ramp sat a Papa John's Pizza. Up the other way, instead of the long-awaited Christ the King that the monks had sought, you could see the luminous glow of a Dairy Queen.

CHAPTER 12

YEAR OF THE DESTROYING ANGELS

You fall in bed exhausted, depleted but satisfied, your head buzzing from all that the day contained. You have used the tub to wash the grime from the day's socks, shirt, and underwear, twisting them to squeeze out every drop so they will dry by the morning. You dream all night of walking but then step from bed, excited, an hour before sunrise, clenching your fists in anticipation of the day ahead. I was off to spend some hours with a family that had walked the same hallways of the same house for nine generations.

Fickleness and fate guide our steps whenever we're on the move. A whirlwind of ghastly forces had landed that family along the banks of Muddy Creek, where they had sunk deep roots. Meanwhile, I knew of that family because of a much different set of forces, perhaps equally odd.

In 1921, an eight-year-old boy named John Collier Jr. had his formal education cut short due to cognitive impairment and hearing loss from a car wreck in Mill Valley, California. His father, later FDR's head of the Bureau of Indian Affairs, sent the boy to live with friends on the Taos Indian Pueblo. That experience sparked lifelong passions for anthropology and photography. The boy bounced between New Mexico and Mill Valley and turned to art, and sailing. Paul Strand and other artists who streamed through New Mexico took an interest in Collier. He apprenticed to the Western painter Maynard Dixon and met Dixon's wife, the photographer Dorothea Lange.

In his late twenties, Collier signed on as a photographer for the Historical Section of the Farm Security Administration (FSA). His boss, the economist Roy Stryker, had a broad mission: "Show the city people what it's like to live on the farm."

Collier roamed Lancaster County for the FSA in March 1942, chronicling Amish auctions and barns and the butchering of hogs. Outside of Ephrata that March, he spent a day in and around a tall, whitewashed stone house. His austere black-and-white photos of the house and its interior all bore captions testifying to Collier's fascination with the longevity of those who lived there. "Fry homestead," said one, "which has been in the family for seven generations."

I was walking now along Frysville Road because a few months earlier, I had stumbled on Collier's Fry homestead photos in the archives of the Library of Congress. Those images got lodged in my mind. I couldn't quite shake them. The simple continuity of that family, embodied by that one house, had captivated Collier in the early 1940s. I became captivated, too, not just at the prospect of finding the house, but in discovering what memories, what clues to our past and future, it might still hold.

Surely the house still existed, no? Did the Fry family, now on to its ninth or tenth generation, still live there? I had to find out.

———◆———

There are today, at heart, two American stories: the story of those who stay, and the story of those who go. The land was settled—as far back as the earliest tribes—by people who took great leaps.

Some of us still wander from place to place, and many others of us don't. We have the Somewhere people, who are very much of a place and rooted there, and we have the Anywhere people, who have a faint sense of belonging wherever they are and if they ever had a place, they left it behind long ago.

My life began with rootedness as a fourth-generation Coloradan. I was raised in a town where I could hike up the mountain and see the hospital where I was born, the house I grew up in, and every school I attended until the age of eighteen. But then that gave way to migrations that took me to every state in the country and far across the Atlantic for nearly the whole of the 1990s, before settling in Washington, a city I barely knew until we bought our house on Ninth Street. If I tried to count the places where I have lived for more than a month, it would tally in the many dozens, even if nearly half my life now I have lived in one place. I am an Anywhere person, vaguely at home Anywhere, living in a city dominated by Anywhere people. I have neighbors within forty yards of my house whose names I don't know.

I left Ephrata that morning and walked past Anywhere—the Starbucks, the Arbys, the Taco Bell—and then cut back into the land of the particular along Hahnstown Road. That particular tree in front of that particular house. I turned at the Hahnstown United Zion Church and took Frysville Road across Muddy Creek to where it intersected with Frys Road. There, among a stand of trees along the creek, I found Frysville Farm in Frysville, Pennsylvania. Across the yard stood the house I had seen, and beside it an old mill house where I'd been told I could find Simon Fry. I knocked at the door and thirty seconds later, Simon Fry yanked it open and told me to watch my head coming in. He had been expecting me.

"I'll give you a look around," he said, making no mention of masks or any of that. The virus wasn't discussed much in this part of the state. "There is a lot to see."

Simon and his brother Tony and his siblings are now the eighth generation of Frys to live on the Frysville property. Their children are the ninth. Their children's children are the tenth. No one other than Frys reside in Frysville. I had never been to a ville, if you could call it that, made up entirely of a single family. The cavernous room where I stood was not just the office for the family's booming floral business, but was also the archives for more than two centuries of residency on the land.

Simon, at fifty-three, had a grizzled beard and a weathered baseball cap atop his head. He wore a faded blue T-shirt with a pen protruding from his breast pocket. His family's story he knew perhaps better than he knew the two hundred acres of creek front where he lived.

His people were not Anabaptists but Swiss German Lutherans who migrated into the Palatinate area of Germany after the devastation of the Thirty Years War. They were among the flood who then poured into Rotterdam in the spring of 1738 hoping to pack onto ships and sail to America. The horrors that ensued were such that 1738 became known as the Year of the Destroying Angels, as from Psalm 78, verse 49: "He let loose on them his fierce anger, wrath, indignation, and distress, a company of destroying angels."

Simon talked as if all this happened a decade ago. "You had a lot of pestilence in Rotterdam. Things weren't sanitary. You had all these people packed into refugee camps and if you survived that you were packed onto a ship and had to survive three months across the ocean." It brought to mind the legions that were at the moment streaming up from El Salvador, Guatemala, and Haiti, trying to get across the Mexican border and safely into the United States.

English sea captains spread word of bargains and bogus schemes that swelled the numbers beyond available space. Rotterdam closed its gates to the sickly hordes and packed them into fetid holding camps rife with dysentery and typhus, where they waited months for the ships to come. In all, scholars estimate that 6,490 people embarked from the Netherlands that season, and 4,330 survived the trip.

"Thus are the judgments of God over those who went down the Rhine toward their anticipated paradise to the tune of fiddles and pipes, dancing and jumping, cursing, swearing, indulging in food and drink, with all exuberance and dreams of high living," said one stern account of that year.

Simon's forebearer, Hans Martin Fry, came across with his mother and siblings aboard the *Two Sisters,* which sailed up the Delaware and deposited them in Philadelphia. It was the third ship to arrive among the fleet of twenty-three that brought so many Germans across the Atlantic that year. I asked what month that would have been. Simon pulled out the bottom drawer of a desk and extracted a document, glanced at it, and said, "They arrived on September 9, 1738." He had in his hand a copy of the ship's manifest.

Hans Martin Fry had a son named John Martin Fry and that son survived six battles in the Revolutionary War and crossed the Delaware with Washington's troops in 1776, and then bought the grist mill, where we now stood, in 1785. The maps on the walls, the massive 1729 Nuremberg Bible that Simon held in his hands, the stacks of land deeds on parchment signed by the sons of William Penn—it was as if the room held America's very own birth records. One cabinet, five feet tall, bulged top to bottom with the leather-bound ledgers that recorded the grist mill's every transaction, day after day and year after year, until the mill shut down in 1920.

Simon showed me what he called the family wall, a sea of old framed photos. His great-great-grandparents. His great-grandparents. His grandparents. His parents. The whole line since the advent of photography. They all lived there and died there. The bookshelves held battered editions of Shakespeare, Twain, Kipling, Matthew Arnold, Conan Doyle, *The Popular Encyclopedia of Useful Knowledge.*

We went outside to see the house that John Collier Jr. had

photographed in 1942, so struck then that seven generations of Frys had lived in that house. Simon's father, Morton, was eleven years old on the day of that visit. Simon came along twenty-six years later. When I tracked him down by phone two weeks before my walk, he was surprised he had never heard of the Collier photographs that now reside at the Library of Congress. "Dad never mentioned those," he said.

The old house still stood, of course. Tony Fry lived there now with his wife, Denise, who invited me inside. The interior bore little resemblance to the austere rooms Collier had toured in 1942. The exterior had changed, too, but far less. The original porch had rotted years ago and been torn off. They stripped away the old horsehair plaster and revealed the original stone structure, quarried from just up the hill. The simple pattern of a radiating sun was still there, built into the masonry just below the crown of the roof and to the side of the chimney. The house sported a big TV antenna now, evidence that Tony was no captive to the cable companies.

In all, four members of the eighth generation remained on the property. They in turn had twelve children, who had also begun to have children, marking the beginning of the tenth generation.

Simon's nephew Andre joined us, and as we stood on the yard of the old house talking, I asked about those who stay and those who go. Hundreds of Frys from Frysville had transplanted across the country, of course. Distant cousins and nephews and such. "There are Frys scattered from coast to coast," Simon said.

Of the ninth generation of Frys, Andre was the only one so far who planned to stick around. Both he and Simon had had their years away at college or working different jobs elsewhere. Simon went to Penn State and had a couple of years doing landscape jobs. Andre lived for a few years in Colorado and Texas. Both had every intention of coming back. "There is always just someone who sticks around, I guess," said Andre. "I figured I would make my mistakes elsewhere before coming back," Simon said. "I never entertained any idea other than being here."

If the world really is divided between Somewhere people and Anywhere people, Simon and Andre were as Somewhere as you could find, and they made no apologies for it. A Fry born more than three hundred years earlier had made one wrenching move to cross the Atlantic, to leave everything behind and risk life in a new land on a voyage named for a destroying angel. His son settled along Muddy Creek, and portions of the next eight generations never left.

We heard the cry of an osprey and stopped talking for a minute to watch it circle. Simon described when the osprey come and go every spring and fall, where they nest and hunt. He knew where all the eagles had built their nests. How a guy named Gundy, who he said had worked as a cook for Washington's army at Valley Forge, was buried right up there on that hill. Exactly what day his people had arrived in Philadelphia in 1738, and aboard what ship. He carried all that and would pass it along, as others had passed along the grist mill ledgers, the hefty Bible, *The Popular Encyclopedia of Useful Knowledge,* and the house that Collier photographed.

———◆———

I had arrived at the Frysville Farm about an hour late, as will happen sometimes when you're out walking and stumble on things. I spent the time in a barn making small talk with a Mennonite farrier and the man whose horse he was shoeing. I'd noticed a sign beside the road with the image of a merry trotting horse above the word "Horseshoeing," then heard hammering in a shop up the gravel drive. It was all an invitation to see what might await me there.

The man inside the little barn was bent at the knees with a

horse hoof in his lap and he looked back at me over his left shoulder as he drove a nail through a hole in the horseshoe and said, "Well, what have we got here?" It really was an excellent question.

"Just walking through," I said. "From my house in Washington all the way to New York. Seeing things."

"If you've come to see horseshoeing, you've come to the right place." He was wiry, forty-five or so, and wore a dirty leather apron and heavy boots. He was at work on the first of four hooves and had time to kill.

I took a seat. He told me his name was Matt Strawn.

As he moved on to the second hoof, he used a long shearing knife—a butteris, they call it—to shave the horse's huge toenail to make it smooth and even. Horses need a manicure like this four times a year or so, and new shoes at least that often, he said. "They wear out fast on these roads."

The guy who owned the horse, Amon Burkholder, came in with his young son in his arms. He took the seat next to me. Amon wore a green felt fedora and a light jacket and he wouldn't have been out of place hunting foxes in the horse country of Virginia. His son wore a bright blue knit hat for warmth that surely his mother had made. I have never seen one like it for purchase. Amon's buggy was framed by the open barn door, right out front, square and black, awaiting its newly shod engine.

I took it all in—Amon and his son with their buggy right outside; Matt and the horse huffing in the corner—and thought I would have walked the whole way from Washington just to sit on that stool, a privileged perch from which to see things I'd never seen before.

I had barged into Matt Strawn's barn as if I belonged there. Pretty much everywhere I'd gone so far—the dot that was Young Man's Fancy, the tavern near the Mason-Dixon Line, the Black cemetery in York, the butcher shop outside Lancaster, the Mennonite school, the Hoover family farm—I'd felt pretty much the same way. I knew well that I was drawing on a privilege both of attitude and appearance, and how seamlessly the one buttresses the other.

Pushing open certain doors is infinitely easier when you inhabit one body and not another. Being white and male undoubtedly smooths the path and reduces the risks along the way. Not for a second would I downplay the entitlement that grants.

Being an Anywhere Person also makes you more at home anywhere. I could stride into Matt Strawn's barn and sit on his stool and strike up a conversation because I brought with me a sense of belonging. A sense that I did not feel out of place there.

The feeling that you belong where you are is the ultimate human privilege—the state we all yearn to achieve as we go forward. That sense of being at ease in the place where you stand. That you are respected and trusted and not looked down upon. That you share with the people around you a common sense of relevance, a mutual caring for the other's well-being, maybe even a similar purpose. Or at the least a basic feeling of welcomeness, as Matt Strawn had extended his welcome without pause or hesitation when I came through his door.

Ideally, we learn to expand our sphere of belonging well beyond our family, our clan, our tribe or political party or village or sports team or national identity. When that happens, belonging becomes a transportable state of mind, something that you take with you as you roam. Belonging is something you do—you belong—but also something you have, like a cherished item you can hold in your hand. "He arrived with his few belongings on his back."

The best way to get people to think you belong in the pool hall, the bar, the Mennonite schoolhouse, or the barn with the bearded auctioneer while the snow blows horizontally outside is for you to feel like you belong there yourself. The most durable form of belonging starts, oddly, with solitude. The better you are at being alone, the more comfortable you are as you go and the more effortlessly you belong in the places where you arrive. At the same time, you treat the people you meet as if they also belong as part of your world, that they are themselves a part of your walk.

The word "belong" derives from an old Germanic root with rumblings both of duration and movement. To belong was to go along with someone, to relate to them and accompany them. Which was, I supposed, what all of us were doing now as Matt shoed the horse. It felt natural to accompany him as he worked his way from hoof to hoof.

As I sat there, Amon glanced at me with no surprise or distrust and told me he had owned the horse for a couple of years. "He's a good horse. Speedy. Good endurance." You could hear in his English a touch of the German he still spoke at home.

The horse was a sixteen-year-old bay standardbred who stood sixteen hands tall, Amon said. Sometimes the horse would lean on Matt and Matt would yell, "Whoa now!" and push back. I asked Matt how many horses he might shoe in a day, and he said ten. He charged $75 a horse.

I looked at Amon and said, "Now we're talking real money." They both laughed and I said, "But of course horse-kick insurance can get pretty costly."

"Real costly," Matt said. "Even more costly is when you do get kicked and can't work for weeks."

Whenever a buggy clattered by, they would both duck to the open window to see who it was. They knew everybody. A couple of times Matt trash-talked the buggy drivers, all of them men. "That all ya got?" "Geez. Now where ya heading?"

I drew laughs with stories of the folks I'd met along the way— the Zimmermans at the butcher shop, the kids at the school, Amos Hoover up at the library, the Hoovers on their farm on Crooked Lane. How I was off to see the Frys at Frysville Farm. It was all as familiar as the horse in front of them. I had gathered a lot of local currency in a day, and it would all draw a blank in another ten miles.

I asked how things were going, how life was, and they both said it pretty much couldn't be better. Amon had a warehouse operation that grew produce of all kinds, which was selling well. Matt said everyone he knew had never been busier, and COVID hadn't slowed anyone.

I asked if these were the best of times, or whether times had been better, and they both looked at each other and said these times were pretty much as good as they've been. "In our memories, anyway," said Matt.

"Haven't you already shoed that hoof?" I asked when he was yanking off the rear right shoe with a special pry tool. Matt exhaled loudly at the question. "I may be getting shaky but I'm not outright Alzheimer's," he said.

When he finished with the sixteen-hand standard bay, Matt handed Amon a yellow invoice and then said to me, "I don't know what to make of you exactly, Neil King, but I am going to give you some cookies."

He went across to the house and his wife put four oatmeal chocolate chip cookies in a little bag, and Matt tossed it to me across the yard. I could feel their warmth when they fell into my cupped hands. "Those will serve you well," he said.

I went back down the drive past the sign that had caught my eye and bit into the first cookie as Matt brought the horse out of the shop and we both waved. "I don't know what to make of you, Matt Strawn, but thanks for the cookies," I said.

———◆———

Evening would put me beyond the land of the Anabaptists and into the showier farms and houses of the English in Chester County. I was walking again between nations, as when I crossed the Susque-hanna earlier that week, and was a little mournful to be moving on.

Outside the Terre Hill Mennonite High School, I stopped to watch a group of schoolkids play soccer on a wide field. The school administrator, Dan Rudd, came out after a few minutes to greet me with a lunch cooler in his hand. There was a briskness to his step and a clear squint of concern in his eyes. I could tell he'd come to make sure I wasn't a menace. His expression changed as I told him about the walk and how the kids at the school in Farmersville had sung for me, and how Neal Weaver and I had talked about nonconformity in the basement of the school.

"I will pray for you," Dan Rudd said as I began to walk on. I stopped and asked what he meant. What would he pray for in particular? I grew up Catholic, and occasionally went to church, but I wasn't sure I was keen to be the vessel for just any old prayer. "I am going to pray that during your walk you see Jesus in new ways," he said.

It dawned on me that walkers bring out this sort of thing—passing benedictions and the like. That maybe it's something that goes back to ancient times and runs in the blood.

The week before, in northern Maryland, Ted—outside his house hauling in the trash can—had told me that I was on a holy walk, and that if I did it right, I might get the whole nation back on the right frequency. Near Railroad, Pennsylvania, Ken Keeny in the slanting snow outside his barn had said the country was sinking into evil, but that "the proper sparks," like our talk that afternoon, might make a difference in beating that back. In York, the mayor had told me that we are all God's mirrors, and we exist so God might enjoy his creation. When leaving York, I ran into the woman in a nightgown whose husband had just died of COVID and she blessed me and said that she, too, would pray for me. Neal Weaver had quoted from Paul's letter to the Romans on how one should "be not conformed to the world." And now this guy was heaping a prayer on me, too. I told him I'd keep my eyes peeled for any signs of Jesus.

Farther along, I kept thinking about the whole question of who is doing it right, and what that even means. I know that a lot of us aren't doing it right. That our lives are too cluttered, too filled with distraction. That "getting and spending," as Wordsworth said, "we lay waste our powers." Instead of seeking simplicity, we incline the other way, and take on more possessions, more burdens, more stuff to do. Despite all those pants in my closet, I was never above buying more.

I walked along and came to a woman tending to an explosion of yellow daffodils in her front garden. She was on her knees wearing a simple gray dress and a white head covering. In front of her, on the opposite side of the road, stretched an enormous valley of farms and grain silos and fields. You could see for miles across all that, and in the foreground, you could see a mother cutting across a dirt lane with a small child beside her, pushing a baby buggy.

The woman brightened when she saw me and said, "And where might you be off to?" I told her and she raised her eyebrows, thought about it for a second, and said: "That sounds like a fine way to spend a spring as beautiful as this."

We talked about her flowers, and whether they needed much tending, and then I told her about having quizzed the kids at the school about whether they thought they were doing it right. I told her how they had squirmed and sort of laughed when I asked them that question. And she said, "I'm not sure about doing it right, but I do know that we are blessed. I feel blessed right now."

"Being blessed," I said, "suggests you just might be doing it right."

She smiled and said, "Then I think we probably are."

CHAPTER 13

ROAD TO YELLOW SPRINGS

That night I stayed at an inn, the sole guest there, beside a creek I would follow for much of the next day. I had walked dozens of miles west of Ephrata and could hear French Creek cascading over the rocks outside. French Creek flows into the Schuylkill, which then flows past Valley Forge and from there into the Delaware in Philadelphia. I had left the land where all waters drained into the Chesapeake and would sleep where every rivulet was destined for the Delaware.

A man was dining at the bar—tan sport jacket, jeans—when I descended the creaky stairs that night to get a beer. He put his fork down and asked what had brought me to St. Peters Village on the banks of French Creek. When I told him, and said I was heading to Valley Forge in the morning, he reached into his jacket pocket and handed me his business card. *Wesley Sessa,* it said. *18th Century Restoration Inc.*

"I have a house to show you that will be worth your while," he said as though we'd been destined from the start of the walk to meet. "It's in Coventryville. That's on your way. Or at least not out of your way."

We say that one thing leads to another—and then another, and another after that, and like drops in a river we end up where we are heading along routes not entirely of our choosing. Wesley Sessa was one of those sentries that pop up along all good walks to point the pilgrim down the better path. I had no planned route to Valley Forge, had given it no thought, oddly, and he emerged to provide one. "You won't regret it," he said.

I wandered into Coventryville on a radiant morning with the forsythia in full flower. I had woken early, well before dawn, to the sound of the creek pounding outside, spent a couple of hours writing about the day before, devoured two granola bars and three cups of coffee, let myself out of the inn, and locked the door behind me. There wasn't a soul to be seen anywhere.

As I came into Coventryville every house along the road had a stateliness that made you want to stop and salute it. All made with a solid virtue of pale stone either plucked from the fields or quarried in the nearby hills.

I had now traversed three small nations and was well into my fourth. I had come from the microstate of Capitolia up through what I called Southlandia, the hinge region of northern Maryland through York County to the banks of the Susquehanna. From there I had entered Anabaptistan with its buggies and flapping laundry and distinct whiff of the eighteenth century. A protective people who could also be startlingly frank and open.

Now I was walking through the outer reaches of Englandia, which began after Morgantown and intensified as I meandered down French Creek. This area gave off a whiff of starchy Federalism with a touch of the Quaker. The stone houses had the feel of summer quarters for the smart set. There were inns and spas for pleasuring the monied people. You could feel the gravitational pull of an urban center not far away.

The whole of Wesley Sessa's hamlet, every stitch of it, was on the National Registry of Historic Places. This "was a peaceful, quiet place in 1700," read the application for that distinction. It had but "a few inhabitants living on small, cleared acreages, separated from each other by virgin forests, and totally dependent on themselves for their basic needs."

Coventryville's old general store served now as Wesley's office, crammed not with canned peas and bags of flour but with old armoires, tables, and chairs. Wesley was waiting outside, a boyish seventy-one-year-old, sandy-haired and limber. A former high school English teacher, he had restored eighteenth-century houses and estates and landmarks—hundreds of them, all told—all over the Delaware Valley.

"Let's head up the hill," Wesley said. "I will tell you the story." We walked up a narrow road through a stand of sycamores and Wesley could barely contain himself in telling of all the forces that came together in this small place where the birds of early spring were chirping.

Romantic heartache, pig iron, the first flickers of America's industrial might, Ben Franklin's famous stove, the Battle of the Clouds, cannons straight from the furnace, George Washington marching through with his bedraggled troops—it all merged and swirled right there in humble Coventryville. And Wesley unspooled all of it for the wanderer passing by.

A Quaker named Samuel Nutt, he said, arrived in these hills from Coventry, England, in 1717 with a plan to turn the abundant surface ore into iron, which he did with a series of forges built along French Creek. The first steel ever poured in America came out of his Coventry forge. The Nutt empire expanded even after Samuel's death when his wife, Anna Rutter Nutt, built the famous Warwick Furnace nearby. Many a cannon forged to fire on the British sprang from that furnace.

But Wesley, above all, wanted to show me a house, and he threw open his arms in introduction as we came within sight of her. She wasn't a stunner exactly, but an austere stone Georgian perched on a hill overlooking a pond. Wesley had primped and perfected her over twenty years for two different owners, and he was smitten. A man in love. "With that façade, that south-facing exposure, the raised paneled parlors inside, god is she ever a beauty. This is as good as it gets from that era," he said as we stood outside. "A colonial Philadelphia house built right here in the country. Such a sight."

The house was built of fieldstone covered with coarse ashlar cut sandstone, he explained, and its oldest section, built in 1733, was the spitting image of the Potts house that Washington commandeered as his Valley Forge headquarters. "You will see that house when you get there," Wesley said. "We call them side-passage halls."

Back then, this original modest structure was about as grand as a house got, with a few exceptions, like William Penn's huge manor house in Philadelphia. A kitchen and living area downstairs, a couple of bedrooms upstairs. When Pennsylvania became one of the United States in 1787, nine of ten Chester County houses were still made of logs. It was a flashy house then. Today it would be monkishly small.

One of Ben Franklin's closest friends, a fellow named Robert Grace, had lived here. He moved in after he married Samuel Nutt's niece, Rebecca. Franklin and Grace founded one of the country's earliest cultural organizations, the Library Company of Philadelphia, whose Latin motto reads: "To pour forth benefits for the common good is divine." Its early shelves were heavy with science, geography, and accounts of voyages, but light on theology.

Franklin had had a thing for Rebecca, Wesley told me. They were secretly in love, but it was never to be. "When both lost their spouses, he proposed to her. She turned him down—too much of a rake," he said. Still, she traveled to Philadelphia when Franklin was dying and was among the last to sit beside him.

Years earlier, Franklin had given Robert Grace the specs for his newest creation, known now as the Franklin stove, to settle a debt.

Franklin designed it not for cooking but to improve the heating of chilly houses. The first such stove was made in the town forge and tested, legend has it, right here in the Grace house.

Wesley led me to a window and told me to peer inside. "Okay, now cup your hands around your eyes and let them adjust. See that fireplace? Pretty sure they tested the first Franklin stove right there." Growing up in Stamford, Connecticut, Wesley had served as an altar boy at William F. Buckley's wedding. But this, for him, was more exciting. I could see a modest little sitting room with a fireplace. Franklin had warmed his feet there while pining for Rebecca.

When Washington and his troops came through this way in the early fall of 1777, en route to wintering in Valley Forge, their mission was to check on the Warwick Furnace, which was vital to the army's supply chain. Wesley took me to the furnace along a stretch of French Creek. The trees on the hillsides all flashed the most subtle shades of red, green, and yellow, the earliest stirrings of the summer shade. An astonishingly huge sycamore stood bare-limbed in front of the manor house across the road from the old furnace, now little more than a ruin. We stopped for a moment to take in that tree, which dwarfed the house in size and beauty. Its infancy and that of the country may well have overlapped.

Along the way, Wesley mentioned that Washington had ordered a military hospital be built not far away at a place called Yellow Springs. "It's just over that hill a bit. The ruins of it are still there," he said. The mere mention of Yellow Springs—the hospital ruins but also that it had been a resting place for native tribes, and later an artsy oasis to revive the city folk—stuck in my head, much like the Collier photo of the Fry house. I had to go.

The Lenape and tribes before them had considered the springs sacred ground. One bubbled up infused with iron, another with magnesium, and a third with sulfur. People had been drawn to those waters for centuries.

"It's such a beautiful walk," Wesley said. "I envy you the morning you're about to have." And with that Wesley gave me a soldierly salute as I went off down the road toward Yellow Springs.

———◆———

When I entered the little spa town an hour or so later, a group of women were hanging pictures on the wall inside a sprawling wooden structure called the Lincoln House. They invited me inside, but when I took one look at the paintings of trees and farms, I recoiled and turned back into the sunlight. Better an actual sunflower than the painting of a sunflower.

Down through the woods stood the spring houses built in the early 1900s to draw tourists and convalescents to come take the healing waters. They were not quite the standard of Marienbad. The water in their deep basins still bubbled up with the smell of their added element, but the gated entries were held firm by lock and chain. Moisture and grime had stained their plaster. Weeds and saplings were moving in. Give the forest a decade and it would take it all back.

What remained of the old hospital, called Washington Hall, clung to the hillside across the road among an exploding splendor of fruit trees and white maple. It was the first U.S. military hospital built in America and the only one established during the whole of the Revolutionary War. Its designers didn't skimp. When finished, the building stood three stories high, 106 feet long and 34 feet wide. Nine-foot-wide porches ran around two of its floors.

Nothing remained now but the stone foundations, where grass grew in what had once been the hospital's cellar. Our earliest sick and wounded soldiers were tended to here, and many died in their beds. "These fieldstone ruins stand as a witness," read a sign nearby, "to the brave Continental soldiers whose spirits stand silent guard from the unmarked graves around the hospital site."

I sat on the stone of one wall with the sun at my back, listening to the wind in the trees, a human basking in April warmth. Just being there on such a morning paid small homage to those deprived such pleasures.

All the art ladies were sitting on the wooden stairs eating lunch when I went back down to the Lincoln House. They told me that at the end of the Civil War, orphans from both sides had been put up in that house, and the house next to that, and the one after that. The mere mention of orphans added a residual tinge of sadness to the afternoon, like a small shift in the atmospheric pressure.

I asked where I could find lunch in the area, and they started ticking off various possibilities on the way toward Valley Forge. Several of the places sounded to be in shopping malls, suggesting the beauty of the past three days was about to end. I was, after all, sneaking toward Philadelphia through a back door and had caught the faint whiffs of its outer sprawl. The distant murmur of traffic. The sense that just beyond those trees were acres of asphalt.

"So is the sprawl of the city just right over there?" I asked, pointing behind me.

"Oh absolutely," one woman said.

Her friend disagreed. "No, no, no. There is still a lot of beauty on the way to Valley Forge."

As I wished them well and set off, one of them hollered after me: "And you can always grab a sandwich down the road at Hallman's General Store."

———◆———

I was sitting in warm sunlight at a picnic table behind Hallman's General Store when an older woman came from the house just up the hill and walked toward me across the sloping lawn. Spread before me was an Italian sub with hot peppers and layered with provolone cheese, onions, tomatoes, the works. I had a cold can of Pennsylvania Dutch Birch Beer pulled straight from Hallman's fridge and a packet of Herr's Kettle Cooked potato chips plucked off the shelf. The perfect lunch for that exact moment.

As I chewed my Italian sub, Mrs. Hallman, the widow to the store's namesake, approached and stopped to gaze at me like she'd found an exotic animal resting in her yard. She looked at my pack on the bench across from me, then at the sub, and then at the man eating the sub. She was tall, slender, highly skeptical.

"Passing through?" she said, one brow raised.

I told her what I was doing, and she was even more perplexed. Had I walked all the way from Washington along roads and highways? Wasn't I worried about being run over? What was the purpose of this walk? Was I sleeping outside? Did I not know there are ticks in the woods? Did I have a wife and kids? What did they think of all this? Was I walking alone?

"You have to do a walk like this alone," I told her. "Another person would just get in the way. And you can be sure my wife had no desire to come along."

"I can imagine she didn't," Mrs. Hallman said.

All her questions were the questions of a mom, and there was so much about her—her height, her proud posture, her quizzical skepticism—that reminded me of mine, tucked away in Colorado and doing her own share of worrying. My mom, too, had fretted over all the things that might happen to a son out walking busy roads.

I told Mrs. Hallman that she resembled my mom, and she let the mention pass.

"All I can say is I hope you aren't walking along the roads after dark," she said, like a mother, and went into the store.

A few minutes later she burst back out holding aloft the fancy water flask I'd left inside. The smile that splashed across her face confirmed she was indeed my mother's double. In a merry singsong she said, "Forget something important, by any chance?"

"That confirms it. You really are my mom."

"If I were," she said with a smile, "I would tell you to go back home."

———◆———

I still had three hours to walk to my day's destination when I came down the road and stopped to watch Pickering Creek flow under a bridge. It was a small creek, nothing grand, but I could see riffles and pools and nice little runs, and a path took me from the road up into willows along the banks. I had to fish.

Tucked into my pack was a twelve-foot Tenkara fly rod, which telescopes down to about a foot and a half and weighs almost nothing. It's a Japanese form of fishing that is basically a long and very sensitive and active rod with a line at the other end. No reel, no spools of weighted fishing line. Just a long stick with a long line on the end.

I had flies of different sorts, maybe forty in all, a spool of No. 5 tippet, a little bottle of flotant, some clippers, and a pair of those surgeon's forceps—called hemostats—to extract the hook from a trout's jaws. My one indulgence was a pair of neoprene Patagonia wading socks that extended to just below the knees. Right there, pretty much all you need.

I tied a tiny dry fly to my tapering line, slipped on the socks, hung my backpack on the limb of a tree, and stepped into the river. One of my shoes, left on the bank, had sprouted a hole over the big toe.

The blend of time and space shifts subtly when you step into moving water. I was no longer a walker on a road but a fisherman on a river. The world before I stepped in the river moved as I walked and now it moved as I stood still. I had fished parts of French Creek the evening before with a friend, Ed Baldrige, who had overlapped with me on the river and afterward for dinner. We caught a few small trout and white perch but were glad mainly for the stillness and the motion.

On Pickering Creek, named for an English counterfeiter deported in the eighteenth century, I skirted the edges of three beautiful pools that took me up several bends in the river, treading along in those booties and letting the fly float in each of the obvious seams. I switched up to a zebra midge and let that drag deep through all the holes. Then I switched up yet again, to a colorful nymph in case that might be more appealing. Still nothing.

I let the fly float while thinking about the fussiness a fisherman brings to the river—his hyperfocus, his meticulous attention to detail. Then I stopped to look around and was overcome by the grandeur of that small creek.

You might think there is nothing more human than our deliberateness: the precise knot, the finicky adjusting of the cast so that the fly floats just right. But as I stood there, knee-deep in the water, I realized that that meticulousness is not at all our special gift. It is not what sets us humans apart. The trout, the spider, the mosquito, the tiny crustacean, they are no less focused or precise or deliberate in what they do. The trout sips passing nymphs with machinelike precision. The spider weaves the perfect web. The mosquito detects the scent of blood from hundreds of yards away and goes straight to it.

What we bring to the river and to the world that is supremely human, or so we think, is this ability to stop, drop everything, forget the fishing, let the line go slack, and just stand there in awe. Perhaps our ability to behold is what sets us apart. Our ability to feel the immensity and power of the river as it washes over us, to turn all our senses not to detecting danger or eyeing prey, but to absorbing wonder.

Our ability to step out of our deliberateness may be our greatest gift. Our ability to be distracted. To gawk in awe at the river for four or five minutes—tingling, all but holding your breath, reverential—before getting back to fishing.

But what do any of us know? Maybe deer and raccoons and squirrels also stop and say "Wow." Maybe they, too, come to the top of a hill on a late afternoon and look across fields to the watercolor wash of a stand of trees in bloom, and gasp. For all we know they live in a perpetual Wow while we are the ones who are distracted from that Wow by our very deliberateness, who feel that wonder only in spurts, when we pause from going about our business.

I started casting, less mindful now, while thinking about the possibility of perpetual awe. Could that even be a thing? Our psyche and even our spirit, our entire emotional wiring, really, is built for bursts—bursts of speed, bursts of words, bursts of passion or inspiration or epiphany. But could one achieve a state of perpetual joy, perpetual wonder, perpetual elation? Would you even want to? My moments of rapture so far along the way—could they last for hours or a week? Wouldn't that be draining and exhausting? Don't we, for that matter, need the contrast, the blur of bland days that make the moment of awe more vivid? The shock that I might be deprived of whole decades surely made the years I am now getting that much richer.

I sat on a rock with the water washing around me and just studied the river and forgot about fishing. A recent conversation with my brother Kevin came to mind. He'd always been gifted at turning common obstacles and castoffs into art. No fan of those who railed against trespassers, he'd once perfectly twisted the strands of a barbed-wire fence erected to block a hiking trail into a swooping *Welcome!* sign, complete with the exclamation point, and hung it outside the door of his mountain house.

Later, he became an awed student of his own malady. As his language skills ebbed, words reared up with greater power and mystery.

"I was trying to write an email and got completely lost in the word 'beauty,'" he told me over the phone. "All those vowels and how they worked together. It made no sense and just swallowed me up." He described the dream he'd had on the night of his first brain operation. It consisted entirely of scenes of perfect harmony, one after the other, until he yelled out, "There is love!" and terrified the nurses.

My fishing line as I sat there had spilled over a small waterfall and swirled for too long in the foamy current. When I retrieved it, the tippet was hilariously tangled in a thousand loops around the fly. There was no unraveling that knot, so I clipped it off and slipped it into my shirt pocket, a memento of infinity made of monofilament.

———————◆———————

On toward Valley Forge I marched with eighteen pounds on my back and my water socks, still wet, strapped to my pack. The terrain got hilly with the road swooping up past mansions stuck in the woods, then down again, then up, like an asphalt roller coaster. My calves and the small of my back got to complaining, louder as I went. The sunlight streamed horizontally through the trees. A man threw open the gates at the end of his drive to fetch two wheeled garbage bins nearly as tall as him. He was a wealthy man with a very large house behind a high fence. He had a right to possess and fill very large garbage bins. Those bins were emblems of his status and achievement.

"Just coming through on my way to Manhattan," I said, cheery as a wandering jester, just so he had something to tell his wife when he went back. "Have a good evening," he said, unmoved.

My bed for the night was in a small Airbnb unit above a garage overlooking the driveway of a house tucked in the hills just west of Valley Forge. An hour's walk from any restaurant, I ordered chicken parmesan from an Italian takeout place near the freeway, which had it to me by car in thirty minutes. I sent a note to my host, Penny, who lived next door, pleading for a beer. She brought two, straight from her fridge, and handed them to me in her drive. I gripped them like golden icons.

Penny leaned in and whispered that she'd read about my walk online. "I saw the stories and I turned to my husband, and I said, 'Gary, we have a celebrity staying with us tonight.'"

"An achy wanderer who can't wait to open these beers is what you have," I said.

I trod back upstairs with that bounty of food and drink and sat reading a yellowing account from 1876 of Washington and his men braving it out that grim winter at Valley Forge a century earlier. "Soldiers in rags and undisciplined, half fed, with fevers eating out their life and strength, doing duty barefoot in the snow." The Red Coats having their way with Philadelphia, gobbling up the best of the harvest, billeting plump in warm houses a day's march away.

I stashed my leftover chicken parmesan in the little fridge and thought of the shivering remnants of the Continental Army as I sprawled for twenty minutes in the hot shower trying to wash those hills from my legs. Then I drained the last of my beer and crawled between crisp sheets in a bed large enough for four. Too drowsy to read anymore, I girded myself for the next day's hike to Washington's winter quarters.

CHAPTER 14

ONE WINTER LONG AGO

Baron von Steuben arrived at Valley Forge to the jingle of little bells aboard a sleigh pulled by a team of black Percheron horses brought all the way from France. He wore a silk sash studded with medals and had beside him an Italian greyhound named Azor. Two horse pistols dangled from his hips. Among his retinue were an aide de camp, a military secretary, and two young advisers, any one of whom may have been his lover. He was, one soldier wrote, the personification of "the ancient, fabled God of War."

I arrived in Valley Forge that Friday morning on foot, coming down fast through the woods on the Horseshoe Trail wearing shorts with a pack on my back and a right shoe still sporting a hole where the big toe poked through. My sole sustenance a warming slab of the previous night's dinner and my water-filled Hydro Flask, from which I sipped.

What von Steuben found upon arrival that day—February 23, 1778—was a forlorn scene bordering on the grotesque. Melting snow, oozing latrines. Horse carcasses protruding from slush among denuded hills. Hundreds of timber huts housing soldiers short on clothing with not much to eat but hard tack. The bloody footprints left in the snow by the shoeless would later become legendary.

This was Washington's Continental Army, midway through a

winter that morphed, a century later, into our prime symbol of national grit and resilience. A winter that was a turning point in the war, thanks in no small part to the imposing von Steuben.

We were a poor, pathetic, naked infant of a country then. Without swift and significant help, Washington wrote Congress that winter, his army "must inevitably be reduced to one or other of these three things. Starve—dissolve—or disperse." Congress had no money, no reliable way to raise funds. Shoes, pants, jackets, gunpowder, blankets, saddles were almost all nonexistent. Why should farmers supply the rebels, for nothing in return, rather than the British in Philadelphia for silver and gold? Washington wrote that a third of his men were "unfit for want of Cloaths."

Such was the forlornness of what von Steuben found on arrival that day at Valley Forge.

What I found upon arrival was the historian Lorett Treese, climbing from the driver's seat of her Honda Civic in the parking lot of the Valley Forge Post Office, a period piece of gray fieldstone with white shutters and a Stars and Stripes flapping high atop a flagpole.

"This post office," Lorett announced, before anything else, "was built in the 1930s pretty much just so people could post letters from Valley Forge. Its purpose was really just the postmark."

We hadn't even said hello and she was singing my tune already.

Lorett had driven two hours to show me around a place she'd written a whole book about. Except her book, *Valley Forge: Making and Remaking a National Symbol,* wasn't about that foul winter when Washington's men nearly starved in their huts. It was about when and how we Americans decided to care about that winter, which is what I wanted to hear about. When I called a month earlier asking her to be my guide, she didn't hesitate.

Tall, thin, late sixties, dressed in heels and with a cinched belt around the waist of her jacket, Lorett was a snappy former archivist at nearby Bryn Mawr College who now just writes books. She is what you might call a microhistorian, meaning she goes deep on very specific topics and extracts abundant meaning therein. She's written profusely on the Ohio Valley Mound People, multiple histories of different railroads, and about the collapse of Quaker rule in Pennsylvania on the eve of the Revolution. And, yes, about Valley Forge.

"Let's go see Washington's Headquarters," she said.

We walked down from the high ground to where a stone house stood in a wide clearing. A railroad track ran along the Schuylkill to a station perched above the stone house where Washington spent that winter. Lorett's heels clicked on the flagstone. She sketched the story.

No sooner had the Continental Army left in the spring of 1778 than fresh saplings began to sprout. The farmers moved back to replace their fence lines and haul away the huts for firewood. The fields were replanted. The Potts family that owned the house where Washington had quartered retook the house and rebuilt the forge. Washington himself dropped by nine years later, in the summer of 1787, to give the place a wistful look. Over the decades veterans would sometimes return teary-eyed to poke among the ruins. When the aging Marquis de Lafayette made his triumphant tour of the U.S. in 1824, he thought about dropping by, but sent his regrets.

Lorett mentioned a forgotten newspaper writer, Henry Woodman, who helped plant the seed for remembering Valley Forge as an important place. Woodman grew up in these hills and along the banks of Valley Creek. His father had camped there as a soldier that dreadful winter. In 1850, as the country was again preparing to tear itself apart, Woodman wrote a series of letters for the *Doylestown Intelligencer,* one every week for thirty-two weeks, April to December. He told of the place and what had happened there and all the development and boom times since then. And how that valley deserved far more attention.

"I now request some of my readers who have never visited these places to visit," he wrote in his final letter. Readers should come to stand on a hill with a view of it all and attempt to imagine, he advised, "the cold, chilling wind and driving snows, and other accumulated sufferings." And while you do that, "while you figure to your imagination the state of things then existing there," he wrote, "contrast it with its now prosperous condition." That was us then, and this is us now.

Valley Forge, he concluded, is "worthy of being rescued from oblivion. And this small section of country will always occupy a conspicuous place in the history of our national existence." I had had very similar thoughts myself when standing in that forlorn Maryland field where Frederick Douglass had his famous fight.

Woodman's letters rippled across the country and within the halls of Congress, but it still took a quarter of a century—and another civil war—before his sentiments took hold.

"Woodman promoted this as a place to come, as a place to care, but it wasn't until the Centennial in 1876, that people really did," Lorett said.

Lincoln gave his famous speech at Gettysburg four months after that battle. The cornerstone for the first major monument at Gettysburg was laid in July 1865. In Montana, the government erected the first monument to the Battle of Little Bighorn in 1881, five years after Custer and his men fell on those grassy hills. It took a century, by comparison, for the Centennial and Memorial Association of Valley Forge to acquire Washington's Headquarters and to begin to memorialize those grounds.

Multiple forces converged to begin converting Valley Forge into what it is now. People had leisure time and actual weekends and a desire to break from the city. The Centennial sparked an awe for America's colonial past at a time of economic expansion but also seething ethnic and racial friction. The state created a park here in 1893. A decade later, an ambitious Episcopal priest laid the cornerstone of a large church that was to blend religion with military patriotism.

A fancy train station rose eight years later along the Schuylkill to bring the day trippers out from Philly. Six years after that they dedicated a huge arch in the style of the Arc de Triomphe. In the 1950s, after years of archaeology and close study, the state began to erect rough replicas of the log huts the soldiers built—huts that also began to rot over time and needed to be replaced. I ducked into one of these huts, dark and dank inside, with wooden bunks along both sides that no soldier ever slept in.

"It's when they built these huts that they really tried to make Valley Forge look like Valley Forge looked to the troops," Lorett said. Sometimes, people really want the present to look like the past, as though the past could remain forever new. The layering continued when, in 1976, President Gerald Ford came to dedicate the place as a national historic site and federal park. It had finally won that status.

Toward the end of our morning, Lorett took me to one of her favorite places in the park, the place she said truly captures the binding element that made Valley Forge such a potent and durable symbol. In the late 1860s, a series of paintings and etchings swept the country of a pious Washington bent on one knee in the snow, praying by himself in the dark woods of Valley Forge for

God to protect and redeem his troops. Washington was a sporadic churchgoer, and not known for his piety. The story of him kneeling in the forest is almost certainly apocryphal.

"But for the Victorian sensibility of the late nineteenth century, that's what this place became: a symbol of Christian suffering and perseverance," Lorett said. "If you have faith in your darkest hour, God will get you out of it."

Those images inspired Reverend Herbert Burk, a local Episcopal minister, to build what became the imposing Gothic spires of Washington Memorial Chapel. "And voilà, presto, here the state, the military, and the church all merged into one," Lorett said as we walked up the drive to the Chapel. We stood on a rise with much of the valley sweeping down before us, much as Henry Woodman had advised the visitor to do.

At the entrance to the church, which was locked, an ornate iron gate bore a small statue of a patriot soldier, musket in hand, along with Jesus's Four Evangelists: Matthew, Mark, Luke, and John. The army marched in league with the Apostles.

In 1904, President Teddy Roosevelt came here to praise Valley Forge as a more important and lasting symbol than Gettysburg. The Civil War site had been a place for just one heroic burst, Roosevelt said, while Valley Forge spoke "to a more difficult thing—constant effort."

"I think as a people we need more to learn the lesson of Valley Forge than the lesson of Gettysburg," Roosevelt said. One was merely a battle. The other, an epic story of endurance.

And that, Lorett said, had been the lesson ever since, a lesson both national and deeply personal. "If you don't give up, you will make it through. The one big message is perseverance."

To continue on, no matter how severe the forces that are pushing back. You don't have to be shoeless in the snow to have your own dark winter. I had had my little version. We all have them, and we push on.

I was set to fish in the afternoon with a veteran from the Battle of Brandywine but had an hour to kill after Lorett drove off, so I hiked up Valley Creek until I snuck past a NO ENTRY sign and emerged into a meadow on the park's outer edge where the Marquis de Lafayette spent his months at Valley Forge. I tossed my pack on a lone picnic table and dug into the leftover chicken parmesan from the night before and pondered what we preserve of our past, and how.

In front of me stood Lafayette's two-story stone house where the fighting Frenchman had once strutted and feted his troops. It was missing a shutter and the mortar was popping from around the windowpanes. The house had two other houses tacked onto it, accordion-style, one covered with plaster and the other with clapboard siding. Both sported cheap screen doors and little illuminated doorbells, like suburban houses from the 1970s.

Twenty yards behind me through a thin band of woods you could see the blur of passing trucks on the Pennsylvania Turnpike, also named I-76 in honor of that gallant year. I ate my lunch, sandwiched between the faded memory of 1778 and the active amnesia of I-76. The dish had warmed nicely in my pack and made for a splendid meal.

You can examine just one winter from a hundred angles like a foggy chunk of crystal in your hand and not exhaust its intricacies. The physicality of the place, which both is and isn't what it seems. The contrived authenticity of the log huts or the restored stone houses. The serene vistas that were hardly serene at the time. The woods where Washington didn't pray on bended knee. The little soldier with the Four Evangelists. The memorials that capture in stone the fluidity of our efforts to remember.

In front of me once slept a twenty-year-old French aristocrat who helped convince the twenty-three-year-old French king, Louis XVI, to enter the war against Britain, which France and its mighty navy did, to decisive effect. Not far away were the parade grounds where a gay Prussian who spoke no English had taught the unruly Americans how to act like a modern army.

Baron von Steuben was the best sort of American contrivance. A seeker and an outsider like Hamilton, like Thomas Paine and Lafayette himself, but like them also a man of true talents. Rumors of his sexuality had derailed his career, and he hadn't moved among troops in fifteen years. With borrowed money, a letter of recommendation from Ben Franklin, and an inflated résumé, he sought his fortunes in America. He traveled all the way to York to present himself to a rump Congress, which then sent him on to Valley Forge with a promise of payment if he did well.

And he did do well, very well. He taught the troops how to march properly, how to reload quickly, how not to crap in their own water supply. He later wrote the army's first training manual. The order and discipline he instilled in the troops changed the course of the war. Washington wrote to von Steuben in December 1783, "the last Letter I shall ever write while I continue in the service of my Country," thanking him for his "faithful & meritorious Services." The baron wrote back: "Having received this last public testimony of Your esteem, there remains nothing for me to desire."

Valley Forge serves now as a sprawling testament to American grit in the face of profound hardship and want, but running through it is the tale, too, of how we could easily have lost it all but for the foppish but essential services of Europe's aristocracy. The British evacuated Philadelphia that spring not out of fear of the reconstituted Continental Army, but because the might of the French navy made them reorient their forces to defend British sugar holdings in the Caribbean, which were more important to them than these unruly northern colonies.

I wrapped up the remains of my lunch and walked to the ridge to see the world rip by. There went an Amazon Prime van, then a two-trailer FedEx truck, mere molecules in an endless stream of commerce. When I'd seen enough, I backtracked over the little footbridge to find Brian McGuire, a friend of a friend, striding my way decked in waders and wading boots, a baseball cap on his head, ready to conquer Valley Creek.

"Finicky fish on this one," Brian said. "Beautiful wild trout, but not easily caught. Let's see what we can do."

Like pretty much every run, stream, brook, creek, or river in all of eastern Pennsylvania, Valley Creek had its decades of agony and hardship. Its waters flow down into the famous valley from Mount Misery and Mount Joy mainly from cracks in the crystalline rocks, thus keeping the flow plentiful and cool. But toxins seeped in from sources upstream: PCBs from a train yard, fertilizers and pesticides from abundant backyards, petroleum drippings from cars in parking lots and on freeways.

The creek where Washington and his men once cast for trout began losing its fish. Brian and his friends at the Valley Forge chapter of Trout Unlimited rose to the rescue. They fought for years to revive and protect the stream. It's a natural wonder now, a thing of beauty just twenty-two miles from the Liberty Bell. The same goes for most of the area's streams, brought back to life after long stretches of misery. It's easy to forget what brutes we once were when it came to our treatment of the land.

Brian is a onetime U.S. Senate staffer and a longtime lobbyist for AARP, now retired. We were meeting, riverside, for the first time. He had a thin scruff of gray stubble on his chin and a "More Hockey, Less War" sticker on the back of his Kia Soul. You could tell by how he talked that he didn't mind silence. His Soul bore one emblem for Joe Biden and no fewer than five for his love of trout.

I pulled on my wading socks, unfurled my Tenkara, and tied on a small royal coachman, having little notion what might tantalize the native browns. We walked downriver, toward where Washington had slept and where his horse had slurped water from the stream. We could see Henry Knox's Quarters through the trees as we conferred creekside. Brian waved his rod over the waters below us. "You can take this stretch. I will start fishing upstream. We can hopscotch each other as we go."

I made my way slowly through riffles and around various bends, dropping one fly and then another delicately above rocks and into all the promising pockets. So lifelike, so convincing. But the browns of Valley Forge are a discerning breed. They sniffed and swam away.

Brian and I gave it up after an hour or two and sat on the riverbank with our feet in the water as Brian told of his service in the West Jersey Artillery unit, a hardy band of Revolutionary reenactors. His company has a perfect solid brass replica cannon named Thundering Barbara, and she has fought many a battle since 2012. She's one of the finest cannons "ever constructed for the Revolutionary War living history community," says the group on its website.

Brian's last big battle was at Brandywine, 240 years after Washington and his men got outfoxed there at the hands of the British in September 1777. That would put Brian's battle in 2017, the first year of Trump.

Brian remembered it like yesterday. How the late-summer sun beat down hard on Thundering Barbara. The puffs of smoke. The crackle of musket fire. The tall grass. How everything turned foul so quickly.

"We were trying to get up a long hill and we just stalled out," he said. "They basically overran us."

Brian fell silent.

I had to ask. "Did you die?"

"I did," he said, as though reluctant to revive the memory. "Not far from where Lafayette took a slug in the leg. We were trying to push the cannon up a hill and were set upon by guys with muskets." Two shots to the back, right between the shoulder blades.

I could see it all as if in slow motion. His arms flailing wide. His tricorne flying off. The sweat and surprise and agony on his face.

"It was all pretty dramatic. We all went down in the high grass. We didn't stay down for long, though. You know, because of the ticks."

Even the heroic dead live in fear of the ticks.

Dying in front of so many people, Brian said, had been a thrill. There were a thousand or so people watching. "I've always considered myself pretty good at dying."

I clipped my fly off the end of my line and tucked it into my little fishing pouch as Brian told me about his postmortem and postbellum disenchantment with his artillery service. His beautiful, handstitched uniform with the brass buttons still hangs in his closet, but he had recently resigned from the West Jersey Artillery. He'd come to realize, he said, that the rest of his unit was just too Trumpy.

"They were all pretty right wing. They really loved their guns." The more he had thought about it, and about our own historical events of late—the surge in gun sales, the splintering of the country into hostile factions—the more squeamish he felt about his membership in the group.

"They just tolerated me, truth be told. After a while I felt I didn't quite belong anymore. We all did love our explosions, though." The explosions weren't enough to hold them together anymore. Putting Thundering Barbara behind him gave Brian more time for trout, which was a net plus to the nation, I thought.

As we left the park, I kept trying to create an image in my

mind of George Washington fishing. I'd heard he'd once fished Valley Creek but couldn't quite bring the image to life. It's just not how we see the man. We know him as a slaveholder and a voracious acquirer of land. We see him powdered and imperious on the dollar bill. Or in that little boat on the Delaware. Or astride his white horse. But casting a tapered length of maple knee-deep in a stream? Nothing could quite airbrush that image into existence.

In the heat of late July 1787, a decade after his stay at Valley Forge and three days after the Constitutional Congress voted to create the office of president, Washington fled steamy Philadelphia to revisit the setting of that not-yet-famous winter. His mission, he jotted in his journal, was "to get trout" and to see the state of the place where he'd spent those months of freeze and thaw, muck and muddle.

"Visited all the Works, wch. were in Ruins," he wrote in his odd shorthand, with a whiff of melancholy. Some of the encampments still stood "in woods where the ground had not been cultivated." But he knew it was all going the way of the plow, the ax, the termite, the worm, the general rot.

That process, he and I and the rest of us know, takes so little time.

CHAPTER 15

THE EYES OF GOD

I spent the night snug on the top floor of a house owned by a friend first met in Albania and last seen in Uzbekistan. Such are the ways of the world for us Anywhere people. A heap of laundry straight from his dryer, everything I had, lay beside me on the floor. Outside were wine shops, cafés, universities. I was back in the lap of it again.

We set off in the morning from Haverford into the wilds of West Philadelphia, my friend Charlie Walsh and I, our bellies full of coffee, eggs, toast with jam. Charlie loped beside me and insisted this was the old Lincoln Highway, Route 30, the same road I'd followed on Easter out of York to Wrightsville and then across the Susquehanna to Columbia.

"Doesn't look like the same road, Charlie," I said.

"I'm sure it doesn't," he said.

Within blocks of Overbrook High School—where the towering Wilt Chamberlain racked up an average of 37.4 points a game during his three seasons there—the neighborhood deteriorated into a tableau of decaying strip malls, collapsing churches, grimy corner stores, garbage piled high in empty lots.

You can go look at old America, the taverns and roadhouses and grist mills and churches from long ago, but you find our true decrepitude in patches like this. We flatter ourselves as a young country still, innovative, prosperous, ever renewing, but we excel in the art of selective decay. Ahead of us the city's downtown towers gleamed with morning sunlight, but here it was hard to detect even the hint of lost youth. Valley Forge now is what it never was before, with its meticulously kept make-believe huts and granite monuments, while chunks of West Philadelphia sink into the mire. As we neared the river we could see where the town fathers lavished the love and polish and public investment.

Crossing that bridge into Philadelphia proper is to traverse a divide far vaster than the river itself. Fleets of rowers in long sculls left yawning wakes in the river. Along sidewalks dotted with sculptures and statues came a steady stream of runners. We had entered a land of fitness and wealth, another micronation along the way. Folks here wanted you to know they were on the move. It was hard to know which side of the river better captured our future.

I had arrived in Philadelphia and felt a surge of disbelief and a tingle of accomplishment. It had taken me twelve days to get across the Schuylkill and almost as long to learn how to spell it. I said goodbye to Charlie and kept on, past the boathouses and toward the famous art museum where Rocky pumped his fists. I had just one destination in mind.

◆

During the era of Europe's deepest fascination with America— from around 1820 to 1850 or so—few travelers and writers who streamed across the Atlantic were so foolish as to give Philadelphia a pass. Boston was of interest, as was bustling New York. Baltimore mainly appalled, while Washington was more an idea than a realized thing.

Philadelphia, though, was truly new, a city unrecognizable from anything on the planet with its rectilinear grid, its numbered streets, its public parks. A Quaker city organized from scratch according to a higher rationality. Philadelphia was doing things—in town planning, in medicine and science, in new forms of governance and social hierarchy—that the curious just had to come examine and assess. The world offered nothing more novel than what was happening here.

And when the scholars, reformers, novelists, philosophers, adventurers, and preachers arrived, many made a beeline to one place, as I was now myself: to the hulking stone walls of the city's Eastern State Penitentiary. Cherry Hill, as many knew it, was by far the century's star attraction for anyone interested in new forms of imprisonment.

Alexis de Tocqueville didn't sail to America in 1831 to extol and admire and investigate the state of our democracy. His book on that subject made him famous four years later—and a darling in America. What brought Tocqueville to America were its prisons, and especially this shining new model to extreme incarceration called Eastern State.

When the young novelist Charles Dickens came eleven years later, he devoted fifteen pages of his *American Notes for General Circulation* to his brief time in Philadelphia. All but three of those pages describe his day wandering the corridors of Eastern State.

More than Valley Forge or Independence Hall or the steamboats on the Hudson, this prison is what sets America apart. "The U.S. has no literature, no eloquence . . . no fine arts," Tocqueville sniffed in a letter to a friend in France. "A fine prison therefore looms as large as the pyramid of Cheops . . . What is greater than a prison? If we told Americans that only a handful of people in France had ever heard of a penal system, they would no doubt be astonished."

I turned up Fairmont Avenue and there she was, dour and gray, like a fortress castle dropped here from the Middle Ages. They'd emptied her of prisoners long ago but have done little else to spiff her up.

Opened in 1829 within a ten-acre, thirty-foot-high circular

wall, the prison relied on a wagon wheel, hub-and-spoke design, with each cell block radiating out from the center. In theory, a single guard standing at the center could keep an eye on the door to every cell by peering down their long, arched hallways. It was Jeremy Bentham's eerie panopticon—that eighteenth-century concept of the modern surveillance state—made real in stone and iron. Worldwide, dozens of countries went on to model more than three hundred prisons on Eastern State's design.

It was the height of modern efficiency, and all toward one end: the absolute isolation of the prisoner.

"No prison in the world was more studied, more visited, or more imitated," said Matt Murphy, a lumberjack of a tour supervisor who came to escort me through the prison's cell blocks, operating rooms, psych wards, and death row. I had reached out to the prison a week or so earlier, and Matt had thrown up his hand. "It was one giant social experiment—the most expensive public building in America at the time and the costliest prison in the world, bar none."

With a shock of black hair and a bushy beard, Matt had worked as an interpreter of history at Lincoln's birthplace, Alcatraz Island, Independence Hall, and now twelve years within the walls of Eastern State Penitentiary. He laughed when I pointed out that he'd done democracy on the one hand, prisons on the other, rather like Tocqueville himself.

Matt threw open the gate to Cell Block One and we began to walk past tiny cells on either side. "Philadelphia," he said, "was the Athens of America in the 1820s and '30s, the site of the Revolution, of our founding documents, but our real obsession then was not liberty and freedom but new forms of incarceration."

What drew Tocqueville, Dickens, and others here was the novel "Pennsylvania way" of reforming the prisoners inside. In a penitentiary, the inmate would learn to be penitent. Prisoners were escorted to their cells with a sack over their heads and then kept

in total solitary confinement. The cells had a single circular opening to the sky, the Eye of God, and a small solitary exercise space
in back that also had an opening to the sky. Meals were passed
through a trapdoor.

The surest path to penance, its Quaker designers thought, was to
have each prisoner left alone, to contemplate their deeds without
distraction or interruption, for years on end in some cases. The
sheer weight of solitude and unbroken introspection would create
such deep anxiety that it would remold and reform the prisoner's
psyche.

I stepped into a cell. There was a cot in the corner, a small table
and chair, and a sink and toilet: all confined within whitewashed
walls and an arched ceiling that made it feel like a tiny cloister.
You could stand looking up into that luminous oval with its mere
hint of the day outside and close your eyes and attempt to imagine
entire years passing within that single space. But you'd fail. I did
that, pinching my ancient coin as I squinted at the sky. And I was
glad to step out.

We see such confinement as barbarous now, but this was an emblem of enlightenment when it opened. Tocqueville's assessment
of Eastern State—he and Gustave de Beaumont spent a week there
interviewing inmates—was largely positive. Dickens thought it in-
humane, and let Tocqueville know as much. Either way, America's
long history of mass incarceration was underway.

The two Frenchmen interviewed forty-four prisoners here.
They had already spent time at New York's Sing Sing and Auburn
prisons—which hewed to a very different system of forced group
labor—and would visit many others around the U.S. By their cal-
culation, at least half of all American prisoners were Black, while
Blacks at the time represented just a sixth of the U.S. population.

Their book, *On the Penitentiary System in the United States and Its
Application to France,* contains brief transcripts of dozens of inmate
interviews at Eastern State.

Ques. *Do you find it difficult to endure solitude?*
Ans. *Ah! It is the most horrid punishment that can be imagined!*

Eastern State's first prisoner was Charles Williams: "Burglar. Light Black Skin. Five feet seven inches tall," say the prison records. When the two Frenchmen sat with him, he read to them the parable of the good shepherd, who left his flock of ninety-nine sheep to go find the one that was lost. The story, they wrote, "impressed him deeply—one who was born of a degraded and depressed race and had never experienced anything but indifference and harshness."

At Eastern, the ultimate punishment was to deprive the prisoner of all fellowship, all community. To leave him to his own mind and body, with no other warmth. The Frenchmen interviewed one prisoner so bereft that every insect became a friend. "When a cricket entered my yard, it looked to me like a companion. If a butterfly, or any other animal enters my cell, I never do it any harm."

Tocqueville found much to praise in Eastern State's stern moralism. But in his other works where he examined all of society, including *Democracy in America* and *The Old Regime and the Revolution,* he warns of the despotism that springs from eerily similar conditions. Eastern State was a place of strict equality where every inmate was cut off from the other and cared only for their own well-being—not unlike the soil, he noted elsewhere, from which despotism springs.

"Despotism," he wrote in *Democracy,* "sees in the separation among men the surest guarantee of its continuance, and it usually makes every effort to keep them separate." "It immures them," he wrote in *The Old Regime,* "each in his private life and, taking advantage of the tendency they already have to keep apart, it estranges them still more."

Tocqueville warned of the perils that could flow from a general estrangement in American life, a dissolving of common interests and a common space, creating a vacuum that despotic forces would then rush to fill. In walking from my house and turning north, I felt that I had entered a sliver of that common space. The very idea of a common ground—of a set of people standing, despite our differences, in the same place—had taken on new meaning. I could glimpse both its vital importance and its utter fragility, as Tocqueville had.

———◆———

Eastern State is a fine place to mull the nature of time and how infinitely slowly—and swiftly—it passes. More than seventy-five thousand inmates spent a portion of their lives here. Some experienced many decades beneath their own Eye of God. I calculated that 1.2 million inmate hours were spent in just the lone cell I stood in, from 1829 up to the prison's closing in 1971. An eternity by most human standards.

But there was another clock at work here. You could shudder over the horror of years spent alone in a cell while also marveling at the speed with which gravity and water and plants were chewing away at the structure itself. The prison lay abandoned and neglected for more than twenty years, and whole sections of it still haven't been refurbished in any way. Those sections are essentially returning to earth before our eyes. Give it another century or so without help and the place will be a mound of stone being devoured by trees and vines.

We emerged into a small open exercise yard off death row where a whole section had fallen to the ground. Trees had feasted upon the crumbled brick and mortar and now lay in a tangle of deracinated trunks and limbs, decaying among weeds and vines.

"We call this a stabilized ruin," Matt said. "At some point, this will all be gone." *This*—in this case—being the entire penitentiary.

I laughed when he said that. Everything human is a stabilized ruin. Every person, house, bridge. Every condo building with sweeping views of the beach. Entropy lurks. Things fall apart.

For a thousand years the Roman Colosseum was a riotous jungle of crooked elms and pear trees, overgrown with figs, wild roses, and strawberries. The new rulers of Rome tore all that out in the late nineteenth century in a bid to reclaim their classical past. That forestalled the Colosseum's eventual collapse.

"In the grand scheme of things," I said, "everything will be different from what it is. It will all come tumbling down."

Matt pointed later to a tangle of trees growing in another tumbledown section of the prison. "Paulownia trees. Among the fastest growing and most aggressive trees in the world. Paulownias love ruins."

We stood there for a moment thinking about trees that love ruins. Trees that are slowly tearing apart a prison.

"I really dig what you're doing with this walk of yours," Matt said before we parted. "My brother died suddenly this year, and I've been doing my own smaller versions of what you are doing, you know, to try to come to terms. I think you know what I mean."

I told him I did know what he meant. I told him about how my own brother was wrestling with a brain cancer that was slowly taking his mobility and speech and would take his life before the end of the summer. This journey of mine—out walking, out talking— was in part an homage to him. I was covering miles and telling tales that Kevin could no longer cover or tell himself, and keeping him updated with the occasional call as I went.

Matt and I spoke of the moments we all have, however brief, to slip through doors, perfectly ordinary doors, that open onto paths offering a wider freedom to move and to think. That you may not be able to prolong such moments forever, but while you can, they are free for the taking. We talked about human freedom, and how we all strive to obtain it, as we stood within the high walls of a building designed to cure people through extreme confinement. When I pointed out that irony, Matt noted another obvious one, that the Land of the Free has, by far, the world's highest imprisonment rate.

———————

I entered Philadelphia through the Eyes of God at Eastern State, so it seemed fitting that I should leave it while sprawled on my back on a bench at a Quaker meetinghouse, peering up at Heaven through an eight-by-nine-foot rectangle cut from the ceiling.

It was dusk—a sun setting through clouds—and the sky through that box blazed so many colors and performed so many optical tricks that I had trouble keeping up. I was stretched on my back in a house of worship and the sky was telling me that the human eye and the human brain are both theaters for wonder and connivers of illusion.

What we see—a sky as green as spring clover or as orange as an autumn leaf—is brilliantly real but also profoundly not what it seems. The whole of that slice of the sky could change by the slightest alterations in the hue of the ceiling itself. We are not what we are alone, but a blend of our surroundings. The leaf is green because chlorophyll doesn't absorb that part of the light spectrum. What we see, in a sense, is what isn't there.

All this deserves some explanation.

I had met—again, that best of all things, a friend of a friend—the brilliant editorial cartoonist Signe Wilkinson. Signe had worked for decades in cartooning at Philadelphia's *Daily News* and later the *Inquirer*. Her work earned her the Pulitzer Prize in 1992. A Quaker and a Texan by birth, she knew every inch of her adopted city and had the natural inquisitiveness and nosiness of a true reporter.

Lean, short, seventy years old, with icy blue eyes and a boyish mop of sandy hair, Signe darted through the city in her cluttered

Prius with the precision of a veteran cabbie. When we drove past the soaring alabaster building on Broad Street where she worked most of her career and drew maybe four thousand cartoons, she said: "There it is. The white tower of truth." She whipped to the curb to point out Underground Railroad basements, old meetinghouses, intersections where mass shootings occurred.

"This is a great place to be shot," she would say. Or: "This is one of the city's prime drug corners. Need anything?" Or: "Battle of Germantown fought there. Didn't turn out well."

We went to the Fair Hill Burial Grounds in North Philadelphia, one of the earliest Quaker cemeteries in America. Signe described the devastation there when she and other Quakers joined with neighborhood leaders to bring the cemetery back to life in the 1990s. Metal thieves had stolen half the old iron fence. Brick thieves had ripped up some of the sidewalk. Weeds and saplings and high grasses had taken over the entire hill so that it looked like a forest within a torn fence. Drug dealers used the property as an open-air drug mart.

"Everyone called it the Badlands," Signe said as we circled the cemetery, trying to find the lock that would accept the combination she had scrawled on a piece of paper.

Many of the nineteenth century's most famous feminists and abolitionists are buried there, luminaries like Lucretia Mott, Harriet Forten Purvis, and Mary Ann M'Clintock. No gravestone stands higher than a few inches off the ground.

"Some people in the neighborhood doubt the dead here can be so important with gravestones this small," Signe said, once we'd unlocked the gate and wandered inside. "They think it's a pet cemetery." The stones stood in uneven rows, barely visible among the trimmed grass.

Restoring the cemetery hadn't healed the area's many wounds; it remains among the city's most dangerous police districts. But with the help of other nearby projects, the work had created an oasis and a wider pocket of calm. As we left, you could see across the street a three-story-tall Harriet Tubman peering down from a high exposed wall, her regal dress painted a vivid blue.

Before, the cemetery and its immediate surroundings "had looked like a Bruegel painting," Signe said as we left. I thought of the *Triumph of Death* or maybe *The Fall of the Rebel Angels* with Bruegel's grotesque fish falling from the sky.

◆

The real object for our outing that late afternoon was the Chestnut Hill Friends Meeting, a plain fieldstone meetinghouse with a tin roof in a spruced-up enclave north of the city. There the gifted and prolific California-born light and space artist James Turrell had turned the main meeting hall into a Skyspace, one of eighty such installations that Turrell has built across all continents.

Turrell has scattered the globe with his studies of space and light, places where the human eye takes in a vastness of color and sky and creates, through the blend of interacting colors, its own reality. His most famous is in a vast crater he spent years seeking and now owns in the Arizona desert. I would like one day to walk there.

For the first time since the pandemic struck, Signe had convinced the meeting hall board to reopen the hall and retract the roof fifteen minutes before sunset so that a small group of us could lay on our backs and watch wonders unfold. Above us was the arc of the white ceiling, across which would play out subtle shifts in color and brightness—all orchestrated in absentia by the artist himself. And within, peering through an open rectangle, was the sky itself, the main attraction.

Quaker meeting halls exist for silence and informality, so no one hesitated in finding their place on a pew or stretched on the floor, a folded coat or sweater tucked beneath heads for comfort. No promptings needed to keep quiet.

I scrawled six pages of notes in my little notebook as I lay on my back, knowing I'd be lost without some record. I was drug free, in case you wonder at the following scribbles, because this is an accurate description of what I saw through that space when the lights went off and the show began.

A clothlike fabric of oceanic green, luxuriantly
    smooth . . .
begins to turn blue and impose itself, pushing inward . . .
a radiant periwinkle blue . . .
as the ceiling went slowly pink, the sky turns intensely
    green, clover green . . .
there is no sky, only color . . .
then splotchy gray to monochromatically gray to
    radiant purple . . .
it is now the softest gauzy baby pink . . .
as the ceiling goes blue the sky turns pale gray . . .
it becomes a greenish yellow like old newsprint . . .
then back to oceanic green . . .
the sky becomes so solidly green you're convinced
    there is no sky, none at all . . .
burnt orange now and protruding into the room . . .
the ceiling turns taupe and the sky, a light pale radiant
    blue . . .
all of it in Rothko hues . . .
you want to see a star or passing plane to prove it is the
    sky . . .
the eye creates stars where there are no stars . . .
finally, just a solid, intensely black black . . .
and it is over

We'd been there fifty minutes or so, supine and still as the sun set and the darkness came. Then someone turned on the lights and broke the spell. "And that," Signe said, sitting up from where she was sprawled, "is a James Turrell sunset."

With the silence shattered, everyone chimed in. Some of us rubbed our eyes or stood to shake our limbs.

"You can see it dozens of times, and it's never the same," someone said.

"I may have dozed off," said another.

"It's all about impermanence and transience. It tells you: don't trust your eyes."

Signe asked if I had any questions.

I laughed. "I have only questions," I said.

We had stretched ourselves out in a house of worship for a lesson in doubt and profound relativism. What we saw outside had everything to do with the prism through which we saw it. The color of the near altered the color of the far. It was all one vast interplay. You could come away perplexed, your certitude challenged, or you could come away soothed, gladdened by the complexity.

The Quakers believe in silence, simplicity, egalitarianism. They abhor hierarchy. They value the inner spirit and believe it moves in all of us. When it does, it can make us quake with joy, hence the name. Their thinking was the inspiration for the reform-minded solitary confinement of the Eastern State Penitentiary, which seems so ghastly now. And it saturated the worldview of James Turrell, himself a Quaker.

I wondered if any prisoner had ever been transported into a rapture, however brief, by the light coming through his ceiling at Eastern State. I wondered if a chance shift of light or hue through that little opening to the sky overhead had ever offered a prisoner a new view on life. Perhaps its own kind of penance. And if it had, shouldn't that have been sufficient grounds for his imprisoners to set him free?

CHAPTER 16

THE SECOND NAIVETE

Like a hobo, a newly arrived settler, a soldier returning home, I had planned to camp for a few nights here or there along my walk. I would tuck into my pack the bare minimum of gear—a thin sleeping bag, a rain guard—and sleep under stars or in the woods along some old battlefield or farm. I wanted to curl up in the woods at Valley Forge.

What changed those plans? What had me, the morning I was heading out of Philadelphia, ascending nine floors of a downtown high-rise to consult with a doctor? That minuscule deer tick did. The same one that squirted its *Borrelia burgdorferi* bacteria into my bloodstream the previous August. The one that gave me Lyme disease, which then paralyzed my left vocal cord and had me talking within days in a gravelly whisper à la Miles Davis.

How routinely do bits of microscopic matter reroute our lives or the arc of a nation. Cellular aberrations had created a cancer in me and ripped up my calendar. An airborne virus from China had rocked the world and hit pause on billions of lives. A bacterium from a tiny tick had turned my voice into a wheezy whisper and sent me up these stairs one morning in April to consult with a specialist who hoped to fix me. You get to where all this feels ordinary, and of course it is. Expect, the sages say, the unexpected.

"You did what?" the good doctor said, wide-eyed, when he

nearly stumbled over my backpack on entering the examination room. "You walked all the way here?"

My appointment with Dr. Robert Sataloff was perfectly positioned for my passage through town, so the same man who once ministered to the pipes of Luciano Pavarotti, Liza Minnelli, and Julie Andrews was now peering down my throat and asking me to squeal. "O sole mio," I said.

He stuck a tiny camera past my tongue and examined the moist quaverings of my vocal cords on a big screen. They looked like naked oysters mating in a briny pool.

"Still no real sign of improvement," the good doctor said. "Come see me again in six weeks. Next time by car."

———◆———

When you root around in the dusty archives and let one strand lead to another, you stumble on ideas and people and moments that astonish and electrify. You want to call your friends and say, "Can you believe this person existed?" In planning for the walk, I experienced so many of those little discoveries, daily eureka moments that have you obsessing over long-dead eccentrics. Now I was heading straight north from Philadelphia to pay homage to a few of them. A couple of days' detour, in essence, to tip my hat to a few oddballs who represented long-buried slices of the American experience I wanted to resurface. One of whom had lived in a concrete castle he built himself and the other two in caves beside rivers far apart.

I'd rested for a couple of days in Philadelphia and dutifully seen my doctor. Shailagh had driven up for an overnight visit, and it was a joy to be together. I was heading north now with fresh legs to the Wissahickon Valley about six miles up along the Schuylkill, past the Rocky statue at the foot of the museum stairs and along the tree-draped drive named for John B. Kelly, father of Grace Kelly and one of America's great rowers. I wanted to see what the inner edges of the American wilderness looked like in 1694.

I'd heard mention of a hermit's cave up the Wissahickon. Something about how a certain Johannes Kelpius from the deep interior of Transylvania had brought a doomsday brotherhood to those woods that year, in the very early days of European settlement, when Philadelphia was just a few blocks deep along the Delaware. He had gone there, to a high ridge above a roaring creek, because those woods then were the deep, dark beginnings of the American frontier. He took his group of forty there to await the Second Coming and the end of the world.

When Kelpius and his followers sailed up the Delaware that spring, Philadelphia was a dusty place just twelve years old. Its role as a magnet for religious oddities was just beginning. The twenty-six-year-old Kelpius and his Society of the Woman of the Wilderness were the embodiment of a thread that ran back to the monastic mysticism of the Middle Ages and up through thinkers like Paracelsus and Jakob Böhme. They brought with them astrolabes and telescopes and a magnificent refractive sundial later owned by Benjamin Franklin.

Kelpius was a Pietist, a writer of hymns and a book of prayers. Cave life, it turns out, didn't suit him well. He put great value in the theory of mystic numbers, the number 40 above all. He died of consumption at forty-one, eleven years after he arrived here and well after the world failed to end. His band of brothers disbanded but their practices and progeny helped spread an aura of mystical thinking that grew and lingered in pockets of eastern Pennsylvania for centuries. Some of his acolytes went on to help establish the Mystic Order of the Solitary in Ephrata, whose abandoned cloister I had visited the week before.

Today, Kelpius's woods spill down into a ravine through which a major thoroughfare flows along the Wissahickon Creek. Houses with grand terraces and porches rim the park. As I cut down from the houses and approached the cave along a trail, a mountain biker flew by and howdied me in passing.

The cave was more of a stone grotto carved into the hillside topped with a tangle of bushes and vines. It had crude stone walls and an arching ceiling that dripped water onto a dirt floor strewn with stones and pieces of wood. A tall memorial stone stood outside, "lovingly erected by Grand Lodge Rosicrucians AD 1961"—an offshoot, evidently, of an esoteric mystical order that went back to the early seventeenth century. Someone had written in white paint along the side of the stone, in Greek, the word "Nefeli," the name of a cloud nymph created by Zeus, though I had no idea what that could possibly mean.

These woods and the river that bent through them had been a muse to many for centuries. During his Philadelphia years in the 1840s, Edgar Allan Poe often scrambled along the rocky banks of the Wissahickon. It was, he wrote, a river "of so remarkable a loveliness that were it flowing in England, it would be the theme of every bard, and the common topic of every tongue."

We don't think of Poe as a hiker but more as a gaunt drinker and a haunter of urban alleyways. But he was also an apostle for walking. "In America generally," he wrote in the same essay, "the traveler who would behold the finest landscapes, must seek them not by the railroad, nor by the steamboat, nor by the stagecoach, nor in his private carriage, nor yet even on horseback—but on foot. He must walk, he must leap ravines, he must risk his neck among precipices, or he must leave unseen the truest, the richest, and most unspeakable glories of the land."

I sat in dappled sunlight on a fallen tree by the mouth of Kelpius's grotto, and with a plastic fork I consumed an entire tub of Trader Joe's curried chicken salad picked up that morning near the doctor's office. Surely a tastier dish than any Herr Kelpius ever had. Then I leaped ravines and risked my neck among precipices to head to the place of the day's second cave dweller, the fiery and incomparable Benjamin Lay.

He was a hunchback, barely four feet tall. The hunchback dwarf, they called him. The Quaker Comet. He may have been the most obnoxious man in colonial America. The most in your face. The least forgiving. Also, the most driven by conscience. The clearest eyed. He made Thaddeus Stevens look like a pushover.

Born in 1682, Benjamin Lay had convictions like others have fingers or toes. He was a fervent pacifist, an inflammatory abolitionist, an ardent vegetarian and proto-environmentalist. He shunned anything that sprang from slavery—sugar, tea, coffee—and urged others to join him, making him the father of American boycotts a century and a half before that was even a word. He believed passionately in animal rights at a time when horses were horribly mistreated.

He was perhaps America's first ruckus-maker, a performance artist for political causes without equal. He went to a Quaker gathering and hurled clay pipes against the wall to protest the use of tobacco, another slavery-derived product. He took his late wife's fine china to the Philadelphia market and smashed the cups and saucers as he fulminated against slavery and tea-drinking.

Franklin's *Gazette* described that incident as follows: "On Monday about Noon, being in the Time of the General Meeting of Friends, Benjamin Lay, the Pythagorean-cynical-christian Philosopher, bore a publick Testimony against the Vanity of Tea-drinking, by devoting to Destruction in the Market-place, a large Parcel of valuable China, &c. belonging to his deceased Wife."

His most famous act came in 1738 when he disrupted the Yearly Meeting of Quakers by driving a sword through a Bible that splattered a bloody red juice in all directions. He had hidden a bladder inside the book filled with berry juice. He was routinely tossed from Quaker meetings—and in four cases officially disowned—for calling out those who owned other human beings.

His *All Slave-Keepers That Keep the Innocent in Bondage, Apostates* brims with invective and isn't an easy read, but his friend Ben Franklin published it in 1737. The book was by far the staunchest text against slavery published to that point in the young America. "The sound of his words constitutes an autobiographic scream," one scholar said of a book that made the Quaker leadership hate Lay even more. He was disowned from his local meetinghouse the same year.

I made it to Lay's hometown eight miles north of Philadelphia in the middle of the afternoon and found George Schaefer—another friend of a friend—seated in his car in front of the Abington Quaker Meeting House, a large stone building whose origins stretch back to the late 1600s. "Welcome," George said as he strode across the driveway. "Let me show you around."

George served as clerk of the Abington congregation during a tumultuous stretch in 2017 when the Quaker Comet came roaring back in the oddest of ways. The property's caretaker, David Wemerling, was rooting around in an upstairs closet when he found an old etching of the little giant stashed on a shelf. The etching showed a wild-eyed Lay standing with a simple walking stick on spindly bare legs, a book called *African Emancipation* in one hand, the other raised in midfulmination. Wemerling turned the framed sketch over and found on the back a water-stained and barely legible description of Lay's tumultuous life and passion for ending slavery. "His remains were interred in Friends' burial ground at Abington," it read. A brief inscription at the end said: *The root of righteousness yieldeth fruit.*

Wemerling was shocked. He had worked there for years but never heard of Benjamin Lay. How could Lay's memory have been so erased? His discovery led to a surge of interest in Lay's life and legacy. The meetinghouse leadership voted to restore Lay's standing as "a Friend of the Truth" and to acknowledge him with a proper gravestone. An official marker along the highway soon followed. These moves rippled far and wide, so that soon all the other groups that had disowned Lay—one in Philadelphia and two in England—passed similar resolutions of solidarity with Lay 260 years after his death.

George led me to the simple gravestone set there for Lay and his wife, Sarah, amid some pomp in the summer of 2018. "Exact location of grave unknown," it said. The marker rose up barely six inches high. "Pretty sure he'd be perturbed by this," George said of the stone. "Too showy."

As we stood in the tree shadows, George told me how Lay's antecedents and intellectual pedigree borrowed from the Greek Cynic philosophers, who also engaged in ruckus making, as did Jesus. "Prophets are rabble-rousers, but they are not telling us any-thing we don't already know," George said. "They are holding us to the values we already profess, as Martin Luther King did."

George and I talked about the oddities of the Quakers, a group so crucial to the country's founding. Without them—without their truth-telling and their cooling influence, without Quaker Pennsylvania itself wedged like a keystone between the opposing fires of North and South—we'd be a different place now. Their numbers are tiny—not even fifteen thousand or so in the entire greater Philadelphia area—but their influence has been large.

Lay died in 1759, just months after the Philadelphia Quakers finally began to move toward disciplining and disowning anyone who traded in slaves. "I can now die in peace," Lay said when told of the news. Not until 1777 did the whole of the Quakers ban slaveholding within their ranks, a move that still made them a rad-ical vanguard in opposing an institution accepted then by nearly all white Americans. Lay was perhaps the brightest early spark in lighting that fire.

Lay lived near the Abington meetinghouse in a cave with his wife, a fellow dwarf; his library; and a grove of apple trees outside. George took me south of the meetinghouse and dropped me along a creek. "The cave is over that way, along that ridge," he said as motorists behind us blared their horns. I grabbed my pack from the back seat and jumped over a stone wall. I soaked my shoes crossing the creek and searched every which way along the embankment and the rocky outcroppings as a commuter train swooshed past, but I couldn't find the opening.

I went on, north toward Doylestown now, hoping to run into a Lay acolyte who would steer me back to his cave and tell me how kernels of his feistiness still sprouted among the people. But the houses, the roomy garages, the cars parked in the driveways or zipping by on the road instilled little confidence that Lay had left much of a mark. Our greatest men and women may have moved the dial in their time. May have nudged the course of our history this way or that. But do even the slightest traces of their DNA live on within us? They were castoffs and oddities and misfits then and remain so now, and we flatter ourselves to think otherwise.

◆

The neighborhoods had names—Cedarbrook, Edge Hill, Ardsley—but you couldn't tell one from the other as I went up the old Limekiln Pike, built for carts to carry lime to the local kilns and the first official road from Philadelphia into the American wilderness. *Burgers. Fries. Shakes. Ice Cream. Water. Ice. Sundaes.* I couldn't resist all that, so I stopped at the roadside Richman's burger joint and sat in the shade with burger, shake, fries, and felt the first whiff of summer coming on..

My belly got to grumbling forty-five minutes or so later when I came upon a small walled cemetery for the Fitzwater family stuck on a lot between two 1970s tract houses. I went inside and crumpled in the grass, my back against the low stone wall, exhausted, the burger and shake not settling right. Some of the graves went back to the early 1700s and were just wisps of stone with dates and nothing else. It's funny to find yourself resting in a final resting place. You slip through the iron gate and introduce into the eternal hush of a spring afternoon all the carnality of a living human being. Achy tendons, unhappy lower back, riotous gut, swirling brain. You imagine the gravestones saying to one another: "We've got a live one here."

I sat leaning in the shade against that rock wall, mulling how any of us apportion our lives, and remembered a phrase that George Schaefer had tossed out a couple of hours earlier as we stood beside Lay's gravestone. "A second naivete," he said.

We were talking about the essence of Quakerism, which George described as "basically a rational mysticism, a primitive form of Christianity." No priests, no hierarchy, no set doctrine to follow. "We all have an inner light. People basically wait for the spirit to move them."

Then George mentioned the people who stumble upon Quakerism later in life. "They are often going through a second naivete, as some philosophers call it."

I stopped him when he said that and asked him to elaborate. The French philosopher Paul Ricoeur, he said, had first floated the concept of a second naivete. On the other side of adult critical thought, Ricoeur posited, resides a place where ancient symbols and myths and stories can regain their power to instill hope and wonder. A second childhood of sorts—but of a higher order, if one is so fortunate.

The phrase, when George said it, lit up in my mind, not unlike when Neal Weaver mentioned the line from St. Paul about renewal and a transformation of the spirit. Years earlier, after my cancer diagnosis blurred my future prospects, I put a lot of thought into how I should fashion my sixties if I were so lucky as to have them. I imagined a period during which I attempted to shed my hardened conceptions and to look at things anew. A time to revel in what I didn't know while trying to fill in those huge gaps. I would aim again to greet things as I found them and savor the complexity, which only grew as one saw and learned more. A recapturing, as I saw it, of a much younger phase in life when the limbs and mind and spirit were much more fluid and more limber. I had no name for this approach, but suddenly, "a second naivete" fit quite well.

I naively trudged on.

The road came to a defunct golf course where the fairways and greens were returning to meadow and grass sprouted from the old bunkers, a fine form of redemption that mixed decay with renewal. As I neared Hole #7, my bowels bellowed, and I dropped my pack and scrambled for the woods to lean against a tree, my shorts crumpled now around my ankles. Trees are helpful in moments like that when you make deposits among leaves and twigs. Reemerging into sunlight I felt mightily relieved, at one with the infinite lineage of open-air poopers who preceded us all. Long walks teach skills that were once second nature. The crustiest of colonials did nearly all their life's business in the woods.

I sat for half an hour on a bench a mile or two up the road watching two middle-aged Korean men smack tennis balls across the net on a municipal court. They spoke to each other in Korean but all their tennis terms—*love, deuce, add in, long*—were in English. They laughed and thanked me when I inserted myself a time or two as an informal line judge for close calls.

"Just wide," I said, when one of them scorched a forehand that hit an inch shy of the line. They immediately deferred to the impartial one.

When they were toweling off and stashing their rackets, I decided to step a little deeper into their world, curious if one of them might be willing to bend a small portion of his evening to accommodate a stranger. I walked around to the backside of the court and asked through the fence if either of them cared to play a little longer.

"I've been walking all day," I explained. "I'm on my way to New York on a long walk from Washington. I would love to chase a tennis ball for a bit if one of you has the energy. I'd need to borrow a racket, of course."

They glanced at each other and then at me, a strange man with a raspy voice, six and a half feet tall, no racket, a toe hole in one of his walking shoes, and no known address. Then they glanced at each other again.

"I need to get home," said one, shouldering his bag. You could tell he didn't know quite what to make of the new arrival.

The other one looked at me for a second and smiled. "Sure, why not? I'll play." When I came onto the court, he handed me a racket and said his name was Eugene. "I do software," he said, before I even asked.

Eugene wore a sweatband like John McEnroe and had an aggressive topspin forehand and a floating backhand that ran me ragged. We didn't do much to keep score. My legs were wobbly from the day's walking and my gut still aggrieved from that burger and shake. But I gave it my best, pleased to be on the run.

"Nice rally," Eugene said, after one point where I lunged from side to side and then stood to watch his backhand float gracefully down the line. He chuckled on the next point when his dropshot had me huffing to the net and then gasping to the baseline as his lob arced in a perfect parabola over my head. But mostly we just hit, back and forth, which is what I wanted most. That, and convincing a stranger to lend me a racket and play.

I thanked Eugene for taking the time. "Enjoy the walk," he said.

At the Hilton Homewood Suites off the Pennsylvania Turnpike and across the street from a Lowe's, the clerk at the front desk peered at me through his glasses, looked at my backpack, heard what I was doing, and turned to pull two bottles of cold pale ale straight from the fridge.

"On the house," he said. "The least we can do. Seriously." It was my first and only act of corporate sponsorship.

The plastic key the clerk gave me became a wand that magically opened the door to a room with a sofa, four chairs, an endlessly hot shower, and a five-foot-wide bed with starchy sheets and six fluffy pillows. It was no cave.

CHAPTER 17

THE FOUNDING TOOLS

Who were the founders? Who built the foundations of our early republic? Who made the country possible? Without whom, let's say, could it not have happened at all?

You think about who did the original spadework when you walk the roads, the railbeds, the canal towpaths, when you cross the expansive bridges over the biggest rivers or the small but elegant bridges over mere creeks. You think of who built what while admiring the barns, the stone houses, the tumbledown grist mills, the fields under plow that someone cleared of trees, and then of the stones turned into walls that snake beside the roads you walk. I have stood to admire such walls, just trying to imagine the exertion it took to build them.

We have founders who wrote declarations, who helped conceive of constitutions or offered amendments, who trafficked in ideas and gave speeches on liberty or death. Founders who put their looping signatures at the bottom of solemn documents. We give primacy to such thinkers in part because it's the thinkers who have the power to grant primacy. They are the ones in the framed portraits, on the covers of books or peering from our currency in part because the portrait painters, the book makers, and the printers of currency had the power to put them there.

I was walking to Doylestown up Limekiln Road not to diminish those founders but to look at the works of a man who obsessed over other founders—the makers and builders, the users of tools.

Henry Chapman Mercer looms as a great curiosity from a stretch of the late nineteenth century that produced many passionate eccentrics. Mercer, like many of them, was a multitude of things rolled into one: archaeologist, wanderer and traveler, cultural sociologist, artist and renowned tile maker, keeper of lore, architect, and builder of big and extravagant buildings. Few of us have so many facets now.

Most germane to my walk, Mercer was a great hoarder and rememberer of the lost traditions of America. The industrial age brought the first sustained wave of mass forgetting, and Mercer became obsessed with pushing back. As the whole of the country swapped out its methods and tools for doing nearly everything, Mercer went in search of the artifacts of a vanishing America. He roamed the countryside of the Delaware Valley and then the wider Mid-Atlantic, and soon the whole of the country, poking around county fairs and old barns in search of tools and implements whose function had been all but forgotten. The founding tools, he called them.

Treading toward me along the roadside, south from Doylestown, came an old friend, Woody Woodhull, who had driven up that morning from Washington to meet me for the day. Woody had made the trip, like me, to pay homage to a person he knew nothing about months earlier, but whose life he now knew in all its bizarre twists and turns. The minute we met and set back the way he had come, Woody was spilling over with Mercer lore and talk of future walks we had to take to honor other places and other people.

Woody had nudged open his own small door, ventured out, and his eyes were alit with discovery and adventure. "C'mon, give it to me," he said, grabbing my pack and shouldering it for the remainder of the walk into town. "I want the full experience." He was bursting with essential questions. "So, have you shat in the woods?" he asked. Many times, I said, and told him of my squat the day before beside the defunct golf course. What a joy to be among pals.

Woody produces radio shows and podcasts, and a steady stream of verbal content pretty much wherever he goes. As we came into proud Doylestown—hometown not only of Mercer but also of Margaret Mead and James Michener—Woody went full swing into a sustained Mercer monologue. Woody's a born monologuist.

Mercer was a curmudgeon. An irascible loner. Devoted to his own opinions. "Okay, here's just a little indication of his personality," Woody said. "In the margin of his copy of *A Farewell to Arms* he'd scribbled, 'As charming as a bottle of dead flies.' That's how much he liked Hemingway." Woody howled over that.

Mercer went to Harvard and studied law. "But that wasn't his thing," Woody said. He quit and hurled himself into archaeology and engaged in digs across the States and all the way down to the Yucatán, trying to pin down the origins of humankind in the Americas, until he'd had enough of that.

"One day all of a sudden," Woody said, stopping in his tracks, making sure I heard him, "Mercer had this epiphany. He said to himself, 'This is stupid. We're doing all this examining of things from thousands of years ago at the same time as we're losing all these artifacts right in front of us that we hold dear.' So, he set out to collect everything."

Woody and I were heading toward the hulking great fortress of a museum that Mercer built on the edge of downtown Doylestown to hold all the things that he went into the world to find.

Mercer bought enormous cider presses, grain threshers, whale boats, stagecoaches, Conestoga wagons, cigar-store figures, the heads that protruded from the bows of great ships. Every implement ever used by a carpenter, blacksmith, hatmaker, weaver, gunmaker, Mercer acquired. He amassed enormous numbers of early American guns, knives, hatchets, saws, ropes, fishing poles, traps, harpoons. That Franklin stove that was supposedly first tested in that house I peered into in Coventryville—the last-known version of that stove resided inside on a high floor of Mercer's museum.

Mercer bought and installed there the Doylestown gallows. He brought down from New Bedford, Massachusetts, a perfect thirty-by-six-foot whaling boat, complete with all the harpoons and coils of rope. When you looked at it you could imagine Queequeg thrashing in the swells and a white-faced Ahab on the bow, possessed, yelling at him to hurl the harpoon.

Henry Mercer and I had crossed paths twice already along my walk. In May 1885, at twenty-nine, he'd taken his own springtime walk from Doylestown to the Susquehanna, guided by rumors he'd heard about ancient petroglyphs carved on giant rocks in that river. The designs he copied from those rocks—the same rocks I'd stood upon with Paul Nevin that Easter afternoon—he later used in his famous mosaics on the rotunda floor at the Pennsylvania state capitol. One day, I had to go see those.

I'd come upon Mercer, too, nearly a week later at Valley Forge, when Lorett Treese took me to what little remained of the long-reburied Port Kennedy Bone Cave, where Mercer in 1894 had led an archaeological dig. Over several summers he had unearthed the remains of dozens of extinct species—mammoths, tapirs, bears—from the mid-Pleistocene epoch 750,000 years earlier. Miners had found the bones in an ancient sinkhole while digging for limestone.

In the same place where we had forgotten and then remembered the winter of 1777/78, this bone cave had been revealed, reburied, discovered anew, paved over by a state highway, rediscovered yet again, then made part of the same national park established to remember that famous winter. "It's over there, past those railroad tracks," Lorett said that afternoon from her car. "But you aren't going to see much."

So goes the true layering of our history, the eternal washing back and forth of remembering and forgetting. Mercer was
disappointed—hurt, even—that for all his weeks of digging, he'd
plucked no human remains from among the jawbones and spines
of those tapirs and mammoths.

———◆———

Woody's soliloquy came to a head as we neared the museum.
"What Mercer said of all these implements and tools is that they
murmured with a greater resonance than any shouts from the
Declaration of Independence or the U.S. Constitution."

The museum stood seven stories high across a moat of grass like
the medieval residence of some sadistic count, its sheer walls of
gray concrete studded with little paned windows. You expected to
hear groans and the clatter of chains inside.

Woody went on. "To Mercer, the ingenuity and singular purpose
of ordinary people created this country at least as much as, you
know, 'When in the course of human events, blah, blah, blah, blah.'"

We went inside and gaped at it all from the ground level, looking
up. "He built it like this, 115 feet up, so we could see everything
from all angles," Woody said. The baskets, sleighs, harnesses, yokes,
carriages, looms, wagon wheels, bellows, canoes, all hanging helter-
skelter this way and that. And then from the top floor, peering
down.

Taking it all in, I was struck by how wooden and leathery and
metallic our past was. Instead of the sounds of torment I imagined outside, the objects inside summoned the clang and scrape
and groan of sweaty men and women working. You are struck by
the naturalness of our recent past. How, if you left it outside for
very long, all but the steel and iron of it would be gone in so little
time. It sprang from the earth and was of the earth. How many

devices we needed to grind and press and mash things down to flour, to grist, to cider, to wine. How many different axes and saws we needed to fell the forests and turn trees into planks.

A museum to the past that was so irrevocably of the past, antique and distant, and a hundred times more so to anyone who grew up entirely in the age of plastics and carbon fibers, of polyester, polystyrene, and polyethylene. When the container that held your chicken salad the day before outlasts you by a thousand years.

Mercer had a particular passion for axes, those most brute of instruments, and for the work they did. He devoted a whole wall of the museum to them.

"You may go down into Independence Hall in Philadelphia and stand in the room in which the Declaration of Independence was signed and there look upon the portraits of the signers," he wrote in his book *Tools of the Nation Maker,* complete with photos of every conceivable ax. "But do you think you are any nearer the essence of the matter there than you are here when you realize that ten hundred thousand arms, seizing upon axes of this type, with an immense amount of labor and effort made it worthwhile to have a Declaration of Independence by cutting down one of the greatest forests in the North Temperate Zone?"

One small room in the museum contained some of the stone scrapers and grinders and arrow heads Mercer had dug up from his days as an archaeologist. The floor showed a tile mosaic, Mercer's own handiwork and bursting with color, depicting Columbus's ships setting sail to cross the ocean blue. "Today we realize," noted a sign nearby, "that rather than discovering a New World, Columbus's voyages unleashed a collision between the cultures of two worlds, both already old."

Yes, those two worlds and cultures were both already old, but as Mercer's museum and all the land around it illustrated, they were both being made new daily. They were being looked at fresh and seen differently. The museum itself was pushing to remember things—old tools, old practices—in the face of the stronger force of forgetfulness.

————◆————

The whole of the walk kept bringing delights beyond the bounds of any rightful expectation. Where I slept that night was evidence of that. A gas fire sputtered in a stone fireplace large enough to sit inside. An arching, twenty-five-foot concrete ceiling soared overhead, hung with baskets and old farm implements. Along one wall the paned windows reached equally high. The room looked like the dining hall for some Mystic Order of the Knights Templar. Our host had laid beds on the floor for me, Woody, and a second friend, Judge Michael Ryan, who drove up late from Washington to walk with me in the morning to the Delaware.

I hadn't planned to sleep in Mercer's famous Indian House, a twenty-minute walk from the museum and just down the hill from his towering residence, Fonthill Castle. Indian House was where he first began making ceramic tiles in the late 1890s and did so until his death in 1930. I wouldn't have dreamt of sleeping there. It wasn't even a place where people slept.

But my sister-in-law, just weeks after I decided to detour to Doylestown to immerse myself in Mercer, sent a note to say that a friend of hers, a woman I had met decades earlier at their wedding, was about to take over Mercer's Moravian Pottery & Tile Works. Katia McGuirk was herself a tile artist, a Mercer devotee, a passionate Bucks County booster. And for three years she had tussled with the county commission and the historical board to have her own nonprofit take over operations of the tile works. She had finally prevailed, and exactly a week before I arrived, they had plunked the keys to the place in her hands. It was hers now to do with as she pleased.

I dropped Katia a note to say I was coming. "Bring it," she

wrote back. I told her a couple of friends might join us and asked where we should stay that night. "I have just the place," she said. "We are setting up camp for you and your compadres." In the Indian House? Yes, she said. Three mattresses loaded with blankets and pillows arrayed around the enormous fireplace. It was all too much to believe.

The high concrete pillar at the start of the long drive leading to the residence said FONTHILL. It was chipped and cracked and only partially legible. Woody and I walked down the puddled drive between towering sycamores naked of leaf. Mercer's manor house, built entirely of poured concrete, was a dour gray, a sort of modernist medieval. "Decorate construction but never construct decoration" was Mercer's stern motto, taken from the English architect Augustus Pugin. You expected to see Norma Desmond peering from a high window.

Down the hill on the back of the property he built his sprawling tile works, which looked like an ancient factory attached to a monastic cloister. There, for decades, he and others told the story of the New World, which was actually Old, through colorful ceramic tiles made of the mud dug from Bucks County riverbanks and then hardened with fire.

The three of us—me, Woody, and the good Judge Ryan—sat for hours around the studio's gaping fireplace drinking beers Woody had brought up in a cooler from Washington. "Want another?" Woody would say, then disappear into the gloom of the back studio to fetch a few. The fireplace was so expansive it had an inglenook, a stone bench that allowed one of us to sit inside the hearth, so we swapped places as the evening wore on. We debated things— the causes of homelessness, the condition of our cities, whether the axmen or Madison were more central to our founding. Frederick Douglass, Thomas Paine, Ben Franklin, Abraham Lincoln—they and others hovered briefly by the firelight. We resolved nothing. Occasionally we went to examine the stars and pee.

"It was a rare and fine alchemy that brought us all here to-night," Woody declared, beer raised, and to that we all agreed with a clinking of cold bottles.

We stumbled into our beds with the fire muttering at our feet, thinking of Mercer and the world he scrambled to gather up before it was gone, and how scraps of it—baskets, threshers, scythes—now hung ominously over our heads.

CHAPTER 18

SAUNTERING ONES

I used to subscribe to the linear life. Back in my twenties when I was a philosophy student at Columbia and a New York cabbie, and when righteousness came naturally, I scoffed at vacations. Only cowards took trips with preordained outcomes. When two women spilled into my cab one night buzzing about their upcoming week at a Sandals in Jamaica, I told them they were doing it all wrong. "Quit your jobs and head out, not knowing if you will ever come back," I told them. They thought a madman was behind the wheel.

I later saw that Thoreau in his essay "Walking" issued the same trumpet call, only more grandly: "We should go forth on the shortest walk, perchance, in the spirit of undying adventure, never to return—prepared to send back our embalmed hearts only as relics to our desolate kingdoms." How I howled when I read those lines: Thoreau, whose longest trip was to Minnesota toward the end of his life, saw such infinitude in the near at hand.

We set out, Judge Michael Ryan and I, from Doylestown on a gray misty morning heading for the Delaware along Swamp Road, which became Forest Grove Road, and then Lower Mountain Road. Those eleven miles to New Hope cut through rolling farmland and along curving lanes past settlements with proud stone houses and barns that made you stop to praise them. The Continental Army marched this way with Oneida and Tuscarora warriors in the ranks. They were heading to the Jerseys in June 1778, after their long winter at Valley Forge, chasing the Red Coats as they hightailed it to New York.

Michael shared my stride and had a good feel for the art of walking along the road's shoulders and staying clear of the few cars that came our way. We talked when we wanted, but when we didn't, we just listened to our steps on the wet road or to the crows cawing in the woods.

A federal judge in Washington, Michael deals with all the hardships life serves up there—street shootings, fraud, juvenile crimes, grim battles over custody. He put his docket aside for a day to walk to the Delaware and brimmed with enthusiasm over the magnitude of that one morning. We talked about his work but also about the trees and how differently they were blooming mile to mile. We would walk into a valley where the maples were just flowering and then up a hill where they weren't and then back into another valley where they were again. Such was the fickleness of the blossoming line at that moment in mid-April that the season wavered from early spring to late winter, and back again, as we went. We talked about the variety of the old stone houses along the way, and how almost all of them told a story of change and modification over the centuries, from log to fieldstone to quarried stone. Some even bore more recent additions, often regrettable. A single house could speak to the evolution of humankind.

We talked, too, about the linearity of the true walk. How a walk like this, from one point to another far away, is so incomparably different from any daily walk when at home. Not because of the distance alone, but because you will never retrace your steps. When you traverse a beautiful rolling stretch of Bucks County, as we were that one Thursday in that one April, you know it's a road you will never walk again. Even if you did come back, it wouldn't be on a day like that, with the weeping cherry trees exploding in the yards and the forsythia lining the roadways in brilliant yellow. That feeling of traversing territory once and only once makes the long walk a dramatization of life itself.

Etymologists differ over the origins of the word "saunter." Most say it evolved from a Middle English word in the 1300s meaning to muse or daydream. Thoreau wishfully thought it derived from the holy pilgrim off to the "la Sainte Terre," the Holy Land. The fussy Adam Smith in his *Wealth of Nations* described sauntering as what country laborers did as they turned their attentions from one task to the next. It was, in other words, a waste of time: "For some time he rather trifles than applies to good purpose," Smith sniffed of the saunterer. John Muir picked up Thoreau's whimsy and told a fellow walker that he hated the word "hike." Too deliberate. Too Point A to Point B. "People ought to saunter in the woods—not hike!"

We talked without much knowledge about the word "path" and whether it bore some family tie to the "path" in words like "empathy" and "sympathy" that denote forms of feeling. Whether you had to walk a common trail to get to where you could feel something for the strangers you passed along the way. The late Japanese American theologian Kosuke Koyama called the walker's pace "the speed of God." Love moves, he wrote, at three miles an hour. "It is an inner speed. It is a spiritual speed."

The roster of inspired saunterers runs long. Beethoven took long walks between the hours spent composing. So did Kant. The shared past between walking and thinking stretches through the ages. "I can only meditate when I am walking," Rousseau wrote in his *Confessions*. "When I stop, I cease to think. My mind only works with my legs." Nietzsche, known for his walks along the Côte d'Azur, agreed. "A sedentary life is the real sin against the Holy Spirit," he wrote in *Twilight of the Idols*. "Only those thoughts that come by walking have any value."

If you're a runner, you will know that the longer the run, the deeper you will venture into certain thoughts. You arrive at places in your mind that are accessible only to the runner. You will find yourself saying, "I was thinking the other day, while out running . . . ," and then describe a thought that came to you only because you'd been running. Often the best thoughts come only after the seventh or eighth mile, as though it takes that long to get the brain engaged.

The same physics applies to walking. Some of it is just giving yourself the time to think without distraction. But it has to do with blood flow, too, and the rhythm of one's legs and the happiness of the animated brain. The longer you run or walk and the richer the blood flows, the freer and nimbler the thoughts. Now I was coming to realize that if you kept going, the lucidity granted to the walker deepened over the days. It had the power to cast a more lasting spell.

Michael and I came to things we couldn't understand. A stone house half covered with vines, graceful but awkward at the same time, with two front doors that lacked all symmetry. A weathered barn that was stone on two sides, wood on the others. The crumbled foundations of what was once an inn or maybe a roadside saloon, and the elaborate patchwork of its cornerstones, some quarried, the rest pulled randomly from the ground. We would poke among such ruins and attempt to re-create them in our minds. Failing that, we would try to fathom how time had so meticulously broken them apart.

For a week the forecasts promised sheets of rain for our walk to New Hope, but the storm fizzled or took a different path, giving us a morning of low, moist clouds but nothing more. We were both a little blue as we came up the Old York Road into town. "That went too fast," Michael said. We wanted those eleven miles to last much longer.

You can't arrive in a river town and not head straight for the river, which functions as a magnet. The Delaware River was a silvery gray like the sky when we got there. It flowed strong beneath the steel trussed bridge that took cars across to Lambertville. A small flotilla of skiffs bobbed at anchor just down from the bridge with men aboard casting for shad, I assumed. The Delaware flows free for the whole of her length, undammed for all 330 miles, the longest and most majestic unimpeded river east of the Mississippi.

There was a time, as with the Susquehanna, when this, too, was the rough frontier, the beginning of the beyond, a demarcation line for the Dutch and a buffer against the British. I just stood there, hands around the rail, taking it in.

This gash in the earth has gone by many names. Different tribes called portions of it the Mariskitton, the Lenape Wihittuck, or the River of the Lenape, among many other names. Europeans gave rivers a single name for the whole of their length while the native people, seeing a river's many parts as distinct places, would often know a river by multiple names to honor the stretch where the waterfall broke into a white foam or where the bear had died or where a fallen tree had created a natural bridge. The Dutch unimaginatively called the Hudson the Noort Rivier and the Delaware the Zuyd River or South River, as though the essence of those rivers derived from the location of the one who saw them.

The English were lamer still, giving the entire river, its two main branches, the bay it flows into, the native people who lived along it, and finally an entire U.S. state all the same name, plucked from the hereditary title for a dubious aristocrat, Thomas West, otherwise known as Lord De La Warr, who never even sailed the bay named for him or floated its main river. The lord who gave his name to the Delaware didn't fare well in the New World despite his large footprint. During his ten months in Virginia, he ordered the first English massacre of native Americans and suffered from "scurvy, fevers, ague, dysentery, malaria, flux, cramps, calenture (yellow fever), typhus, and gout." Some historians think he was poisoned when he died on his trip back to Virginia in 1618, and that his corpse was then tossed out to sea.

We found a table overlooking Thomas West's river and ordered our lunch. Three times I picked young ticks off my legs and tossed them in the water as ducks and geese circled below us on alert for a French fry or crust of bread.

"Those things have an affinity for you," Michael said of the ticks.

I had crossed the Susquehanna on Easter, then the Schuylkill six days later, and now running at my feet was my last mighty river before arriving at the Hudson late the next week. We heard a grumble, then a light patter, and the waiter announced it: "Here comes the rain." After lunch it began to fall in earnest when I gave the judge a quick hug, wished him a good trip home, shouldered my pack, and set off downriver with fat drops splattering at my feet.

At a café on the edge of town I ordered a cappuccino; when the owner heard where I had come from and where I was heading, she pushed the cup my way and gave me a brownie, too. "This is on me," she said. Nothing I said would get her to take my cash.

I went on, thinking about how differently people perceive the person who is walking through to a faraway place. Yes, there was the man who couldn't see fit to fill my water bottle. But at so many other stops along the way—the bakery, the coffee shop, the hotel bar, the sandwich shop—people had given me things for free. Cappuccinos, pastries, beer, a sandwich of bologna and cheese. I accepted the gifts and thanked them, while wondering why they did it. It's not because they thought I was short of money or in need of some pity.

I think the long-distance walker taps some primordial urge within us to respond to the pilgrim, to urge him on, to hope a little of whatever it is he or she might be seeking will rub off on us.

Pilgrims as they go often carry a token or a relic of some sort to touch to sacred things so that some spirit might be imparted on it. My Greek coin with the face of Athena served that purpose, and I confirmed as I went that it was still there in my pocket.

In the Middle Ages, arriving in Jerusalem or Canterbury or Compostela, the pilgrim would chip away a piece of the stone crypt to carry back, as though what they had gone to find was embodied in the stone of the shrine itself. When this became a problem, merchants sold tokens to bring back. The token for those who walked the Camino to Compostela took the form of a scallop shell. In Arles, along the route to Compostela at the Cathedral of Saint-Trophime, a stone depiction of Luke's Journey to Emmaus shows one of the disciples walking alongside the unrecognized Jesus with a scallop shell sewn into his headgear. The message: you never know who you might meet along the way.

In a similar fashion, people who encounter the walker often have the immediate inclination to give some small part of themselves, an act of kindness to the one they detect is on a pilgrimage. It's almost as if they are saying, "If you are on your way to Rome, remember me along the way. Bring a tiny bit of me with you."

I got the feeling as I went that this prompting runs deep in many of us, a thread there at birth. People want to urge you on and fortify you. But they also want, in an affirmation of the oldest roots of the word, to belong to your walk, to have a part in something that will go along with you. The shopkeeper's day is the ultimate in circular repetition, while the walker is going one way and never coming back.

I saw the flash of envy in her eyes when I mentioned my walk to the café owner in New Hope, that her day would keep her there, inside her shop, while mine would take me for miles down the river amid a light rain, and then on for days to a faraway place.

"Take care," she said. "Enjoy yourself."

———◆———

For two hours I walked from there along the Delaware Canal towpath, south toward where George Washington and his men crossed the river in a desperate bid to rebuff the British. I would get to that crossing in the morning.

On summer weekends this path surely teems with bikers and clusters of walkers, but on a drizzly Thursday afternoon in April there was just the odd fisherman, the occasional runner or idle stroller, the stray mallard, goose, or bald eagle on a limb, and not much more. The perfect reflection of the oaks, still bare, would make you stop and gape. For a long stretch the only thing separating the canal from the river itself was the path where horses once pulled the barges up the canal, and it was gloriously beautiful, especially when the sun peeked from the clouds and lit up the puddles on the path.

To the left of me, three hundred yards across to the other side, flowed the Delaware with big boils disturbing its otherwise smooth surface. To the right was the almost stagnant canal, a tamed version of the river, dug and constructed and maintained by thousands of men over thousands of days. You walked and marveled at the thought of all those shovels, pickaxes, crowbars—the founding tools, in Mercer's eyes. The sweat and toil it took to build these structures that were useful for barely two decades until the train made them irrelevant. The canal was dug to replace the river but now, for human purposes, neither of them mattered much. The unpredictability of the one created the necessity of the other, but now they were both an afterthought. Adornments, but no longer vital channels of commerce.

Below New Hope, I passed what were once a fearsome set of rapids. Rivermen bringing cargo down from upriver in their hefty Durham boats—stuffed with furs, coal, whisky—paddled in fear of the Wells Rapids, and would stop at the boathouse just beforehand to reconnoiter and trade tips. The rapids were still right there, little changed probably, spilling over rocks, tossing up foam. But they were unimpressive now to the man with uncalloused hands, without an oar, walking a tow path no longer used to tow anything at all.

Still farther south, late in the day now with my legs beginning to ache, I saw off to my left across an expanse of grass twenty-three simple white gravestones, all lined up neatly overlooking the Delaware. It was the simplest of memorials, easily missed, with nothing but a flagpole to draw your attention. Each stone marked the grave of a soldier buried there who never made it to New Jersey on the night Washington crossed for his sneak attack in Trenton.

These men all died of disease, exposure, or earlier injuries and were buried there on Christmas Day, 1776. Only one bore a name, that of James Moore, a twenty-four-year-old artillery captain from Alexander Hamilton's New York company. Moore died on Christmas Day, Hamilton wrote a few months later, "of a short but excruciating fit of illness." All the other markers simply said: UNKNOWN SOLDIER, CONTINENTAL LINE, REV WAR, DEC 1776.

I felt a little self-conscious afterward thinking of the young James Moore as I ordered a delivery calzone and a few bottles of cold Budweiser to my bed-and-breakfast two miles downriver. I ate dinner in my room as darkness fell behind the curtains, sitting on my bed, knowing I wouldn't have lasted well on a winter's night like that. And how good the shower would feel when I was done eating. And how, in the morning, there would be a hot breakfast of bacon, eggs, and oatmeal in the parlor before I set off for my own personal crossing of the Delaware.

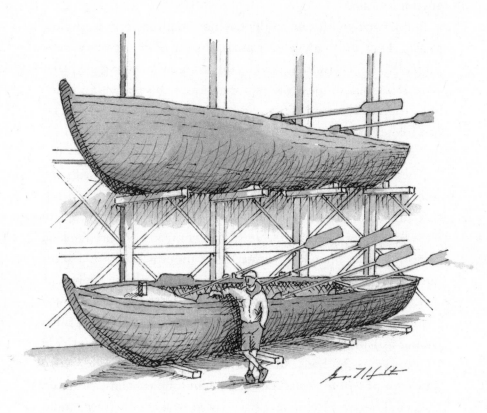

CHAPTER 19

CROSSING THE RIVER

I have a friend, Susan Hockaday, who would put me up the next night well east of the Delaware, not far from Princeton. She would hand me the yellowing typescript of her great-great-great-grandfather's descriptions of Christmas night, 1776, when he crossed the Delaware as a young fifer in Washington's army.

Her long-ago ancestor, John Greenwood, wrote the memoir "from memory in New York on Feby. 14th 1809," when he was fifty-one. He gave those scribbled accounts of his early life to his son Isaac, while his other son, Clark, made a handwritten copy of the memoir and handed that down to his daughter, Marion, who made a third copy by hand, and passed that down through three generations until a typewritten copy of that copy, typed on an old manual typewriter in 1935, ended up with Susan, who pulled it from a shelf in her dining room and passed it to me to read for the night.

"The family's own fifer," Susan said. "I haven't read it myself in years."

Memories scribbled long after the fact, in a New York long gone, transcribed and retranscribed and passed along, generation to generation to generation, but still vibrant and surprising on the page. Just that morning I had crossed the river where John Greenwood had crossed. And that night I huddled in my bedroom to read what he had written of his early life and of the historic river crossing he made that Christmas morning.

John Greenwood says he saw signs of the Revolution coming as a kid. A great blazing comet had cut across the sky and everyone had seen "armies of fighting men in the Clouds, engaged in battles, over our heads, and it was told that the day of Judgement was near at hand, when the Moon would turn to blood, and the world would be set on fire."

He was fourteen when he saw "the tea when it was destroyed in Boston which began the disturbance—likewise several people tarred and feathered, and carried through the town." His bunkmate, an apprentice to his father, died "when the British troops had fired upon the inhabitants and killed seven of them." He wished a church near his house might fall and crush him to death, "so as to be out of pain quickly," before the troubles came, he said.

He was sixteen the night he and the rest of the Continental Army crossed the Delaware. "When we got to the river it began to rain," he wrote. "Over the river we went in a flat-bottomed scow, and when on the other side . . . we began to pull down the fences and make fires to warm ourselves, for the storm came on fast, so that it rained, hailed, and blew a hurricane."

On a flat-bottomed scow, long gone, the boy made the famous crossing. And as a much older man, he wrote of it—the cold, the freezing rain, the bonfires that offered scant warmth—so that someone curled in a bed centuries later might know of his particulars on a night that stood out from all the others.

———◆———

As you walk, there are many roads and paths that will get you from Washington to New York City. But the more you study the matter, the stronger the pull becomes to cross the Delaware where Washington did on that Christmas of 1776. In your own watercraft, paddle in hand. You go with a sheaf of images in your head, cartoons almost, of the gallant white man standing, one knee raised, snow-dusted tricorn on his head, in a little boat packed with motley soldiers picking their way through the ice. That image of *Washington Crossing the Delaware* was lodged in the American psyche from the day its German-born painter, Emanuel Leutze, put the massive canvas on display in New York in 1851.

That painting has been copied, parodied, deconstructed, and lampooned ever since. One of its critics emerged from nowhere in a black Nike tracksuit as I sauntered south along the canal path, on the way to my own crossing. He was on his phone, midconversation, when he saw me and said, "Oh, damn, I gotta jump." He stashed his phone in his pocket and said to me, "Aren't you that dude who is walking to New York?" He'd seen chatter about my walk on the internet.

His name was Travis Manger, late thirties, a onetime star high school quarterback and former college football coach at Morgan State University in Baltimore. He turned to walk with me, and for twenty minutes he put me right on the reality of that crossing and what was wrong about Leutze's painting, as though he'd been sent by some higher power for just this purpose. I glanced over my shoulder, suspicious.

Travis wore bright, brand-new white sneakers and a close-cut dark beard. He grew up nearby and had stood on the riverbank since childhood for the big reenactments they do every Christmas. He'd seen the hefty Durham boats crossing the Delaware multiple times, in all sorts of weather, to take Washington and his troops to rout the nasty Hessians in Trenton. He had heated opinions about how people got the whole thing all wrong. They failed to fully understand the situation.

"Everyone's like, 'It was this super treacherous crossing and there's Washington standing up front with all that ice flowing by in a tiny boat packed with a million people.' They think it was all a lot of rowboats and canoes. It wasn't. The boats they took across were like sixty feet long."

Travis, the heaven-sent instructor, set the scene. All summer and into the fall, the British army, the world's mightiest military power, had routed the rebels in battle after battle from Long Island all the way down through New Jersey. Washington had fled across the river, commandeering all the boats to keep the British from following. Now everyone was settling in for a grim winter, and the ragtag Continental Army was at wit's end. Broke. Dispirited. Without a victory to stoke their spirits. The big dream of independence lit that July looked set to be snuffed.

Washington needed a win. His plan: a sneak attack when they least expected it, at dawn on Christmas morning, against an outpost in Trenton of hired Hessian troops. If successful, he would then march for Princeton and try to push the Red Coats back north.

People don't realize, Travis said, how dicey the whole thing was. How it could have all gone up in smoke, possibly snuffing the American cause. How tenuous Washington's hold was over his own troops. How dubious they were of the whole mission. How little some of them even wanted to be there.

"These guys were standing in the bitter cold and saying, 'Dang, this guy's gonna make us cross this river on Christmas. My enlistment's up. Like I can literally go home in, like, less than a week. And I can get myself out of this bad situation and back with my family. And now I am standing here, and I am freezing and I'm waiting for three hours as everyone else crosses the river. And I'm wondering what it's all for.'"

As the two of us wandered toward where it all happened, Travis in his spiffy tracksuit and sneakers was channeling the discomforts and hesitations of a freezing band of men that night 245 years ago.

Before he left, Travis said he appreciated that I was taking it slow, getting to know the backroads that others just flew down in their cars or avoided altogether. He'd done much the same when he'd recruited football talent from every high school between D.C. and New York. "I've been down every road," he said. And he was taking it slow again, he said, as he figured out the next step in his career and whether to stay in athletics or go a different direction. "Thinking of all that is what put me on this path," he said.

As Travis wandered off to his car, I sat on a bench overlooking the canal and laughed at the weirdness of how one man's career meditations had turned him into an advance guard for my crossing of the river where Washington had.

———◆———

Were you to concoct the perfect day for a Delaware crossing, you would brew a morning like this. No ice and driven snow on a December's night but an April morning that was crisp, sunny, the river flowing strong but not ornery, a sharp breeze coming downriver with the water.

I arrived at a broad park that well-meaning people had studded with markers and statues, as we do when we finally decide a place matters. As was the case at Valley Forge, it took more than a century for anyone to really care about a riverbank where some men spent a wintry night and then crossed over. In 1895, exactly 119 years after that river crossing, the authorities in Bucks County erected a granite marker, and twenty-two years later they made it a park.

I found my friend Phil Kuntz, a fellow *Wall Street Journal* veteran, at the boat launch on the edge of that park with two camo kayaks on a trailer. I hadn't seen Phil in years, but he had heard of my walk and asked if he could chip in, maybe by helping me cross the Delaware by watercraft. I said yes, absolutely, I would accept all available reinforcements from the north. So he had driven down from outside New York City, and there we both were at the appointed hour, giving handshake hugs and preparing for our moment.

We had stewed for weeks about how fearsome the river might be when we got there, and whether we might perish in the icy drink. We'd debated whether we might need neoprene tops in case we turned over—a comfort, I pointed out, that Washington's own men lacked. But after standing on the riverbank to study the river's currents and eddies, and then steadying ourselves in our little boats, we grew so confident we forgot our life preservers and set out with reckless excitement.

Our disembarkation point was sheltered from the main thrust of the current by a long island on the Pennsylvania side of the river. The full current began just around the point where a small branch of the river ran between that island and a much smaller one. Our plan was to nose into the full current there, paddle full thrust up that narrow channel and around that little island, and then head for the other side a couple hundred yards away.

I was not standing in my kayak as I set off. Nor did I have my left hand placed solemnly upon my chest. No soldier stood behind me protecting the Stars and Stripes in his arms. I did not have a phallic sword dangling from my belt. Nothing hinged on the success of my crossing.

Strong paddling got me up that narrow channel and into the thrust of the full river, swollen with spring runoff. Phil was not so lucky. He kept getting knocked off course and dragged downriver. Several times he called out from the other side of the brush. "I'm getting hung up," I heard him shout.

I was making good progress cutting diagonally across the strong current, feeling steady, jubilant. Should I loop back to assist my distressed comrade? I paused over that question until Phil emerged triumphantly from behind the island shrubbery and onto the main river. We both fought our way across, whooping as we went. To prolong the journey we performed a few curlicues in the river or just sat there, paddling against the current to stay in one place and take it all in. Then we turned our noses to New Jersey and brought ourselves ashore.

My first patch of Jersey soil was a dark, semisolid mud that enveloped the soles of my shoe as I stepped ashore. There was no enemy about. No Hessian soldiers for hire. No ragtag fellow infantry shivering around fires made of torn-down fences.

We dragged our boats ashore and gave each other rowdy high fives. Two weeks since crossing the Mason-Dixon Line into Penn's Woods, the Keystone Commonwealth, I was in a new land now on the edge of a state named for an island, Jersey, in the middle of the English Channel. I wasn't sure what this micronation held, but I knew it would be the sixth along my course. I had departed Capitolia and crossed Southlandia into Antibaptistan, and from there into a corner of Englandia, and thus into Greater Philadelphia. I ducked back into the eastern edges of Englandia, and to the river's edge. I didn't know what to call this place, but it felt different from the land I'd just left.

From this riverbank, Washington and his men began their nine-mile wintry slog to Trenton, but Phil and I had to trek back across the bridge so Phil could grab his car and trailer. When we got across the bridge we came upon a party of fifteen middle-aged hikers, huddled near the stone McConkey's Ferry Inn, all in matching yellow shirts that said "Enjoying the Outdoors Together. Hunterdon Hiking Club." They had heard I was coming their way and had gathered to meet the passing pilgrim. When I approached, the group began to applaud, and a woman in a puffy down vest stepped forward to present me with a box of cookies and another of spiced nuts, each box handmade of intricately folded origami. I felt myself blushing, unworthy of such attention.

"A token of our appreciation for your walk," she said.

Another member of the club, a man wearing a tricorne hat with a hatchet in his hand, handed me an honorary brass Washington's Crossing lapel pin, the only spare he had. His name was Dan McAuliffe, but he introduced himself as Captain Daniel Bray, his 1776 nom de guerre. "I'm the guy who procured the boats for Washington to get across that morning," he said in a proud sotto voce. What he meant was that he plays Captain Bray in the annual Christmas reenactment.

I had entered, perhaps, a more virus-conscious part of the country, so Dan had a black face mask to block any errant COVID molecules but also to match the color of his tricorne, from which a white feather protruded. "I left my musket on the Jersey side. They wouldn't let me bring it over to Pennsylvania."

Down the lane came Dianne Breen, a park ranger whose full-time job was that one wintry day a long time ago. You could tell she was pleased to see such a crowd gathered on a crisp morning even before the official opening time. Once she heard what had brought us there, she threw open the cavernous boat barn and invited Phil and me to go inside, past the rope, to get up close with the huge Durham boats that the reenactors use every December to make the chilly crossing.

"These are the real deal. Well, as close as we can get to the real deal," Dianne said. The mighty wooden beasts—eight feet wide, three feet deep, and up to sixty-five feet long—were stacked two to a side on steel I-beams. "Their steering oars alone weigh seventy-five pounds," Dianne said.

These were the long-haul truckers of their day, the boats that brought grain, iron ore, pelts, whisky, over rapids from far upriver in the decades before the canal. I stood there and imagined the thrill of the downriver trip, but couldn't summon the grinding tedium of getting that boat back upriver.

"Give it a feel," Dianne said as she gave the black wooden hull a firm pat. I knocked it once with the fleshy side of my fist. The boat responded with a dull thud.

"Boats just like this brought Washington and his men across," Dianne said. The canons, horses, and many of the rank and file crossed on wide, flat-bottomed barges. No one, she made a point of noting, had gone across in a kayak.

In his memoir, the young fifer tells of his discomfort after he got to the other side that night and tried to keep from freezing around a large bonfire. What warmed him, he writes, was the commotion of it all. "The noise of the soldiers coming over and cleaning the cakes of Ice from off the boats, and the rattling of the cannon wheels over the frozen ground, with the cheerfulness of my fellow soldiers, cheered me up beyond expression, and as big a coward as I acknowledge myself to be I felt more pleasure then than I do now in writing it."

Once they had all mustered, his unit began to march "in the old slow way," as did I back across the steel bridge with the Hunterdon Hiking Club flanking me on all sides, north through the high woods toward my friend Susan's converted barn outside Princeton, New Jersey. The club led me to the end of a park and showed me the right way to walk to where I was going, and off I went up Pennington Road.

I was now firmly in my third state, the Garden State, settled by the most solid of middling English folk. "Weavers, tanners, carpenters, bricklayers, chandlers, blacksmiths, coopers, bakers, haberdashers, hatters, and linen drapers," as one historian put it, "they were in no sense adventurers, gold seekers, cavaliers, or desperadoes." You think New Jersey and you think Turnpike, Pine Barrens, Jersey Shore, Springsteen, Sopranos, but I managed to slip north toward Princeton through a rolling landscape—I know few will believe it—dotted with horses and cut through by a trout stream.

Susan and her husband, Maitland Jones, gave me a room off the kitchen with a washer-dryer just steps from a shower. I couldn't have imagined a better arrangement. I put all my clothing and my shoes in the washer and then myself in the shower. After dinner, I crawled into bed to read of Susan's forefather, the fifer John Greenwood, and how he crossed that river on a flat-bottomed scow many years before.

CHAPTER 20

THE HEART OF AMAZONIA

The sun was barely up when Susan came into the kitchen with the morning paper and dropped a palmful of pale-yellow maple flowers on the breakfast table. Day to day, week to week, she collects all manner of natural things and turns them into art. "Aren't these lovely?" she said.

Over a plate of eggs and biscuits, her husband, Maitland, a chemist, got to talking about entropy and how within all the physical sciences it is among the few forces reliant on a past and future, on the passage of what we call time. That decay by definition had a past and a present. He took a ghoulish pleasure in listing the natural phenomena—white dwarves, the red giant, a slight shift in the Higgs field—that could make the world go boom. I buttered my biscuit and listened.

The Higgs field, scientists think, is the force that gives all particles mass. It was created at the instant of the Big Bang and is assumed to have been set, upon creation, at its lowest point of energy, with no room to fall. All of creation has aligned with that setting. But if the Higgs field is itself susceptible to entropy, even in the slightest degree, and decides one day to shift a notch, Mait explained as he nibbled his biscuit, "Then it's lights out." He said that with great glee.

I thanked Mait and Susan for their hospitality—I had spent two whole nights at their place laundering and resting up—and walked east toward Princeton thinking what the "lights out" of a shift in the Higgs field would feel like, all of us sharing in the disintegration of everything, all at once. "I wouldn't want to miss out on that," I had told Mait. Better to go out with a bang, in voluminous company, than to wink out all alone, I figured.

I cut through the woods on a spring morning, with a loose stride, taking New Jersey as it came. I was not shooting north or south across the state as we usually do on our way elsewhere at whatever velocities a car, train, or jet would permit. The state today was not a succession of train stops or Turnpike Exits 6, 7, 7A, 8, 8A, 9, each a way out that the body in motion wants in the rearview. Today it was a host of very particular things, seen slowly.

In the Princeton Battlefield on the edge of town, I stood beside a tree boxed in by a split-rail fence, the site of the famous Mercer Oak whose roots were watered one January morning, 1777, by the blood of the freshly bayoneted Brigadier General Hugh Mercer. Cars streamed past on Mercer Road. Princeton resides within Mercer County. The huge Mercer Oak collapsed "of old age on March 3, 2000," said a nearby sign, but still stands tall on the Mercer County seal. The current tree within the protective fence was its offspring.

Leaning against that fence was Larry Kidder, yet another friend of a friend and a true authority on the Battle of Princeton. He's written books about it. He'd given many tours of these grounds and agreed to meet for an early-Sunday-morning walk-through of the battlefield. Larry looked fore and aft and then whispered to me, "I hate to say it, but the Mercer Oak is a myth. It wasn't a witness tree to the Revolution. There was simply no oak here for that battle."

It was across this field, astride his steed, that George Washington led, I like to think, the one gallant charge of the entire grim slog of that war. It was the third of January, nine days after he crossed the Delaware and thumped the Hessians in Trenton. He caught the British by surprise in Princeton.

"He threw two brigades at them, the first led by Hugh Mercer, but that wasn't enough," Larry explained as we stood in the battlefield-turned-picnic-yard. A group of parents with balloons bobbing were setting up a children's birthday party. "The British bayonets brought a lot of our men down. Mercer was bayoneted many times just up there. Then Washington came charging in from along that line of trees."

"It's a fine fox chase, my boys," George yelled from atop his white horse, sword raised, before he galloped with his men down the hill. Or so lore had it. The British troops turned and scattered.

"Surely that was the single most satisfying martial moment in all of Washington's career," I said to Larry.

He declined to second my assessment. "I am hesitant to say 'greatest' or 'best' or any of that, but it might have been," he said.

He confirmed there was abundant drama, though. "Some of the soldiers said they covered their eyes with their hats so as not to see the general cut down," Larry said. He had summoned that image many times before—to busloads of students and ladies' auxiliaries—but still he flushed in the retelling.

Larry shielded his eyes from the morning sun and told me about the research he was doing for a big Revolutionary musical that would capture, in all its patriotic glory, how a band of ragged misfits turned the course of the war, and saved America, between Christmas 1776 and the battle fought on this field.

"It won't be all about Washington but more about the common folk," Larry assured me. "We're calling it 'The Crossing and the Ten Crucial Days—The Musical.'"

Larry declined to hum me any tunes.

———◆———

On I went past Einstein's white clapboard house with its little black sign on the gate—PRIVATE RESIDENCE—pondering the relativity of truth and history and how it all depended on where you stood. Marian Anderson spent a night there as Einstein's guest in 1937 after she sang for thousands in town but was refused a room at the inn. You can see photos of Einstein sprawled on the steps of the porch, much as he was in that statue I'd passed my first morning, heading out of Washington.

I went past the PRESENT DAY CLUB, ESTABLISHED 1898, and through the university, where streams of earnest students bisected all the campus's neat rectangles. Town gave way to country, dissolved into farmlands and fields.

It was the third Sunday in April and along Washington Road, fathers were mowing their yards of the first spring grass. The forsythias were now half green, half yellow and the tulip magnolias had dropped in a wide arc around them the blossoms they'd once held aloft. The maples were still in flower, but the plums had all leafed and the sycamores still had weeks to go. The smell of fresh-cut grass trailed me for miles.

At Princeton Junction a bridge spanned five sets of tracks and a New Jersey transit train shot beneath me, on its way elsewhere fast. A tall four-sided clock at the corner announced it was 2:30 in the afternoon. I took a left on Cranbury Road.

At the junction of three roads where some guy named Grover once had a mill, Louis Mok was cutting his grass on a tractor mower. The house behind him had a big white porch and beat-up black shutters that looked ready to fall off. When I saw the guy on his mower, something about him and that house told me I had to talk to him, so I waved, and he cut the motor.

"Welcome to Grovers Mill. This is Grover's House, where Grover himself lived," Louis said. "The mill is right over there." He pointed across the street. Dressed head to toe in black Nike sweat-shirt, black jeans, and black Nike sneakers, Louis told me that Grovers Mill had two claims to fame. One was that Walter S. Grover had been a big deal back in the day, so when fancy people came through town, they tended to bunk with him. "Two presidents stayed here," Louis said, pointing his thumb to his house. "Woodrow Wilson and Grover Cleveland. At least that's what they say."

The hamlet's other big moment was when Martians landed there in 1938. They had sought a place to terrorize the humans on Earth and decided to do so right outside Princeton in the utterly plain and all-American setting of Grovers Mill. When news of the Martian landing hit the nation's airwaves on October 30, 1938, people panicked, including the residents of this tiny burg.

"Good heavens," said a supposed reporter on the spot, describing what he saw to a rapt audience. "Something's wriggling out of the shadow like a gray snake. Now it's another one, and another. It's large, large as a bear and it glistens like wet leather."

Then came an urgent bulletin, all written and narrated by the devilish Orson Welles: "I have been requested by the governor of New Jersey to place the counties of Mercer and Middlesex as far west as Princeton and east to Jamesburg under martial law."

"Radio Listeners in Panic, Taking War Drama as Fact" blared the next day's *New York Times*.

"Did you see that weird water tower in my backyard?" Louis said, getting off his mower. He was a stocky fellow, a retired architect, likely in his midseventies. He led me around the side of his house to where a swimming pool still had its cover pulled tight and a water tower jabbed into the sky with strange wires sticking out like a primitive rocket ship.

"Never seen a water tower quite like that one," I said. Louis explained it was a one-house water tower, to draw water for his house and hold it aloft in that big wooden barrel. "But you can see why it scared people, right? People thought it was the Martian landing craft. There are pictures in old books of a guy with a shotgun taking shots at it, but some dispute that ever happened."

Orson Welles's producer for that fictitious radio show, *War of the Worlds,* claims to have hit on Grovers Mill by randomly dropping a pencil onto a map of New Jersey. Louis has his own version. He said Welles picked the place because it was right near Princeton, which had an observatory that features in the drama, but was just far enough away to be Anytown America. Louis now lives in the house built by the man who gave that town its name.

Mercer Oak, Einstein, Grover Cleveland, Martians, old water tower that may have been shot at, pencil drop. You just take it in and wonder.

Louis was proud of the house but even more proud of his Series Y Tesla sedan tucked away in the garage. By a strange twist that Orson Welles himself would've loved, Louis was mowing the grass wearing a black cap with the word "SpaceX" emblazoned across it.

"No confusion intended," Louis said, when I asked about the hat. "I just happen to like Elon Musk."

———◆———

I had picked that day's destination with a deliberation more exacting than that of Welles's producer picking Grover Mills. For three weeks I had hiked a wide arc to the northwest, knowing that all along, somewhere over there toward the rising sun, was that great sucking force of the East's premier north-south conduit, known here as the New Jersey Turnpike, but farther north and south as Interstate 95. Its construction starting soon after World War II made the freeway an emblem of anonymous speed and convenience from Maine to Miami, the first of the formidable interstate highways.

For months, like a knight plotting his encounter with a distant dragon, I had mulled where and how to approach and cross that wide ribbon of asphalt and concrete. It loomed now less than an hour to the east. It would be a solemn moment, not unlike the crossing of the Ganges or the Nile or one's first encounter with the edge of the Sahara. It had to be done right.

At home, while sketching my approach, I had squinted over old maps and zoomed in on overhead imagery on Google Earth, examining how the roads moved and the rivers and creeks flowed and seeking the ultimate collision of past and present. Suddenly, my heart soared. Here was a tiny town, a stage stop from the eighteenth century largely unscathed by the centuries after, smack on the edge of the turnpike madness. To the west of it stretched miles of verdant farmland. To the east, within barely three hundred yards, yawned acre after acre of massive distribution centers: Amazon, Wayfair, Home Depot, Crate and Barrel. The stationary container ships holding all the world makes and consumes. You could see the gray boxes on the satellite view with the trucks lined up chockablock around them.

For anyone roaring north or south on the turnpike, the town of Cranbury resides just off Exit 8A. You will see it emblazoned right there on the sign: EXIT 8A, CRANBURY/JAMESBURG. Better still, a small river ran through town called Cranbury Brook. I could see its water like a silvery ribbon on the overhead imagery. And up that river lay the warehouses, and beyond those, the turnpike itself. My plan locked into place. I would tarry in lovely Cranbury and talk to the little group that tends to its history. Then I would walk up that river like Henry Morton Stanley slashing back the vines and snakes with his machete. Thusly I would traverse Amazonia.

The rest of the afternoon I skirted fruit orchards in puffy bloom and sauntered beside infant spinach fields and past painted barns, all as though rendered by some quaint landscape painter. Somewhere along that route, I crossed the old dotted line, seen on colonial maps from the seventeenth century, that divided East Jersey from West Jersey. I was on the east side now and the land remained virginal all the way into Cranbury. You could hear the twenty-first century whining along the freeway less than a mile to the east, but not a whisper of it was to be seen or heard as I wandered into town north along South Main Street, the day dwindling into evening and my motel room just up the way.

―――――◆―――――

"We're an island, the hole in the donut," said John Chambers, a cheery eighty-four-year-old Rutgers professor, as we sat in sunlight the next morning in the backyard of the Cranbury Museum, tucked in a tidy clapboard house with two rocking chairs on the front porch.

Birds flitted everywhere in the trees overhead. Dogs barked in other backyards. With us in the sunlight sat other town dignitaries, who had also agreed to meet that morning, beaming with pride over their little burg. "We may be the best-preserved nineteenth-century town in all of America, for all I know," John said.

I'd walked down Main Street an hour before to get breakfast. Elderly gentlemen-turned-crossing-guards protected the schoolkids from the cars that hardly existed. Half the houses bore historical markers telling me who had built what or slept where, and when. It appeared most of the Founders had at least paused for lunch here. A few had spent the night. Yes, Washington had dozed here one night, a catnap really, on his way to the Battle of Monmouth Courthouse. Jefferson, Hamilton, Lafayette—they'd all tarried in Cranbury. Ben Franklin had walked through as a boy, heading south to become a printer in Philadelphia.

At the counter at Teddy's café, where I stopped for coffee and a blueberry muffin, a local named Tom told me how he'd once upped and walked one morning to his beach house on the Jersey shore, thirty-one miles away. What had he learned from that stroll? "Nothing, really, except every time I drive that way now, I have a different respect for those thirty-one miles."

The group in the museum's backyard laughed when I told them that story. Teddy's, they assured me, was an institution. I was on the Old Post Road now, John said, the route that ran from Boston all the way down through Washington, D.C. Cranbury was a changing station, the halfway point from New York to Philly where the riders would leave the mail at the tavern and turn back.

John and the others who wanted to tell me of Cranbury's glories explained how the village had been left alone and overlooked as the earthmovers and steamrollers had wreaked their havoc all around. In the direction I was heading, John said, "we're the last gasp of small town, bucolic America."

Cranbury wasn't what it was by sheer chance. No, the town had fought back against sprawl in the 1960s and then more recently cut a deal to industrialize the town's eastern flank in exchange for protecting all the farmland to the west. Hence the creation of the warehouse wilderness through which I planned to walk, and the beauty of the farms I'd passed the day before. The selling out of the one had saved the other.

The mere mention of my plans to forge up the brook sparked immediate crosstalk and concern from the group. One late arrival to our session was Peggy Brennan, a brassy eighty-one-year-old who had grown up in Cranbury and seen the farmhouses leveled as the turnpike plowed through. Peggy was the most insistent in expressing her view that my plan made no sense.

"That simply won't work," she said, squinting into the sun. "Too swampy. No room to walk under the freeway. It's all water up there." Then she said with the authority of a four-star general: "I have a better idea."

She pulled her phone from her pocket, stepped around the side of the house, and called her son, a local elementary school teacher named Tim. Her inquiries wafted back, muffled but urgent. "He's on it," Peggy said when she returned.

Tim Brennan arrived twenty minutes later wearing white bucks, pink socks, pink shorts, and a seersucker shirt with a blue tie. His tie had what looked like tiny white canoes all over it. Today was his school's picture day—all on Zoom—and he wanted to make an impression. But first, Tim had an even more pressing mission. He wanted to give me his kayak so I could paddle up Cranbury Brook and navigate beneath the turnpike. He was so caught up in my expedition that he hardly paused to explain his attire.

He began to note the obstacles and impediments in exacting detail. "Okay, you are going to go under the Highway 130 bridge and then make your way through a wide swampy area filled with lily pads and after a while you will come to several fallen trees you will have to squeeze under before you get to the first of two large logjams that you will have to haul the kayak over. If you can do that—and you may also have to cut through the forest a little— you should be good to go. Getting under the turnpike at that point will be a breeze."

I stared at him. I tried to digest the white bucks, the pink shorts, and everything he just said. I tried to understand how Tim with his canoe-dotted tie had emerged from nowhere filled with such conviction on how exactly I would get up Cranbury Brook. I tried to imagine myself hauling the kayak over multiple logjams without tumbling into the swamp or encasing the only shoes I had in mud. And then there was the most obvious issue.

"Tim, where will I leave the kayak? How will you get it back?"

"Oh, don't worry about that. I'll go back upriver later in my canoe and haul it back."

"Are you serious?"

"Couldn't be more serious."

He went around the corner, dragged the kayak from beneath

his house, and strapped it to the roof of his car. Off we went to the shores of Brainerd Lake, a few blocks down the road. It was a narrow lake in the center of town where lovers might paddle of an evening or Boy Scouts might fish with earthworm and hook. We went to the little floating dock and Tim plopped the kayak in the water and said, "Here you go. Ready and able."

I tucked my shoes and socks into its back hatch, and Peggy, Tim's mother, stepped up to haul my backpack to her car, promising to deliver it to me—my laptop, my few clothes, my notes—when I emerged on the other side. I was agog at all this charity. An eighty-one-year-old woman had just stuffed my backpack into her car. "Call me when you get to the other side," she said. Suddenly, the bunch of us—John, Peggy, Tim—were like a small commando unit orchestrating a vital mission.

Minutes later the entire delegation of Cranbury notables stood on that little pier waving goodbye to the strange man who had just walked into town with some silly notion in his head and was departing now by borrowed kayak. It was like they'd gotten my joke before I even said it. "Bon voyage," one of them yelled.

———◆———

I closed my eyes and laughed as I paddled. My fixation on crossing under the Jersey Turnpike via Cranbury Brook had found its willing agent in Peggy Brennan and her son, Tim. Desire has a funny way of getting others to join in.

Once I paddled under the Highway 130 overpass with the trucks roaring overhead, the town of Cranbury vanished and the lake became a wide estuary filled with huge lily pads and tubular vines with something resembling a river undulating through it. A huge blue heron eyed me from a fallen tree and lifted off gracefully as I drew near. Turtles plopped into the water. Geese and ducks, surprised, made a racket as they relocated upriver. On either side

I could see through the trees the huge warehouses and the trucks shoulder to shoulder alongside them, taking on cargo.

I was paddling up the Amazon through Amazonia, toward the heart of darkness, the Jersey Turnpike itself. I came to a few obstructions—submerged trees, a tangle of vines and limbs—just shallow enough to push my way across with the paddle. The whole of the place had a presence like a body exhaling.

Around a bend, ten minutes up, with the hum of traffic from 130 behind me and the fresher din of I-95 up ahead, I came to a tangle of fallen trees, just as Tim said, and laid my belly flat on the kayak to squirm under. Then I came to a large fallen oak that lay athwart the river five feet high. I brought the boat to a high bank, tossed my paddle ashore, and shimmied out. I dragged the kayak through the woods barefoot and around the jam.

As I paddled up, I wondered how much this little stream had really changed since the indigenous Lenape, the "original people," had lived and fished and hunted along its shores for thousands of years before Europeans ever dreamt of the Americas. In the basement of the Cranbury Museum, a glass case held elaborate spear and arrow and ax heads found along these riverbanks. The water quality had worsened surely, but little else had likely changed for centuries. The forest ferns and the wild cabbage were sprouting, and the brambles were sending up their shoots, all as they had in late April for eons. I was paddling through one form of permanence, a swampy river etched through maples and oaks, surrounded by all the human hubbub of need-it-now deliveries and commerce, barely visible and audible through the trees. I could imagine all that crumbling, nibbled by the rain and consumed by vines, while the brook kept wending through the woods just like this. A home to heron, ducks, geese, turtles.

When I finally caught sight of the turnpike and its steady blur of trucks heading south, I also saw the last big logjam, just as Tim described: a tangle of trees and natural debris higher than the one before, piled there by past storms. Again, I crawled up the bank, hauled the kayak behind me, and tiptoed through the forest, making sure to steer around the spring brambles. The bank on the other side was four feet high, so I had to lower the boat nose first into the water and hold her steady with the paddle as I slid off into the opening. One false move and I would have plunged chest-high into a slurry of mud, twigs, and turnpike runoff.

I now had a clean shot to the deep waters that flowed un-impeded beneath the Great Anaconda. The walker turned rower had long anticipated his arrival at this great swooshing corridor of commerce and dazed travel. "Apart from the pulling and haul-ing stands what I am," Walt Whitman, the bard of New Jersey, sang of himself. The great freight pullers and haulers shot by as I bobbed for a minute to take them in: Roadtex, Swift, Bulk Car-riers, AmeriFreight, Penske, Walmart, carrying what we needed and didn't need from north to south.

I had reached that line and when I paddled into its concrete maw, I saw a young deer illuminated in sunlight on the far side of the tunnel. She waded with grace across the stream and as-cended the opposite bank, her silhouette a thing of beauty.

The freeway ran twelve lanes wide and turned the watery tun-nel into a chamber of howls and groans. I hollered and heard my echo holler back. A flock of terrified pigeons took flight. After every three lanes there was a break in the overpass through which golden sunlight spilled.

I paddled out the other side into a blander, tamer, more hu-manized world. A chain-link fence ran along the freeway, and an energy company had buried a huge oil pipeline with signs every twenty yards warning you not to dig there. A vast billboard adver-tised detergent: TRUSTED BY GENERATIONS. FEARED BY STAINS. I could see more warehouses through the woods, and beyond those, the tract-house subdivisions spilled across what had once been farmland and before that, when Franklin and others came this way by foot, towering forests and grasslands.

The deer that had waded the river still stood on the opposite bank. She looked over her shoulder at me without alarm, but more with what I took to be pity, then loped off into the woods. I did a little dance of triumph with the paddle held high, having crossed under the beast into a new land. I tucked the kayak high on the bank among some reeds where Tim would easily find it, and set off on foot, a mere thirty-eight miles now from the city of New York. Peggy arrived outside a Subway sandwich shop a mile up the road to return my rucksack. She was proud to have assisted, one of many along the way to have opened a magic door.

———◆———

When I crossed the Delaware three days before, I had entered what I later came to call Presbyteriana, a genteel and horsey patch settled by Presbyterians and Quakers with a shiny ivory tower at its heart. From there, as I passed under the Jersey Turnpike, I entered an entirely different nation. A nation of brass-tacks working folk in humble small houses on lots strung along roadways and within planned developments. You saw military insignia on the windows of their trucks or fluttering on banners in their gardens. More Trump flags flew than I'd seen anywhere so far. The trucks and vans along the road suggested most were tradespeople and various forms of construction workers, folks holding on to the third or fourth rung of the ten-rung ladder. I saw people of color, Southeast Asians and Blacks and others, but the stores and such suggested it was an area mostly of Mediterranean and East European stock, people who were still conscious of those origins.

People like Ken Kovacs, whom I met just outside of East Brunswick. I was treading past his house, which was all festooned with little American flags. There was a big blue Trump sign in the yard, and a red pickup with a picture of Trump giving a thumbs-up, and I thought: "Huh, too bad. It's been a while since I've had a decent chat with a member of this tribe." And at that exact moment, as if on cue, out walked this guy wearing a red MAGA hat and camo pants and a U.S. Army sweatshirt.

"Where you headed?" he said when he saw me. I told him and his eyes lit up, so eager was he to engage with a person who had walked all the way from the U.S. Capitol.

"Oh, really," he said, and then he waved his arm toward his Trump display like a carnival barker asking you to step right up and see the bearded lady. "Does this provoke any thoughts?" That was his way of stirring some discussion. He was a wiry, fidgety, rapid-fire type. His accent was 100 percent Jersey workingman, like an extra plucked from *On the Waterfront*.

"Provokes a few thoughts," I said. "Quite a few thoughts."

But before I got to expressing any, Ken switched gears. "Can I get you anything for your walk? Water? Banana? Granola bar? Clementine? Bottle of beer?" It was another moment of privilege that might not have been extended to just anyone. No other stranger on the whole walk had made so profuse an offering.

I told him, sure, I'd love a beer if he wanted to sit for a few minutes in his driveway and talk. It was late in the day, I was beat, and still had at least an hour's walk to my motel. He went inside and came out with a cold bottle of Rolling Rock, two clementines, one banana, one granola bar, and two bottles of water, all tucked in a plastic bag.

I sat in a lawn chair and popped open the beer. That's when he introduced himself. "I'm a Czechoslovakian Hungarian," he said. A union drywaller, fifty-eight, divorced, two kids over twenty-one, just finished paying his ex-wife alimony. He said the divorce wasn't too friendly. He and his wife had both had their feisty moments.

Ken was a classic jumble of irritations and resentments and humorous asides about coworkers, friends, his ex-wife. You didn't
have to poke much to get him started. His antenna was finely
tuned to the unfair perks others might be getting. Cops, teachers,
county workers, city employees. To hear Ken tell it, the fix was in
pretty much everywhere.

He told me of his voting odyssey. He had liked McCain over
Bush in 2000 because he thought McCain was tougher, but then
voted for Gore because he found Bush—the son of a president—
the essence of nepotism. And he didn't like nepotism. "Nepotism
at the police precinct. Nepotism at the union halls. It's everywhere."
He voted for Obama in 2008. "Since the white guy screwed up so
bad, I figured it was time to give the Black guy a chance."

He talked of Blacks and Hispanics using those terms, but others of various European extractions weren't so lucky. His ex-wife,
he said, was half Irish and half Italian—or "half Mick and half
Guinea," as he put it. "The ultimate witch's brew."

He had worked on Trump projects in New York and had no
illusions. "I mean, the guy is a total rip-off." But so it goes with all
the billionaires, seeking their little loopholes. "It's what they do."
He said he had nothing against foreigners, "but the folks coming
over the border now, they're hands type of people, construction.
That's going to seep into every field of construction." He complained that until the year before, he'd been paying $700 a month
in alimony and child support.

The personal, the national, the global—it all blended into one.
Whatever the force, Ken felt impinged, put upon. "You know what
I mean?" Ken would say that after every second or third sentence.
"You know what I mean?" He liked Trump because Trump put his
foot down and in turn irritated the people who irritated Ken. He
got in their craw. Ken liked that. "You know what I mean?"

"And besides, the whole world is going to go to hell anyway

one of these days," Ken said. "It's going to explode from within or be hit by some huge meteorite and boom, that will be it."

The first of the clementines Ken gave me burst sweet in my mouth as I walked on, tossing its peel in the ditch. The signs touting fast food, motels, and convenience stores grew thicker and more abundant, the road wider, the traffic more noxious. After I checked in through a sheen of protective plexiglass, my motel room had a view of parked cars and the dank smell of moist air-conditioning. The couple one booth over at the Red Lobster watched sitcoms on an iPad while gorging on seafood. I examined the bed for bugs and then crawled inside.

A span that began with a chemist over biscuits warning of the collapse of all matter had found its bookend in a Trump drywaller predicting mass extinction by meteorite. In between I had stood where the Mercer Oak hadn't. Where Washington had or hadn't led his most gallant charge. Where Martians hadn't landed. I had slept in a town that had cut a deal with the present to protect its past. Then I paddled up a creek that spoke of permanence amid all our desire for everything, immediately. I had made of those hours a much larger vessel that contained multitudes and then collapsed in on itself, as all days do. You know what I mean?

CHAPTER 21

CRESTING THE GREAT MOUND

I woke in my clammy room at Best Western and could see through the window the flickering lights of an IHOP. My legs ached and something about that dinner the night before still rumbled in the gut. I could hear the groan of air brakes outside and the high whirr of the ice machine down the hall. The shirt I washed with shampoo and hung in the shower was still moist when I slipped it on. I missed my wife, my dog, my own bed, but there was still much to see, with just a few days left.

The walker wakes to an aim, however humble. Even if the landscape might be drab and cluttered, the day's destination stirs excitement. Destinations do that. On their own, they bestow purpose. One day's little destiny. With a little luck, from a promontory that morning, I might see for the first time the faint outline of the place I'd been heading toward over all these weeks.

This walk was built of many walks, journeys within journeys, and this morning's ramble would take me to a high place built of waste, a place that had stirred excitement since even before I stepped from my house. I set out as the sun nudged up behind the McDonald's, behind the Taco Bell, behind the used-car dealer where the mylar balloons shimmied in the wind. I went through Tanners Corner—no Tanners left and no corner, really—and somewhere between the Open Road Mazda showroom and the

Lukoil service station I first saw her wide flank. I saw the curve of her, glistening green.

The mighty Edgeboro Landfill rose to my right, and I was still more than a mile away. My excitement grew.

Turning up Edgeboro Road, I peeled the second clementine that Ken tossed me in his driveway before he sang Trump's praises. I ate it in sections as I watched the huge garbage trucks stream by, and I silently thanked Ken for the gesture, because it was an incredible clementine.

From the minute I had seen that landfill two months before, shooting past it by car south on the Jersey Turnpike and still mulling my walk path, it had lodged in my brain as a must-see attraction. The mound is impossible to miss. It looms over the landscape like a weather-worn pyramid, encircled by birds and crisscrossed by huge trucks, by far the highest elevation in the region. Few can top it among all the newly minted mountains along the whole of I-95. I knew right then I had to reach her summit.

When I emailed the Middlesex County Utilities Authority, explaining my desire to walk to the top of their landfill, I gave my request a charitable fifty/fifty chance of success. I thought they might be suspicious, or unused to visitors. I got a note back from Robert Leslie, Landfill Engineer. "Sure," he said, "what day do you think you will be in the area?"

My heart sang.

When I strode up the exterior stairs to Bob's office at 9:00 A.M. sharp, he'd been waiting for my arrival and stuck his head out the door and said, "Well, good morning and welcome. Give me a minute and I'll be right out." He was a cheery fellow. I handed him my backpack and he gave me in return a bright orange safety vest. Joining us for the hike was Brian Murray, the chatty site manager, also bubbly this morning. I wondered if proximity to trash was a mood enhancer.

From afar, the landfill looked like an anomalous bulge in the earth, buff-colored, topped with soil, and rimmed with a hesitant fringe of grass. A vast plateau on top gave way to sloping sides. Closer in, as the trucks streamed by with the raw material for building the mound, you caught your first rank whiffs of it. The overall impression was one of orderliness, of a civilization doing what it does to add a new feature to the landscape.

"Let's take Route One," Brian said, and off we went up a wide circular dirt road that curved to the top like a pathway in an Escher drawing. Encircling the entire mound stood a high mesh fence, held in place by utility poles, placed there to keep coyotes and varmints and trash pickers out and any blowing trash in.

Other American civilizations—one thinks, for instance, of the Mound Builders of the Ohio and Mississippi river valleys—once created large hills of all sizes to commemorate great events or sacred places or lost heroes. Many of the mounds they built are small and take the shape of bears or serpents or birds. Others are huge and still punctuate the landscape from West Virginia all the way to the outskirts of St. Louis and up into Minnesota. You will find them, too, all the way down in Louisiana.

I took a walk in the winter of 2020 among ancient mounds along the Mississippi River in far northern Iowa. Archaeologists going back to the 1880s have studied those mounds and dug into them and found that they contain nothing in the way of human remains or pottery or trinkets, as do the pyramids of Central America or Egypt—and even other mounds farther south along the Mississippi. For all we know, the Mound Builders of middle America were a people not prone to acts of vanity or grandeur. I could feel their humility as I walked through the snow that January afternoon, how they had left mounds of earth and their own bones but nothing else. They built these mountains to honor animals or to mark certain seasons or to serve as lunar or solar calendars, as with the petroglyphs I saw on the Susquehanna where the carved serpent pointed to the rising of the first spring sun.

As we trudged up around the first bend and gained sight of the Raritan River, I mentioned the Mound Builders to Brian, who jumped right in. Much to my amazement, he was well steeped in the topic. He had studied at Ohio State and visited the mounds nearby. He had gone many times to the Great Serpent Mound, one of the world's grandest effigy mounds, which snakes four football fields long beside an ancient crater in the south of the state. That mound was created by a lost people two thousand years ago or so, a people who, whatever they called themselves and wherever their remnants may be now, built that huge snake with its gaping mouth and triple-coiled tail of enduring rock and clay. The serpent's lack of bones or any human vestiges inside—its lack of old tires or discarded Lunchables—makes the mound even more difficult to date. "Catch us if you can," say the spirits of the builders of the Great Serpent Mound.

"The mound people left nothing behind but their mounds," said Brian over the groan of a lumbering truck. "Those mounds had sacred and religious purposes or told them things about the path of the sun at certain seasons. They are beautiful things to see."

The dust from the truck settled around us. "Us, on the other hand, we're brutal," Brian said. "We leave everything behind. Our mounds just hold trash."

Every day, every resident of Middlesex County, all 825,000 of them, contributes about 4.5 pounds of garbage to the Edgeboro Landfill. That adds up to around two thousand tons a day. Think of that as 2.3 million rolls of paper towel. Or 16 million Quarter Pounders. Or 128 million crushed cans of Coke.

If you've ever been to the Grand Canyon and hiked all the way down to the Colorado River, you will know that you are traveling back in time as you go. It takes only a few minutes to outwalk the sediment of all recorded human history. By the time you reach the bottom you have descended through nearly 1.8 billion years of geologic time, a third or so of the age of Earth. Near the bottom you will pass, but may not notice, the wavering line that represents the Great Unconformity, a gap of missing geological time—rock washed away by forces we don't yet quite understand—that may have spanned a billion years. The river, when you get there, is of course the surging present, carrying with it the day's sediment through canyons of ancient stone. The river is bracing when you dive into its emerald green.

As we walked up the great mound, we were going up in time, from the past up through layers of our recent history. From the early Kennedy administration to yesterday's plastic milk jug.

It was a breezy morning, bright, sunny. The sweetness of that clementine still lingered in my mouth. The redolence of the dump, its perfume of rotting vegetables and meat, came and went in little gusts. "Where do you figure we are right about here, time wise?" I asked Brian when we were barely a third of the way up the mountain and with a couple hundred feet of altitude still to go. Time is thinner at the base because it is spread out across a larger area, but gets thicker as the mountain goes up and narrows.

"Around 2006, I'd say, give or take," he said. That was the second half of the second Bush administration, back when Saddam Hussein was executed, and Enron's Ken Lay went to prison. I joked they should insert little signposts along the way to give walkers some sense of historical perspective as they walk up through the past. *Vietnam War ends. First Apple computer. World Trade Center towers fall.*

The landfill takes everything but hazardous waste, and it takes that, too, if it comes from households—detergents, old gas cans, oil from the car—having no way to sort what any of us toss into our trash cans. It all just seeps in together. Each layer of the dump is then sealed in durable membranes, Brian explained, so as to keep the bad stuff out of the water table. Among the stew are huge amounts of food waste—about a third of all it receives day to day—including entire shipments of spoiled stuff from the county's distribution warehouses. And lots of animal waste.

"If you can imagine it, we've had it," Brian said. "The parks people had to cull five hundred geese from a local park. We got the geese. Trucks wreck on the freeway filled with chickens or cows. We get the chickens and cows."

The Edgeboro Landfill is aptly named because for centuries, this area was a marshy no-man's-land, an edge world on either side of a big oxbow in the Raritan River. I'd been wondering for months why the old travel routes between Philly and New York always took travelers to the Amboys, and then across from Perth Amboy to Staten Island, and then up from there to Jersey City, and then across to Manhattan—my exact route this week. When Ben Franklin came down as a kid in the 1720s, he took exactly that route in reverse. To the modern eye, it made no sense.

Standing on the landfill provided the answer. From here all the way up to the Meadowlands was a patchwork of marshes and low-lands, tough sledding for horses and carriages but much easier to-day with our concrete viaducts to soar above the cattail swamps. The area around the landfill—blessed with deep deposits of sand left by mountains turned to sea—was particularly good for in-dustries like brick making and sand dredging, and thus prime for dumping. First you dig, then you dump. Where the landfill now stood was, in the early 1950s, a huge hole where they dug the sand to build the New Jersey Turnpike. For whole stretches they had to lay down a bed of sand a hundred feet deep to counteract the marshes. Tons more went into making concrete. The modern yin of the sand pit meets the modern yang of the dump.

"It was amazing, high-quality sand, I'm told," Brian said. "Noth-ing but the best for the turnpike."

When we came around the north side, we could see a few fish-ing boats angling for striped bass on the Raritan. We could see an osprey hunting and turkey vultures circling overhead. Then Brian pointed well past those boats and vultures and said, "There you go. Squint and you'll see it. Your destination."

Far in the hazy distance, I caught my first glint of the high towers of Manhattan, tiny jagged spikes of fool's gold lit by the morning sun. It was just a glimmer running across the far horizon, barely visible through the morning murk, but enough to make the wanderer shiver with excitement. I thought of Hernán Cortés in Mexico when he first spied the island city of Tenochtitlán.

Across the river you could see other, lesser mountains, green now with grass and shrubs: the capped and dormant landfills of a previous era. Brian fell into a broadcaster baritone and said with a sweep of his arm like Edward R. Murrow, "Just as Egypt has its valley of the great pyramids, we here have our great valley of the landfills."

Brian and Bob derived great excitement from showing a newcomer what they do day to day. They mourned our excesses, our wastefulness—we are, literally, full of waste—just as they exulted over the grandeur of what they were creating.

The top of the landfill sprawls across the equivalent of a hundred football fields, a vast acreage set to be filled section by section, day by day, as the modern Mound Builders progress ever upward.

We walked across to that day's debris, coming in strong in a motley stream of trucks. "This is the money shot," Brian said. "All of this has come in since just this morning."

The landfill had opened two hours earlier, about the time I left my motel room, and the pile in question already covered an area the size of a large town square and stood five feet high. We got as close as we could to the heart of the action, with the trash tumbling down from above toward our feet. If the mound was a monument to time and its excesses, we were standing now at the redolent present where all matter merged, the site of the great coalescence.

After each truck backed up and dumped its contents, another took its place and did the same, and behind that, another, and then another in a long line that faded as it trailed down the mound. A tractor then pushed the loads up the hill and a huge, ninety-thousand-pound 826 Caterpillar landfill compactor with enormous, spiked metal wheels drove back and forth across the fresh deposits to pack them down.

This was the dump's creative work being done, like watching the Egyptian workers slide another stone in place at the pyramids at Giza.

I stood there and wanted to see distinct, recognizable things and I did, here and there. A brown prescription jar, crushed. A blue latex glove. One of those ubiquitous surgeon's masks, twisted and half indented into the ground. A Snyder's pretzel bag. A KitKat wrapper. A Starbucks cup with *Sally* written in Sharpie cursive. I thought of Sally sipping her latte.

But already the whole of it was becoming an indistinct mass of plasticky substance, the raw material of our daily lives preparing to vanish under still more layers, and layers after that until it returns, many millennia from now, into the molecular soup from which we all arose. What will our contributions amount to in the future fossil record? "Hmm," some distant alien archaeologist will grumble, picking through it all with a trowel, "it appears some form of semi-intelligent ephemera left a deposit here."

We stopped there for a minute taking it in amid the din of the trucks and tractors, the ubiquitous vulture circling on high.

"Kinda makes you think, doesn't it," Brian said. Kinda does, I thought.

Running a huge landfill in one of the most densely populated parts of the country is an elaborate process. Every night they cover that day's deposits with a mesh fabric and a foot or so of dirt to keep the stuff from going air bound and ending up in people's yards. A black pipe, four inches round, coils to the top along the roadway, delivering a sort of industrial-grade Febreze that the dump tenders can dispense by hose to combat odors, when needed. By ordinance, the dump is not meant to stink, but of course it does, especially in the height of the summer and still more after the arrival of a fresh load of overturned chickens. Sometimes a lightning strike or a smoldering ember causes a part of the dump to combust, so the landfill has its own fire department.

Brian had a piece of tape across his vest where he had written in black Sharpie, "Every Little Bit Helps," beneath which he distilled it further into "E.L.B.H." A worthy motto. Every little bit is pretty much the whole of it, wherever you turn. Every time we don't waste that plate or that water bottle or buy that stupid plastic milk jug, he said, makes a difference. The landfill took in a record of 722,080 tons of trash in 2006, the layer Brian had noted on the way up. The year I saw accumulating around my feet would weigh in, all told, at 565,893 tons.

"It's progress," Brian said, "but it remains a monumental task."

◆

From the dump I had to circle back around its wide girth just to return, on the other side, to the reedy banks of the Raritan River. I was wending my way now toward South Amboy, at the river's mouth. But first I wanted to stop by a very different sort of dump, this one along the South River, a tidal tributary to the Raritan, and just a couple of miles from the Edgeboro Landfill.

A local activist and Rutgers professor, Heather Fenyk, wanted to show me this other dump as another of the wounds all the rivers in this area bore from their interactions with humans over centuries. Heather led me through the trees and along an old rail spur that had largely toppled into a gully.

I had tracked Heather down on my phone while walking a day or two earlier and had sent a note asking if we might meet to talk about the river, to which she responded, "YES!" She agreed to meet at the landfill and show me around afterward. She had spent years studying the endless strains suffered by the Raritan watershed. There were so many things we could see, she explained. The ruins of an old power plant, now home to bald eagle nests. Any number of Superfund sites, of which the lower Raritan could rival any part of the country. "Or would you like to see brick beach?" she asked, and I said yes to that.

As we walked, ducking below low-hanging limbs, Heather explained that the quality of the area's clay had inspired the American Enameled Brick and Tile Company in the 1890s to erect a huge brick-making plant along the banks of the South River, which feeds into the Raritan. Kilns, cooling towers, a smokestack five stories high. From the river it shipped thousands of tons of shiny bricks to New York and other cities to build the brownstones and the shimmery skyscrapers and the walls of many New York subway stations. The plant burned down in 1934. Hardly a whisper of it remains.

"Here we are," said Heather, wedging past a tree as we came out onto a long muddy bank of the river. The shoreline was entirely covered with yellowish bricks, all spilled or dropped overboard during loading into barges from a pier that vanished long ago. A soggy yellow-brick road. The bricks squeaked and sighed in the mud as we walked across them.

"At low tide, you can see that the whole of the river bottom is bricked, too," Heather said as I skipped a flat rock across the muddy water. "It has a weird sort of beauty." I had seen so many weird sorts of beauty on the walk and now added another to the roster.

Heather wants people to care about place—about the field beside their house or the river over the hill. To know and understand the many pasts of that one place, its special spirit, and to care about its health and vitality. If people care about a place, they might also care for it, is Heather's philosophy. She is working to map, and even uncover and restore, some of the hundreds of creeks and brooks that once fed the Raritan but have since been paved over or channeled through culverts. The vanished rivers, she calls them.

Place, I said to Heather when we parted, was probably the simplest binding element of this whole walk. The particularity of being in one place. Stopping to look at a place, marvel at it, and care about it, even in passing. All the mysterious, rich, overlooked places.

Heather's devotion to place struck a chord in me, which may explain why I rattled on at such length telling a likeminded stranger what the walk had taught me. How I'd now been out for more than three weeks walking and examining and looking closely. How I had put no foreign sounds in my ears. I had listened to no music along the way, no podcasts or audiobooks. "That wasn't by design or prior edict," I said. "I just didn't want the interference."

My mind and spirit were fully satisfied and entertained by their natural ruminations, the simple act of walking and taking in what I saw and puzzling over what I encountered as I went. The rhythm and simplicity of it, the waking to a purpose every morning, creates a calm in the walker. Over time, a cycle builds, so as you go from place to place to honor them, those places pay you back in kind. Even the landfill, despite the sordid story it tells of us, had a magic to it. "From atop all that trash I saw the beauty of the city faraway," I said. We promised to keep in touch.

———◆———

I walked on through humble, low-rise neighborhoods spotted with corner delis and pizza shops and then along roads that became freeways where the walker felt less than welcome. Twisting viaducts and overpasses left me wondering how I'd get through as I picked my way toward the Victory Bridge, which would take me north over the Raritan River. From high atop that arch, holding my hat, I could see the wind-chopped mouth of Raritan Bay and the sandy start of Staten Island. I could see the wide waters that lured Verrazzano and Hudson and so many others to go farther and sail into New York's Upper Bay, one of the finest arrangements of land and water anywhere on Earth.

Giovanni da Verrazzano nudged into that glorious harbor in the late spring of 1524 on behalf of the French king. Sailing south along the coast, he had met contingents of the Narragansett, the Wampanoag, and many other tribes. He found the whole of the coastline "densely populated." Of the Narragansett, he later wrote, "They are taller than we are . . . and their manner is sweet and gentle, very like the manner of the ancients." Like every explorer for a century, he would have preferred being elsewhere, on the short route to China. The landmass he found was an impediment. He sailed from modern North Carolina all the way to Newfoundland and gave names to all he saw. The whole of the continent he named Francesca. None of his names stuck.

When I got to the other side, to Perth Amboy proper, I found a bench at the foot of the bridge looking across Smith Street to where a gaggle of young men were making cars shine at the Super Car Wash & Quick Lube. The Lenape had called this place Ompoge, for "point." Europeans later morphed that into Emboyle, then Amboyle and Ambo and finally Amboy. Still later it got its first name in honor of a duke from a place called Perth. I needed a moment to digest where I was.

That morning, Heather had mentioned the existence of ruins in Perth Amboy where a place called Eagleswood once stood three stories high with balconies and filigreed iron work around its entrance. She said it had once been home to a utopian society called the Raritan Bay Union, and Thoreau had traveled to the house in 1856 to give various lectures, including a reading of what became his famous essay "Walking." While there, I learned later, Thoreau went to meet Walt Whitman, and the two scruffy writers, both in their thirties then, did not get on well. "Each seemed planted fast in reserve," wrote one witness of their encounter, "surveying the other curiously, like two beasts, each wondering what the other would do, whether to snap or run." Whitman later described Thoreau as suffering from a "very aggravated case of superciliousness." In time, both saw the other's genius.

Just as intriguing, Thoreau had traveled to Eagleswood not just to lecture but to engage in his other profession, as land surveyor. He had come to walk and measure the land, to trace its contours along the river on behalf of its owners. I wanted to find the land that Thoreau had so closely measured and observed.

I sat on the bench and swiped through pages on my phone trying to determine where this Eagleswood once stood. Could the ruins of it still exist? I found a mention that the estate had once occupied a lot at the corner of Smith Street and Convery Boulevard. When I looked at a map and pinpointed the place and zeroed in, I realized with a jolt that the location was barely fifty feet away, behind a chain-link fence laced with vines and overgrown trees, right across the street from where I sat. I threw my backpack over my shoulder and crossed Convery. Down a block of scrappy, run-down houses, I found a narrow opening in the high fence and wedged through. A dog behind the house next door lunged at me from the end of his chain. I jumped from a wall onto weedy ground and was there, alone amid the ruins on a hot spring afternoon. I did a little dance of triumph.

———◆———

We know Thoreau as a cabin dweller and a haunter of Walden Pond. As an effusive observer of nature and the human spirit. As a writer and an apostle for simplicity. But he worked as a surveyor, too, alongside teaching and making pencils. He did his surveying so obsessively at times that Emerson worried he was wasting his talents. He scoured the banks of the Concord River to measure its bends. By canoe he dropped weights to assess the river's depth.

Everywhere he went he was an obsessive seer. He became fascinated by cougars on his trip down to Eagleswood and made a beeline to P. T. Barnum's Museum in Manhattan to see "the stuffed skin of a cougar that was found floating dead in the Hudson many years ago." He went to the Astor Library to read about cougars. The next day, October 25, he took a long walk around the Eagleswood property and noted that the flowers were "almost entirely done," though he did spot "the seaside goldenrod, lingering still by the Raritan River." At dusk, he noted in his journal that he "saw and heard a katydid." Who else keeps track of hearing a cricket? It reminded me of Jefferson noting the spring's first whippoor-will.

On his survey of the property, Thoreau made meticulous observations in a delicate ink: of the vineyard and peach and pear orchards at the base of Fox Hill, and the exact meanderings of the little brooks that flowed into the river.

Thoreau by then had refined and perfected his lecture on "Walking," building it with scraps from journals and letters to friends. More than an ode to walking it was a call to break away, to not confine oneself to society solely. It was, yes, a testament to nonconformity and the renewing of the mind. "I wish to speak a word for Nature, for absolute freedom and wildness," he began that night before the audience at Eagleswood, the first steps of a talk that must have taken two hours to deliver. "When I would recreate myself, I seek the darkest wood, the thickest and most interminable . . . dismal swamp."

The lecture went over well. "Never had such a walk as this been taken by any one before," wrote one listener later in his journal. "And the conversation so flowing and lively and curious." Thoreau, too, was delighted. It was "a rare success," he wrote of his lecture that night. "I was aware that what I was saying was silently taken in by their ears."

The ruins of Eagleswood were now the remnants of that structure and everything else that had risen and fallen on that same property since then, a palimpsest jumble of concrete and brick scrawled over with swoops of graffiti and shaded by weedy trees and vines. There were twisted rail lines and loading ramps to nowhere, fallen towers and broken stairways. If the spirit of Henry Thoreau still wandered there, it was in the roots of the trees that were slowly wedging apart the concrete and brick, as were the trees in the Philadelphia prison and amid so many of the ruins I'd passed, taking back the earth.

Given sunshine, water, and air, those roots over time would turn it all back into Thoreau's preferred swamp.

I sat on a concrete ledge of the ruin to bask in the sun and to listen to the birds and the hum of the traffic spilling over the Victory Bridge. Such a gift, all of this, the riches of a single day.

As I turned to squeeze back through the fence, my phone rang. It was Samantha Dorm, who I'd last seen in York more than two weeks earlier, when she toured me around the Black cemetery there and spoke to me of forgotten people.

"Where are you?" she asked, a hint of alarm in her voice.

"In Perth Amboy," I said. "Standing on the street."

"You might want to get to your hotel room or somewhere quiet," she said. "The Derek Chauvin verdict is coming out in an hour."

Chauvin was the Minneapolis cop who, nearly a year earlier, had strangled the life from a man named George Floyd by kneeling on his throat for close to nine minutes as Floyd gasped and said, "I can't breathe."

Floyd's killing had sparked months of protests and riots in cities across the country. Chauvin's murder trial, now ending, could well enflame still worse anger if the jury cleared him of all charges. I was touched that Samantha even thought of me.

In my motel room on the edge of town, I sat before a TV for the first time in almost a month. Samantha texted me the minute the verdict came down: "Guilty on all counts."

The country had come to yet another fork and had taken, in this case, the calmer route. I heard gasps and whoops down the motel hallway, and the toot of horns outside. More important was the silent, collective exhale.

CHAPTER 22

PUSHING AT THE MATRIX

Because the last of the North American glacial onslaughts pushed all the way to the island now known as Manhattan tens of thousands of years ago, and because the sheer heft and might of that Laurentide Ice Sheet sluggishly gouged and carved the Hudson River valley, and because that mass of frozen water left behind vast piles of rock and mounds of sand in its melting path and sent the Hudson River flowing, long ago, down an ancestral final trough to the west of Staten Island—for those and other reasons I faced a puzzle when I got to the shores of Perth Amboy.

I had to cross the choppy, current-bedeviled Arthur Kill to get from New Jersey to Staten Island. I needed to find a ferryman.

Named by the Dutch for its role as a back channel, or an *achter kill,* the river runs for ten miles carrying water between Newark Bay south to Raritan Bay and was, where I eyed it, maybe a thousand yards across. The Arthur Kill is an orphan river now, abandoned when its mother, the Hudson River, found another way to get to the ocean via New York Harbor and the Narrows, once blocked by the debris heaped there as the Laurentide Ice Sheet pulled back to the north.

As far back as the middle of the 1700s there was at least some form of crude ferry that went across from Perth Amboy to an area known now as Tottenville. Ben Franklin as a teen got drenched when the boat he was in nearly swamped coming south to Amboy on the way to seek his fortunes in Philadelphia. "[We] met with a squall that tore our rotten sails to pieces, preventing our getting into the Kill," he wrote in his *Autobiography*. Franklin and Adams had crossed here in September 1776 to confer with the British over an early peace settlement that wasn't to be. I knew from his notebooks that Jefferson came this way, too, back in May and June 1791 on that quirky ramble with Madison to Lake Champlain. A little wooden ferry terminal still stood along the shore, now a museum. There hadn't been a ferry for years. Yes, there was a bridge farther upriver that one could walk across, but why do that? I was determined to cross by boat.

An old *Wall Street Journal* buddy and fellow Coloradan, Mike Allen, had come down from the Hudson River valley with an elegant sea kayak strapped to the roof of his car. We'd schemed for weeks over this crossing but still hadn't figured out where to procure another vessel. I recommended the evening before that we go poke around down by the Raritan Yacht Club and figure it out from there. I had high confidence that a little pushing on the matrix would deliver us the necessary luck.

The minute we got there I stopped in wonder at the sight of an enormous, sixty-foot-high dead tree, trimmed of its outer branches, that rose in the yard of a house looking over Raritan Bay. A woman was puttering with a trowel in her garden nearby. "That tree must be ancient," I said to her, walking up her little drive, confident already that this magnificent fossil of a tree would serve as the keyhole for securing our passage across the Arthur Kill.

It was an English elm, she said, that went back to the time of the Revolutionary War, meaning that in its youth it had looked across the waterway and watched momentous events unfold in the summer and fall of 1776 when Washington and his troops were routed in both Staten Island and Long Island. If it were old enough, the tree would also have seen the slave ships pulling up by the hundreds after the first one arrived at Perth Amboy's quays in the late 1600s. The town was once a major trafficker in human misery, with ships hauling their human cargo across the Atlantic to where squalid barracks once lined Smith Street. New Jersey was founded on slavery, had the institution built into its land laws, and was the last of the Northern colonies to give it up.

"It's a true witness tree," the woman said. A bolt of lightning killed it a few years earlier, but it still stood at least twenty-five feet around at the base and strong enough to withstand any storm.

The woman's husband came out on the porch to tell us that Aaron Burr had fled down the Arthur Kill from Manhattan in 1804 to the property next door eleven days after he shot Alexander Hamilton. He came looking for a horse. Burr then scurried off to Cranbury where he secured such a horse to take him on to Philadelphia. When I told the couple my story and the predicament we faced, they said they couldn't think of anyone with a boat or an extra kayak to lend us. "But I do know the combination to get past the gate at the Raritan Yacht Club," the man said. He gave me the combination and I thanked him. Bingo.

Mike and I walked up the street and down the exterior wooden stairs that led to the yacht club's porch and from there to a wide pier. At a locked door I punched in those digits and continued to where all the boats still stood in dry dock except for a couple of small craft bobbing beside the pier. I introduced myself to a knot of boaters talking shop beneath the hull of a tall sloop. I explained that a friend had given me the lock combination and had suggested that they might be of service. They peered at the pack on my back and the hole in my shoe and nodded as I said how I needed to get across the Kill in the morning. They brightened slowly at the absurdity of the whole thing, the walk, the need to find a way across, my plan to traverse the length of Staten Island in the morning.

"If someone could just take me straight across, I could jump in when it gets shallow and storm the beach on my own," I said.

They all squinted at each other and then one of them said, "Maybe Stu?" He pulled a phone from his breast pocket and disappeared behind the boat. He came back a minute later and handed me his phone.

"Talk to Stu Conway," he said. "That's his boat right over there."

A few sentences into my spiel, Stu cut me off. "Sounds interesting," he said. Sure, why not, he'd come down the next morning and take me across in his launch. "Just so long as the weather is good. You probably know there's a storm coming in." Would nine in the morning do? I said that would be perfect.

I did a little fist pump and handed back the phone.

Of all the moments of privilege along the way, moments when I acted as if I belonged in places I'd never been before, this one pushed the limits. I had strolled onto that pier with the help of a secondhand code as though protected by some prior right, which I suppose I was. You have every right to wince at my surge of satisfaction.

But there were other forces at play, too. When you wander town to town, you become adept at nudging open little doors and pushing at the matrix. You learn that skill as a reporter, as I had working in many countries. But you learn it also in many other jobs. I had perfected it on this walk, as I gave mind and spirit the freedom to roam, because belonging—as a skill you nurture—is incubated best in solitude. The reality you encounter as you move from place to place is not a given upon arrival. It is not a fixed thing. It contains elastic qualities that you do a lot to shape as you go. You form a space as you enter it, just as you do a conversation. Excitement, enthusiasm, openness, trust—they can radiate outward and stir the same sentiments in people otherwise just going about their day.

Of course, I didn't belong to the Raritan Yacht Club. I'd never been part of any yacht club. But looked at another way, I did belong. It was a club devoted to adventure and wind-filled sails, and I was myself on a sort of wind-blown adventure. So, I figured I would find a warm audience when I punched in that code.

What had brightened the eyes of those guys on the pier wasn't me but the mention of my journey, that I was headed somewhere with a purpose and needed a hand. They responded to that, as did Stu Conway immediately on the phone and the many others who had offered food and drink and all kinds of assistance along the way. Stu wanted to be a part of my adventure, however briefly. He, in his own way, wanted to belong.

———◆———

My captain arrived the next morning under gray skies wearing jeans, shades, a green windbreaker, and a bright blue knit hat that added three inches to his height. He came down the stairs and strode out to the end of the pier where Mike and I stood drinking coffee and said, "Let's do this." His sturdy little launch, *Peanut,* floated ready at the pier.

Mike and I had ordered extra-large coffees from the Dunkin' Donuts to counteract the night before. We'd taken rooms at the Raritan Hotel, previously known as the Palace, a vast, white concrete edifice of fake Greek columns and arches. "DO NOT stay here. Just don't" was a typical online review. After we checked in, a man sucking on a cigarette outside asked, "You here for one of the sex parties? This place is going to rock tonight." I kept my socks on and my door well locked but all night I could hear the bass-beat throb of fun a floor away. At dawn someone walked down the hall yelling, "Everybody wake the fuck up."

"Sleep well?" Stu asked.

"Memorably," I said.

Stu was a retired bond dealer turned cartoonist and artist. He had sailed around the world years before, which helped explain why he would jump to assist a stranger trying to get to the next place. He had been, in a thousand places, a stranger himself. He knew what it meant to belong and not quite belong in a lot of settings. Along to lend a hand was his buddy Brad Henry, another natural waterman who had grown up along the Harlem River in the Bronx. They were both in their midseventies.

Screwed to the pier railing was a small steel plaque honoring what really mattered around there: RYC REMEMBERS THE 58 BOATS LOST TO SUPERSTORM SANDY. It listed every boat, from *Alegria* to *The Zephyr*, with *Desperado, Island Dog, Rainbow Magic,* and fifty-three others in between. MAY THEY HAVE FAIR WINDS AND FOLLOWING SEAS.

Straight across the Arthur Kill, I could see the sandy beach of Ward Point. The wind was churning some chop, and small waves lopped on the far sand. All Stu had to do, I told him, was get me as snug as possible along the shoreline there and I would leap into the water, D-Day style, with my pack snug on my back. "I'm wearing shorts. I don't care if my shoes get soaked. It doesn't even matter if my pack gets dunked," I said. "You just zip across and I jump out."

"Not happening," Stu said, firm of jaw. "Too risky. I could get hung up in the sand or you could fall in wrong and drown." He said he'd drop me at a public pier a bit upriver. I deferred to the captain.

Stu had a little pug of a launch with two feet of draft and the letters "RYC" emblazoned in black on its bow. It had a brassy inboard motor that when he flipped the cover off it and hit the starter, just wouldn't turn over. He kept cranking it, and juicing it, but the belts just couldn't get it humming. Storm clouds were building to the south and some rain began to pelt us, and I thought, "Well, so much for Plan A."

But Stu was no quitter. He got out his tool kit and loosened a screw on the fuel pump. "Let's bleed it a little," he said to Brad as some purplish gas bubbled out onto the deck. When it still didn't start, Stu grabbed some pliers and loosened the bolts on the other side and bled that side a bit, like a medieval doctor engaged in ritual bloodletting. Stu was solidly of the "just bleed it a bit" generation who knew how an inboard engine worked and which way to turn a pair of pliers. I honor those people. The engine finally kicked over and warmed our hearts with a gurgling roar. Propeller boils emerged around the stern. Stu plopped down the cover, unlashed *Peanut* from the dock, and off we went.

Few things stir joy so easily as heading out of a morning with a watery wake yawning behind you. The wind was up and had streaked the sound with froth. Dark clouds moving in from the south trailed below them long braids of rain. Stu took me up the channel for a mile or so talking of how Hurricane Sandy that October of 2012 had "scoured this whole area of boats," including his own treasured *Fog Dog*, bought and kitted out so he and his wife could do the six-thousand-mile Intracoastal–Great Lakes– Mississippi River Great Loop the next year.

It wasn't to be. Stu had put *Fog Dog* to bed early that fall, way up Morgan Creek on jack stands nearly six feet above the median tide level. But Sandy roared in and tossed *Fog Dog* up among a slew of other keel boats in a tangle of mangled shippage. "Crushed her gunwales and stripped her railings all around," Stu said. A sad story told with the gusto and relish of a mishap now long in the past.

I stood looking aft from the stern of *Peanut* and couldn't imagine anywhere better. It was Day 24 and underfoot was the fourth body of water I'd crossed by boat, with the last of those crossings, of the Hudson, just two days away.

Only then did I learn that Stu and Brad had driven an hour to get there that morning. They waved off my astonishment. "What else were we going to do—twiddle our thumbs over a third cup of coffee?" Brad suggested they buzz me all the way up the Kill and across the harbor to Manhattan. No thanks, I said. "That storm could get a little nasty," Stu said, glancing back at the clouds behind us. Despite the threat of a squall, they were both glad to be out with the rain in their face and eager to extend the trip.

Stu came abreast of a dock at the Tottenville Marina, devoid of human form in all directions. As he brought *Peanut* around, Stu gave me directions for crossing the island—go this way, then that way, then under the freeway and along this park. I failed to take in any of it. Stu jumped onto the dock, and we shook hands. "Glad to be of service," he said. Mike stayed on board and saluted as they pulled away, the little Stars and Stripes at the stern flapping stiff in the breeze. I watched them take a wide loop and head back to Perth Amboy. Standing there on that bobbing pier, I was officially in the City of New York, despite it looking like an outcropping of Cape Cod.

All of America, I discovered that day, can be found in that weird place the Dutch called Staaten Eylandt. I had twelve miles to walk to get to the top end of it and even my phone's mapping service didn't know what to make of my intention to go by foot, as if it wanted to ask in reply: *Are you sure?*

Not far from the pier I stopped for a coffee and a toasted bagel served up by Eritreans. I passed a forested patch with a house in the woods and a FIREWOOD FOR SALE sign at the end of the dirt drive, as though this were a backroad in Vermont. I cut through junkyards stacked high with twisted metal and crushed cars and under viaducts painted bright with graffiti like the edges of Detroit. Two hours in I wound through neat subdivisions with looka-like houses, all with neat little yards out front and ornamental trees just beginning to flower. I walked so close to a pair of golfers that I could smell their cigar smoke. Their drives went awry when I stood to watch.

As I neared the Fresh Kills, once a heaping stew of garbage and the largest landfill in the world, a guy named Nick Rizzo came striding the other way to join in the walk. I didn't know Nick, but he'd just driven down from Poughkeepsie to accompany me for a mile or two. He had heard about the walk, knew I was in Staten Island that morning, and messaged me on Twitter asking where I was. I sent him my coordinates, and there he was walking the other way.

Nick was a slight, scruffy, high-strung guy who exuded immediate intelligence. He could quote from Chaucer's *Canterbury Tales* both in the Middle English and in translation. "*When the stripling sun has run his half-course in Aries, the Ram, and when small birds are making melodies . . . Then people long to go on pilgrimages.*" He launched into the details of Patrick Leigh Fermor's extraordinary account of a walk at the age of eighteen across Europe in the winter of 1933, just after Hitler had taken over—books I had read years earlier. He had George Orwell's looping signature tattooed on his left arm. "Not really because of his stand on totalitarianism or any of that," Nick said, "but because he was just such an awesome writer. I love his prose style."

When Chaucer and the word "stripling" came up, Nick, without missing a beat, defined the word as describing a young male not quite a man. "That was before we had the concept of a teenager. Fitzgerald basically invented the American teenager in the 1920s when he wrote that short story about Bernice bobbing her hair." This is what it was like walking and talking with Nick Rizzo, who had—as I said—materialized out of nowhere. Nick was good company.

We came to the bridge that cuts across an inlet of the Fresh Kills—named by the Dutch for its "fresh springs"—and off to the left we saw the high mounds of waste, more than half a century of waste, 150 million tons of it, turned to green space now. This is the landfill that makes people not in the know think that all of Staten Island is a place built upon trash. Once a virgin swath of marshes and tidal creeks, the Fresh Kills after World War II took in the vast majority of the city's offal and detritus, nearly all its old shoes and lemon rinds, until the tallest of its four mounds stood almost as high as the Brooklyn Bridge. The last trash barge was supposed to have arrived in March 2001, but six months later the Twin Towers fell, and the state reopened Fresh Kills to accept 1.2 million additional tons of those shattered remains. It is now both a retired trash heap and a solemn burial ground.

We are meant to see the Fresh Kills today as a strange symbol for humanity's flair for overcoming our worst failures, for turning our ugliness into something resembling beauty. We applaud our ingenuity while excusing our excesses. Grass covered the high mounds and small trees sprouted across them. An expanse that once crawled with tractors, rats, and scavenging seagulls is now a park. You can paddle and hike much of it now. A kayaker creased the inlet and paddled our way. An osprey fluttered high above, preparing to plummet for his prey.

Nick described as we went how he had tried his hand working as a local political organizer but found it a brutal way to make a living. "It's definitely Triple A, and the difference between Triple A and the big leagues is night and day." He was thinking about taking up real estate.

Before leaving to head back to his car, Nick expounded on why he thought the country was pretty much ungovernable now anyway. He said it was all the difference of big and small. Big countries—the United States, Brazil, China, Russia, India—were all suffering problems because of their size. "It's hard enough to get the two ends of this island to see things the same way, much less the Bronx and West Virginia," he said. "We are losing our ability to forge any unity at all from these United States."

Nick said he made the effort to come join me because the whole concept of a pilgrimage appealed so strongly to him, "what with Chaucer and all, and it being April." He wanted to be a part of one at least for half an hour or so. One day, he said, he'd embark on a far longer walk of his own volition.

When he turned back, I cut through a packed Costco parking lot and sat beneath a tree watching people stash box after box of stuff into the trunks of their cars or the backs of their SUVs. A man pushed his cart out, loaded with bottled water and twelve-packs of paper towels. Another man transferred slabs of steaks and chicken legs into the back of a red Highlander. A woman inserted cases of soft drinks and a new microwave into the trunk of her Accord.

In three days, I had seen all sides of the golden triangle: the massive distribution centers; the enormous landfills; and here the insatiable purchasing that connects the two. When I watched the shoppers streaming from Costco with their carts heaped high, I flashed to that huge Caterpillar compactor at the Edgeboro Landfill rumbling back and forth, attempting to smash and break apart all that we cast aside as we build the mountain ever higher.

———◆———

There were places as I went where the sidewalk ran out and you had to creep along the edge of woods among the plastic bags and the smashed beer cans and the little plastic liquor bottles. Carcass of a cat. Busted kite. Mylar birthday balloon wrapped around a tree. A sign as I cut through a park warned of dangerous deer ticks. If the cars don't get you, the ticks sure will.

I went north through the woods until I came to a large soccer field and sat on a bench there. The fuel that had propelled me on the walk was running low. It wasn't at all the surroundings but just a slow accretion of tiredness. Nothing hurt or ached in any chronic or meaningful way, but the duration of this stroll felt exactly right. I had two days left to go, and two days left in me.

A broken road, pocked with holes and littered with fallen limbs, opened to my left near the soccer field and bent into what looked like a cave of arching trees. NO TRESPASSING BY ORDER OF THE CITY OF NEW YORK said a sign nailed to a post. The storm I saw brewing from the stern of *Peanut* darkened the sky and sent the winter leaves skittering. I went down the road to see what was there.

Scattered among the trees and encased in vines like Mayan temples stood a series of high brick-and-stone buildings, a whole village of them, their roofs fallen in, the glass from their windows shattered and missing. A flock of crows lifted from inside one of them and wheeled overhead. The walls of these ruins glowed in places with the spray-painted insignia of lost tribes, words in block letters that were impossible to decipher.

I took an elevated ramp to enter one of the largest ruins and above its entrance loomed a large, white, ghoulish figure with a crooked grin, painted there by some devious artist. One of its eyes was a large "X," the other a "$." The air inside was fetid and damp. Patches of the ceiling had long ago fallen to the concrete floor. The stairway was succumbing to gravity, but I had no urge to take it anyway, either up or down. The wind whistled outside.

These overgrown woods, I discovered, had once been home to the Richmond County Poor Farm, which opened in 1829 to house the island's indigent, who had to work in exchange for housing and food. The site became known in the 1880s as the New York City Farm Colony, a utopian experiment in self-sufficiency less than ten miles from Lower Manhattan. From the fields now forested over, the residents once grew beets, turnips, spinach, potatoes, peas. I was standing now, I learned later, in the colony's dining hall, where nearly two thousand residents—most of them elderly—ate their meals through most of the previous century. The last of them left in 1975. You could still feel their ghostly presence. You expected a revenant to flit across the room or a bony hand to touch your shoulder.

I saw the sky crackle through the gaping windows and then open with rain, sheets of it as I ran from the building and tried to find a pathway out. A chain-link fence ringed the property to the north but I found a small section of it bent open and crawled through it into a subdivision of little houses. The rain splattered the streets and began to collect in the gutters as it streamed around the hood of my jacket and soaked my shoes.

I felt a jolt of freedom to be walking in the rain through so much strangeness past and present, with three miles to go to find my lodging for the night. Twice in two days I had stumbled on the overgrown ruins of forgotten experiments, utopian dreams gone to seed. You walk through decay and see with what speed the vines and roots and rain do their work. You see the fragility of even the most solid foundations. How quickly and easily it can crumble. The patchwork of experimentation and failure, of the bright new home and the abandoned lot, continued as I went. The rain stopped and the sky cleared as the neighborhoods grew rougher. Some blocks were dying and some others being reborn, a torn and mended fabric that stretches all the way to the Pacific. The morning had landed me on a bobbing pier and had brought me through haunted woods to the tattered outer edges of New York City.

CHAPTER 23

RAPTURE ON THE BAYONNE BRIDGE

You must scrounge to find a bed in Staten Island near the banks of the Kill Van Kull. Scrounge as I did, there was nothing within miles of where I wanted to sleep. Then I found a number for an inn, a place called the Victorian Bed & Breakfast on a hushed side street. When I called, a woman answered with a simple "Hello?" She said in an elegant Slavic whisper, "You will be most welcome to stay in my house. It will be just $110 if you pay cash."

I had experienced some curious lodgings along this trail to New York. The room with the high four-poster bed in Maryland, where FDR slept and where the hosts handed me a flagon of warm rosé and a glass of ice. The creaky-floored suite in an old inn just north of the Mason-Dixon Line named for a flinty Confederate, Stonewall Jackson. The plush mattress on the floor beside the fire in Henry Mercer's tile studio in Doylestown, Pennsylvania. The moldering sex palace the night before in Perth Amboy.

But none could compete with the wonders of the Victorian Bed & Breakfast. I straggled there exhausted, long after the rain had cleared. The miles were beginning to accrue and had settled in my legs and feet. The old factories and auto-body shops and taco outlets weren't suggestive of luxurious lodgings around the bend.

When I got to the tall yellow house, there was no sign outside. I double-checked to be sure I had the right place. I rang the bell, and no one answered. I rang again, and again. I sat on the stoop and rested.

"Oh, my Lord, I'm so sorry," said my host, a Polish émigré in her eighties named Danuta Gorlach, when I finally roused her by phone. She'd been in the basement doing laundry. She appeared at the door with sparkly blue eyes and a pixie haircut and invited me into a parlor heaped with antiques and leather armchairs, the coffee tables stacked high with Plutarch, Hemingway, Hammett. I had stepped into a scene from a Merchant Ivory film.

Danuta hadn't had a guest for weeks. She was so delighted at my arrival—and what she called "the romance" of my walk—that she insisted on doing my laundry. "I will wash all of it," she said. She led me upstairs to my room overlooking the street and gave me slippers and a plush bathrobe. She had made soup and salad. "You will have dinner," she said, as if I had no choice.

She had gone to the store to get a perfect suction stopper for the bath in case I wanted to take one, which I did. "There is bubble bath," she said. I filled the tub high and hot and lay there until it cooled, ecstatic for the whole of the day and how it had unfurled.

Danuta handed me my laundry still warm and folded and then served dinner at her huge round table beneath a crystal chandelier. She brought the soup, a hefty chickpea dotted with little tomatoes, then a heaping bowl of salad, and then she insisted on cooking a portobello mushroom stir fry with brown rice. It was the first home-cooked dinner put before me since my stay outside Valley Forge two weeks before. For dessert, she brought a box of dates, then cookies. Hyden quartets streamed in from the other room.

"Danuta," I said, "you are turning your B and B into a B, D, and B. Or a B, D, B, and L, if you include the dinner, breakfast, *and* laundry."

She blushed, then howled with laughter. "I make dinner only

because you are walking. You need to eat. I never make dinner for anyone else. Please finish your soup."

She brought in a bowl of soup for herself and buttered a slice of bread and started telling of her time as a refugee in Vienna in 1970 after she fled Poland, and how she made it to New York as a thirty-year-old architect with no English. She excelled "despite all I could say was 'What is your name' and 'How are you.'" She was evidently a very good drawer of architectural plans.

In describing one of her biggest triumphs, she put a napkin in front of her face and then lowered it, peekaboo style, and said as she blushed: "I did the drawings for Donald Trump's first hotel, the Grand Hyatt." It was like she had just confessed to a naughty affair. She was appreciative of Trump as president and what she saw as his unapologetic nationalism and his goading of the pampered elite.

"You know we are becoming a communist country," she said, assuming I shared that belief. Her ex-husband, also Polish, "could talk of nothing but America before we came here, but now, he hates it. He wants to go back." She threw up her hands when I told her I was a journalist. We got into an argument about the tearing down of Confederate monuments and the rationale for their existence in the first place.

"Are the Europeans now going to go through every town and village and tear down the princes and kings they don't like?"

"If they don't like them anymore, why not?" I said. "History is all about tearing down and building back. We remember, we forget, we reappraise, we celebrate and renounce." She cringed. As a Pole, she was sensitive to the pitfalls of historical erasure. I had no appetite for a fight.

Danuta had run her bed and breakfast for twenty years but was worried the neighborhood was heading in the wrong direction. To keep up appearances she'd been known to weed and mow various neighbors' yards. Just go into their yards and begin straightening up. "They look at me like I'm crazy."

The next morning, Danuta offered me more breakfast options than an IHOP. She had stuffed her fridge with blueberries and raspberries, and brought out pancakes, fried eggs, bacon, fruit salad, toast. She looked at me wistfully from across the table as she stirred sugar into her coffee. "I had one Danish wanderer like you who came back twice on his journeys and stayed with me. He was very handsome. He hasn't come back for years." She was sad my stay was so brief, and so was I.

I had told many people I met along the way that they alone were worth the walk. Danuta, my hilarious Polish launderette, ranks high on that list. She was blunt, honest, warm, trusting, a little outrageous.

"Never apologize for who you are," she advised over breakfast, her index finger raised like Cicero. She'd reddened after I mentioned that we should all be aware of our privilege. "If you have certain advantages, do me the favor of enjoying them. Just please do me that favor."

I agreed we should not diminish or undermine our own strengths. "But we should also be clear about the blessings of our good fortune," I said.

When I came downstairs lugging my backpack, Danuta stood on the landing jangling her car keys and insisted on driving me the mile from her house to the foot of the Bayonne Bridge. I had told her I was determined to head toward Manhattan via that route because it paralleled the path the earliest of travelers had taken. "Fine," she said, "but I want to get you past the bad stuff and straight to the good stuff."

I said no. She said yes. I said my intention was to walk, not get rides. She told me to get in the car. "It will make it all so much better," she said. I relented and squeezed into her cluttered Toyota.

I didn't feel great about giving in to that ride, but her last line to me made it all worthwhile. I was wearing shorts despite the cold, and when I hauled my backpack from the car and began to cross the street, the eighty-one-year-old Polish émigré rolled down her window and said, "You have really great legs." Those were her last words as I trod toward Manhattan.

———◆———

I waved goodbye to my host and turned toward the foot of the Bayonne Bridge, whose mighty steel arch—opened in 1931—soars across the Kill Van Kull to Bayonne, New Jersey. For weeks I had moved as though in a meditative trance, a space both expansive and entirely my own. I set my own course but remained supremely open to all suggestions as to detours or sidetracks. I marked a place I had to be by nightfall, but left the day open as to what path I would take or what I would see along the way. My days had been filled with the purpose of a set destination, but also the ability to just sit on a stump or a bench or beside a river to think or gawk if the spirit so moved me. I had enjoyed in every way the ultimate in personal freedom.

As I went, day after day, opening myself to the people and places I encountered, I became in turn more open to those people and places. More in tune, more in sync, as Ted had predicted in his driveway on that third morning of the walk. Absent the other-world distractions buried in our phones or laptops, I could feel my capacity for awe and wonder grow exponentially with the days. All I came to care about was what I saw around me, the people I met, the little shifts in culture or barn design, the texture of the land I crossed, the nuances of the forests or the farms. I tried to care about that with all the energies usually spent on caring about more distant and abstract things. It was, I suppose, an effort to grant pre-eminence to place, to make the present truly immediate—to have it stripped, as much as possible, of all unnecessary mediation. To have attention, as the good poet said, be the beginning of devotion.

Perhaps that helps explain why—when I stepped out onto the initial incline going up the huge sweep of the Bayonne Bridge—the sight of the Manhattan skyline hit me with a physical force.

I hadn't been looking for the city. I had my eyes at my feet. I was thinking of other things. Then I raised my head while walking the up ramp, the wind coming strong and bracing from the north, and the sudden sight of the city's jagged towers and the sparkle of the river above the Richmond rooftops washed over me like an ocean wave.

I cupped my head in my hands, so it might have looked like sobs but was instead a weird form of laughter. A bike rider who zipped past might have thought I was distraught and planning to jump. I just sat in the sunlight by a concrete barrier, buffeted by the wind, and looked at the city, overcome. The Quakers might have said that I quaked. The Shakers, that I shook. I heaved with a bodily joy.

My delight sprang in part from the satisfaction of nearing the end of a long pilgrimage. It may have been tinged, even, by some fleck of regret that it was nearly over. I had seen for the first time, laid out against the morning sky, an outline of the place I'd been walking toward for twenty-five days. A skyline altered utterly by human hands, with sheets of glass jutting to impossible heights from a sliver of metamorphic schist tucked between two rivers.

This weird rapture, though, went beyond mere gratification. I had seen this skyline before. A thousand times over the years I had caught sight of it from all directions as a cabdriver and a common traveler. But on this morning the sight of it physically astonished and stunned me. The days and all those steps had pried open a part of the human spirit that magnifies the potency of otherwise simple things and grants the commonplace a touch of the divine.

F. Scott Fitzgerald wrote in *The Great Gatsby* that New York as seen from the Queensboro Bridge "is always the city seen for the first time, in its first wild promise of all the mystery and the beauty in the world." That "first time" effect of seeing things with a renewed vividness and punch isn't simply a refreshening power the bridge gives. It's a power Fitzgerald himself had nurtured, and a power any of us can grant ourselves. It comes, I think, from a cleansing of the eyes but also a stripping away of the extraneous things that weigh us down.

"The eye is the lamp of the body," says Matthew's Gospel. "If your eye is clear, your whole body will be full of light."

My own cleansing hadn't begun the day I walked out my door. It began the morning a doctor first uttered the word "cancer" and the trees on the way home impressed me as trees never had before. I thought of my brother Kevin and how he had startled the nurses with his dream-tossed visions of love. I thought back to my conversation in the basement of that school with Neal Weaver, the Mennonite teacher, and how he had quoted that line from St. Paul that had lodged in my head. "Be not conformed to this world but be transformed by the renewing of your mind." I kept rolling that thought back and forth like a lozenge, rephrasing it to make clearer sense of it. You can go out for a long walk and step out of the world with its dutiful rounds. And the walk itself, through all those days and across all those miles, can cleanse the mind and make it more open to the wonders of the world.

When I looked from the bridge back across Staten Island with its white toy houses and little steeples, I could see the varied hues of the trees, nearly all now in their infant stage of leafing. The faintest green of the maples. The deeper tones of the early sycamore. The russet of the oaks coming out. You could see the brilliant puffs of the fruit trees still in flower. The cherries and plums. I had followed the flame of April's forsythia and some of it still flickered, a brilliant yellow amid encroaching green.

The day before, on an avenue in Aspen Knolls while traversing Staten Island, I stopped in shock beside my first full lilacs, as pungent as ever, and thought of Whitman and Lincoln and that more ghastly redolence of a very different April in 1865. "Here, coffin that slowly passes, I give you my sprig of lilac," Whitman wrote.

Over twenty-five days I had tracked the blossoming and flowering and leafing of one spring as I had never tracked or seen any other, and that spectacle was now reaching its crescendo. The view from the bridge put it all on display.

The list is long of things seen or heard on this walk that hit me with similar force as the sight of the New York skyline. Moments that also sparked that rapture that is a cousin to grief. It's a strange inventory: The view from a tavern window in Maryland of rain falling hard outside. The sudden appearance of a brief slanting snow while walking through farms in southern Pennsylvania. The wide sprawl of the Susquehanna on an Easter afternoon. The ripple of laundry hanging on the line. The many hues of the sky through a gap in the ceiling of a Quaker meetinghouse. How the Delaware heaved and boiled as it flowed. The sight of a deer elegantly crossing the creek at the far end of the viaduct as I paddled under the Jersey Turnpike. The moment when a family of foxes scattered before me as I walked up an abandoned railroad track toward South Amboy. When I walked out of my house at the end of March, I knew where I was headed but had no idea what would move me along the way. I had found a rhythm, a stillness, that can transfigure whole days and elongate time. A buried beauty that resides right there on the surface, for all to see.

◆

The walk from the bridge to where I spent the night in Jersey City was about eight miles. It could have been twice that length, or half as long. I walked all of it in something of a fervent daze. Mine was not a conversion on the road to Damascus but more an illumination on the road to Bayonne. As I came off the high bridge into Bergen Point, walking out of the wind into a cool stillness, I felt enveloped in a strange duality that held for days: that I was not of the place but was at the same time profoundly there. That my transience did not diminish my presence but in some odd way deepened it. That transience and depth coexist, as of course they do, in our greatest rivers and in ourselves.

A small café in Bergen offered warmth, a corner table, and use of the bathroom in back. The woman behind the counter handed me a latte and a pastry, both of which were small revelations as I sat at that table. She told me she had begun a forty-day fast a week earlier, her own form of pilgrimage. "The first few days weren't easy, but I feel great now, lit up," she said. People at the tables around me talked of the day, and I felt only partly of it. The ripples and heaves from the bridge continued.

Broadway carried me up through the neighborhoods of Bergen Point, Constable Hook, Curries Woods, Greenville. Carried me past diners, cafés, tire stores, banks, nail salons, taquerias, liquor stores, gyro shops, fitness centers, shoe stores. A good part of me was sated by what had happened on the bridge. I went, but without desire to interact or inquire or find out new things. I beheld but had no desire to hold. I felt as if I were floating.

At times you saw flashes of Manhattan to the right, glitters of it across the river, but this was a humble byway, without pretension. The Polish mortuary. The Italian wine shop. The Colombian take-out joint. The synagogue. The Egyptian grocery. Millions of new Americans had washed ashore here, put down roots or found their way and moved along. They were doing it still. This Broadway felt in every way the perfect entry to the island across the Hudson with its much grander Broadway, an island that had powered our earliest centuries and done so much to forge our national psyche.

At the corner of Thirty-First Street I took a high-top table inside a bar that looked to have dropped in from Tudor England. The bartender brought me a beer while a onetime Bayonne mayor—or so I heard—told stories in jacket and tie to whomever would listen. Poker hands beamed live from Las Vegas flashed on the screen in the corner. I watched a man barely flinch as he pulled a full house to beat another man who had gone all in on a flush.

This long walk would be over sometime the next afternoon, and I got to thinking while sipping that beer of all I had brought with me. Not the shirts, the two pairs of socks, the notebook or Japanese fly rod. Not even the Athenian coin with the owl stamped into the silver. I had found meaning along the way because I had brought some of my own to exchange.

I had set out with a wonder first stirred by a sickness. A jolt of fear had opened a seam of freedom, and I had slipped through. I went out to seek and give meaning, with the giving being a key part of that conversation. When you look at the landscape as a place imbued inch by inch with meaning, with stories to tell and mysteries you will never quite understand, it repays that attention with gratitude. It rewards the respect you give it, just as people do.

For more than a year I had studied the old maps and read the travelogues, the history of the early settlements, the injustices and travesties and triumphs, the decimation and then regrowth of its flora and fauna. All of that—a mere scratching of the surface and never enough—rewards the traveler in kind. You get from a conversation what you bring to it.

My elation on the bridge or elsewhere along the way may strike some as a little delirious, and it should. The Latins coined the word "delirium" to describe the state of mind of a person who has strayed from his furrow—from his rut, his narrow groove. The world forms us to follow a furrow, back and forth. We do it with a sense of duty. We do it dutifully, as though we owe it to ourselves and to others to be so diligent, because duty is itself a debt we must pay. But strange things can happen when you stray from that furrow, even for a month. When you walk from your door not to go to the store, not to go to work, to the dry cleaner, for a run around the park, to pick up dinner, but instead to open yourself to the world for many days on end. Those steps can refresh the spirit in unusual ways. They can create, in the best of ways, a delightful delirium. Those steps can renew the mind.

———————

I went beneath the twisting viaduct of a freeway, my last exit of the New Jersey Turnpike, and past a small colony of tents for men and women with nowhere else to sleep. One sat outside on a crate making coffee over a tiny stove. He nodded as I passed.

Broadway gave way to Garfield Avenue, which cut through a large cemetery that sloped toward the harbor. This was once a plank road with wooden planks lining the length of it to ease the passage of wagons, and before that a carriage path along which travelers passed on their way between Philadelphia and New York. The road led then to a ferry that crossed the Hudson at a place called Paulus Hook, words I had uttered a hundred times on the walk because you had to like the sound of them: "I am going to Paulus Hook, and from there to the city of New York." I had followed some semblance of that antique route for days.

From the cemetery I caught my first glimpse through the trees of the tall green lady with her rippled robe and golden torch. Once a vast oyster bed, later a quarantine station, then a wealthy estate and again a quarantine station, then an asylum for British loyalists during the War for Independence, and finally a fort, Liberty Island assumed its current incarnation on October 23, 1886, when workers finally riveted that lady's curving fingers into place around that torch. The statue was complete, but the fireworks had to wait seven days until a thick fog cleared. She stood small but mighty now in the distance under a blue sky flecked with clouds.

There was a blighted section of the road that lasted for half a mile where the dust swirled in the wind and the walker felt exposed and picked up his pace while glancing over his shoulder, as you would in a war zone when touched by a sense that you really shouldn't be there. I entered Communipaw, a humble burg of little houses and "the first spot where our ever-to-be-lamented Dutch progenitors planted their standard and cast the seeds of empire," as Washington Irving wrote. Only then did they go on to found what Irving called that "city of dreams and speculations," which we later named New York.

Grand Street bent, then bent again, and far down it, through the towers of Jersey City—the long-ago Paulus Hook—I could see the radiant glimmer of the Hudson River. I walked toward it, still buoyant from my crossing of that bridge, and could see across its rippled surface a slice of the tall towers of Manhattan. But I wouldn't go to the river's edge. I would leave the full view for tomorrow.

CHAPTER 24

ANGEL OF THE WATERS

The city was right there now, arrayed along the Hudson with the morning sun behind it splashing a wide glitter path across the water to where I stood in Jersey City. There rose the huge Roman liberty goddess as the ferry boats cut back and forth through the wind. The virus had struck Manhattan and shuttered normal life. It emptied subways and filled hospitals and killed tens of thousands. And yet the city looked brand-new, young, invincible, vibrant, still among the greatest of human creations. So many writers and newcomers had long marveled at the island's ability to prevail. Perhaps everyone who first sees it thinks the same.

Now I just had to get across the river, wind froth and all.

Five weeks earlier I'd gone in search of a ferryman and found Kevin Murray, a free-spirited local—half Irish, half Italian—whose maternal grandmother used to pack toothpaste into tubes at the Colgate factory that once dominated the Jersey waterfront. Kevin was a defense lawyer, but he also owned a kayak operation called Urban Paddle where that factory once stood.

Might he get me across to Manhattan in late April? I asked. His response was swift and short: "Absolutely."

It so happens that exactly 232 years earlier, on the same day in April, George Washington himself crossed these waters to Lower

Manhattan on his way to becoming president. He had come by carriage and on a white horse with polished hooves from his estate in Mount Vernon, barely fifteen miles from my house, on a journey that had taken just a week. Then he crossed aboard a forty-seven-foot barge, rowed by thirteen pilots dressed all in white, one for each new state. The statesman Elias Boudinot described that river passage in a letter to his wife. "Boat after Boat & Sloop after Sloop added to our Train gaily dressed in all their naval Ornaments made a most Splendid Appearance," he wrote. Washington himself was a bit overcome. The boats with bands aboard, the roar of cannons, the clamoring of the crowds, all of it, he scribbled later in his journal, "filled my mind with sensations as painful . . . as they are pleasing."

Kevin announced that our crossing would be much plainer. "I don't like the look of that chop," he said the minute I arrived at his dock. Kevin was in his midthirties, with tousled black hair and the solid arms of a rower. "I'm thinking we'll have to move to Plan B."

We'd been committed for days to kayaking across, but the weather made that impractical. Kevin asked around the boatyard and found a small Boston whaler to serve as our ferry. I had paddled the Delaware a week earlier with my pal and former *Journal* colleague Phil Kuntz, and he dropped in for the Hudson crossing, too.

We set off across the mouth of the river around noon with the Statue of Liberty standing tall at starboard and just two wispy clouds over the whole of Manhattan. You could not have scoured the sky to turn it a more brilliant blue or scrubbed the air to make it crisper. A ferry cut in front of us, and its wake sloshed a large wave over our bow that refreshed our shoes.

As we crossed, we all told our brief stories of that morning in September when hijacked 767s tore into the Trade Center towers, ending the lives of thousands. Kevin saw the horrors play out as a high school sophomore at St. Peter's Prep, blocks from the river right there in Jersey City. He saw the missing towers from the school courtyard, replaced by foul clouds of toxic dust. Armadas of pleasure craft and ferries cut back and forth across the river, rescuing the terrified and transporting them to Jersey. "It was a terrible morning," he said.

In his twenty-seventh-floor hotel room just to the south of the Trade Center, Phil was woken by the impact of the first jet. He was there to discuss a story with editors at the *Journal*'s headquarters, at the foot of those towers. Those editors fled and never returned to that office. Through his hotel window Phil saw the explosion of the second plane hitting and he was outside, blocks away, when the first tower fell, engulfing him in dust. A woman in the hotel lobby had run through the burning debris right after the first plane hit. "There was flesh all over the street," she told him.

"Watching that first tower collapse was the most unbelievable thing I have ever seen," Phil said as the boat cut through waves.

I watched the morning unfold on multiple screens within the paper's Washington bureau, where I was one of just two *Wall Street Journal* terrorism reporters. A horrified colleague called in to say he'd just seen a third plane slam into the Pentagon. Our daughters were evacuated from their grade school blocks from the Capitol. My story the next day led the front page, part of a package that later won a Pulitzer Prize.

The three of us told our thumbnail stories and then looked in silence at that absence in the sky as the whaler cut its path across the river.

Lower Manhattan was like the jaw of a shark for the whole of its modern history, with long, toothlike piers jutting out at the end of every east/west street. "Your insular city of the Manhattoes, belted round by wharves as Indian isles by coral reefs," Herman Melville wrote of it in *Moby-Dick*. But then Manhattan gave up its ships and longshoremen and their huge hawser ropes, all of them gone elsewhere by the late 1960s, and with them over the next twenty years went the piers that had given the city a salty brawn it has lacked ever since. I remembered from my cab-driving days what a bacchanalia those piers played host to every summer as they slowly collapsed into the river, but today the whole of the lower island along the Hudson has been scrubbed of protuberances and indentations. There is but one place to land a boat, a snug little harbor for rich yacht people called the North Cove Marina. I had called ahead for permission to come ashore there and the manager, Mike Revier, shot back a note: "North Cove would be happy to provide you a landing in Manhattan. At no charge, of course."

Our Boston whaler swooped into the marina and up to a bobbing pier. The uniform towers of what we once called the World Financial Center—across West Street from the vanished World Trade Center—glimmered overhead. The whole scene—the runners, the mothers pushing strollers, the people on benches in the shade reading books—had a Technicolor sheen. You expected a director to shout "Cut" and make it stop. I stepped from the boat and did a fist-clenching dance in the manner of Rocky, even though I was still not on solid ground. Kevin and Phil gave me fist bumps and hugs and then stepped back in the boat. The whaler sent behind it a bubbly wake as they curved back to Jersey, and I stepped ashore on the island of Manhattan.

———◆———

In the twenty years since September 11, I had spent astonishingly little time anywhere close to Ground Zero. I had seen the wreckage and the scar that remained after they took it all away. But I had never managed to wander down to see what we had done since then as a nation to memorialize and honor that day and all who died.

The gap where those two towers once stood remains to this day a hole in the sky. I entered the park with its hundreds of scattered swamp white oaks just starting to leaf and went to stand at the rim of the gaping North Tower. The square hole where the tower once soared had an austere, aching grandeur about it, like an Egyptian pyramid in reverse, a mausoleum for the dead that jutted into the earth instead of pointing to the sky. The monument to that horrible day is an anti-monument. It is the marker of a loss, an absence, of something that is gone but still hurts, like a phantom limb.

Arrayed before me were a dozen of the names of those who died there that day: Patrick Sullivan, John Patrick Salomone, Thomas Joseph Cahill. They and all the names as far as I could see had worked as traders at Cantor Fitzgerald. The brokerage lost two-thirds of its workforce on the upper floors of the tower, 658 people, trapped by the flames and debris after American Airlines Flight 11 plunged into the tower two floors beneath them. Every employee who showed up for work that day died.

Patrick Sullivan, thirty-two, was a Brooklyn native with two brothers, both just slightly older. I read about him later. His brother Greg, a cop, scrambled frantically around the base of the North Tower that morning, looking for Patrick. "I just kept looking up at the fires, and at the people jumping," Greg said later. "You never see those pictures anymore, the people jumping. I saw one group of four or five people coming down holding hands." No remains of his brother were ever found.

Dozens of visitors like me stood at the rim and read a few of those names. We looked down, paused, looked up, and moved on. Workmen were pounding big rivets into a structure across the street that will soon become a performing arts center with views of those two gaping holes. The sunlight flickered in the young oak leaves and the sound of their pounding echoed off the other buildings.

Between the two pits stood a Callery pear in full white blossom turning to leaf. A small rail fence wrapped around it for protection. The tree had a story. Workers had rescued the charred tree from the towers' wreckage and then coaxed it back to life in a

Bronx nursery until planting it there again, back where it came from. It's called the Survivor Tree. WITH CAREFUL TENDING, said a small sign, THE STUMPS OF CHARRED AND GNARLED BARK GAVE GROWTH TO LONGER AND SMOOTHER BRANCHES. Once so beloved in America's young suburbs, Callery pear trees are invasive and now reviled by arborists, but that one, with its scars and spring blossoms, was a singular tree.

At the South Tower pit, the rim along the entire east side listed the names of firefighters and ambulance drivers and police officers killed when the towers came down. Six of the firefighters listed in front of me had raced into Lower Manhattan that morning, sirens wailing, nine miles west from Woodside, Queens, all of them part of Rescue Company #4. They were inside the South Tower when it so shockingly fell, the first to fall, at 9:59 that morning, a sight those of us watching on television, those of us who are still alive, will never forget. A solid tower became dust as we watched. Of all six of those men, they found no remains, but only the heavy steel pry tool that one of them, Lieutenant Kevin Dowdell, brought with him as he ran upstairs. Kevin's name was etched there before me in stone.

In all, 415 emergency workers who came to rescue lives lost their own lives instead. Those workers were going up, willingly and eagerly going up, as others came down. If we search for a definition of goodness, that right there is goodness.

I had known all this, the terrible toll among those who came to help. I had covered it as a reporter in the days and weeks and months after. But still it astonished. The years, as they do, had nibbled away at the memory.

My walk had served up so many monuments and memorials, but this was the first that marked an event that had seared the nation's psyche in my own time. An event so many of us had experienced and witnessed in our different ways, that seemed so proximate and yet already—can it really be twenty years?—so long ago. I had seen memorials where we remember more the memorial than we do the event itself. Or where we needed the memorial to remember the thing at all. And I had seen hundreds of inscriptions in dozens of cemeteries testifying, in words often barely legible, to how the person buried there would never be forgotten. This memorial was still fresh, still young, because the events it marked remain so raw in our minds, even now. I tried to imagine what it would look like in a hundred years. Assuming it would still be there. That we hadn't, in some unimaginable way, moved on by then and filled it in.

As I left, I sorted through my own memories of the World Trade Center as a living place. How, one night in the 1980s, I took the elevator to the top of the North Tower with a college friend, a little under the influence, and we stood looking out from the Windows on the World doing Fitzgerald-style thought experiments. We imagined first how that illuminated ferry coming across the harbor was bringing ashore the love of our life after years apart. We let that emotion radiate and sink in. Then we watched a departing ferry, now carrying that same love away never to be seen again. We let that feeling wash over us. I remembered the photos my wife and I took of our daughters, then barely three feet high, playing on the grass at Liberty Island with the towers glimmering in the distance.

———◆———

On a brilliant spring day, after the long COVID winter, it was good to tally the constants, the things that hadn't changed. The mighty St. Paul's Chapel with its ancient tombstones stood behind its iron fence. It had survived the great fire in 1776 that devoured nearly the whole of Lower Manhattan. President Washington prayed there on April 30, 1789, the day of his inauguration, and after the World Trade Center towers fell, doctors turned his pew into a station for healing workers' feet—a tribute to those bootless soldiers at Valley Forge. A sycamore, now gone, had shielded the chapel from the falling wreckage of the towers. Mourners posted memorials to the dead for months on its fence.

There was the elegant City Hall with all its pear and cherry trees in full flower. Sidewalk salesmen were hustling knockoff designer bags along Canal Street, just as you hoped they would. SoHo's cafés spilled onto the streets and teemed with people having lunch. The fountain shot its spray high over Washington Square and the grassy spots were packed with picnickers and people drowsing, despite the brass band playing a New Orleans boogie romp. Whole phalanxes of bench sitters hunched over their phones, but otherwise the place exuded April vitality.

I curved left to make sure the same possessed souls were still pushing pawns around in that fabled corner of the square, and of course they were. Nearly all the concrete tables were occupied, some with solo players awaiting a rival. Many late nights as a cabdriver in New York I had stopped by here to unwind over games of chess under the dim lights before heading home. I could feel that old tug to play.

A young man with an unruly shock of hair smiled as he waved his open hand slowly over his board as a chef might over a table of iced seafood. "Care to play?" he said. It was impossible to say no. I set my pack to the side, sat down with the white pieces all arrayed before me, and pushed my king pawn out two squares.

The kid's name was Aaron Blau, son of an NYU biology professor, Greenwich Village native, and frequent player in the square. He was sixteen. That all added up to scary. I had played little serious chess for years.

Amateur players play chess sequentially, trying to run long threads of possible outcomes through their mind. If this, then that, then this, then that. Gifted players, I've always thought, surely play more spatially, seeing each move as an alteration in overlapping force fields.

I am leagues from a gifted player, but I was loose. I'd been walking for weeks. I decided to go with the less sequential, more spatial approach.

Aaron put his bishop pawn out to the fifth square in the classic Sicilian defense and then followed up a few moves later by bringing his queen out. I asked him what he called that defense and he said, "It's the Taimanov Variation of the Sicilian Defense," and I shuddered. He told me there was a young Russian grandmaster vying to be the best player in the world and was using this defense a lot lately.

"But he knows it a lot better than I do," Aaron said.

"I certainly hope he does," I said, bringing out my knight.

Most chess matches begin with twenty or so grinding moves in which both sides poke and jab at the other while building their defenses. This one got beyond that point quickly to where Aaron was arraying all his forces for some dastardly trap on my queen side, while I was planning to do the same on his. It was a wide-open gunslinger of a game that suggested my opponent preferred flair over careful execution. I went along for the ride. Both our kings had castled to our queen sides, and both of us were soon severely under attack. Aaron sprang a bishop sacrifice on me that didn't impress much, and then I sprang one on him I was sure was more lethal. I was already up a pawn and had the other of his bishops for one of my knights.

I then managed to unfurl a check on him that forced him to sacrifice his queen, and the ghost was up. A few moves later, Aaron knocked over his king. "It's yours," he said. "You got me."

The game had been so freewheeling that one of the savants at the next table had come over to watch, arms crossed, bobbing up and down on the balls of his feet. A nervous type. "You had checkmate in two right there, dude," he said, pointing out a blunder on my part. It still ranked as one of the wildest games I'd ever played, and perhaps the most satisfying.

"Play again?" Aaron said.

"Can't. I have an appointment uptown, and you'd definitely win if we played again," I said.

With that, I hoisted my pack over my shoulder, and strutted triumphantly through Stanford White's triumphal arch. There was a place I needed to be, forty-four blocks north up Fifth Avenue.

———◆———

The last time I had walked that way had been more than a year earlier, on the day the Broadway theaters went dark, and the city realized it was in for a world of hurt. Fifth Avenue was ghostly then, empty of traffic, a few disoriented tourists wandering about. One lone captain of industry walked by in a velvet-lapeled overcoat, a look of shock on his face. The COVID wave was about to hit the island of Manhattan. Now the sidewalks bustled again. The infection and death numbers had plunged; the masks were coming off. People had a snap in their step and a flash in their eyes. Spring had washed over the city of New York, and not just any spring but a redemptive one, a spring that felt like a mighty release.

As the bells chimed four times at Rockefeller Center I cut through a cluster of dawdlers and dashed beneath the mighty bronze Art Deco rendering of Atlas hoisting the heavens on his shoulders. There stood a beaming Martin Indyk, dear friend and fellow cancer traveler, just at the appointed time and place. When days earlier he proposed meeting so we could walk together into Central Park, I had leaped at the idea. "Meet me beneath Atlas, four P.M. sharp," he'd said. We hugged. We high-fived. We were both very glad to be there.

I'd known Martin as a reporter when he was President Clinton's top envoy to the Middle East and later the U.S. ambassador to Israel. Then Martin and I received the same diagnosis, basically a month apart, and our struggles and triumphs had followed in uncanny sync ever since. A cellular aberration had brought us back together.

For the past three years, Martin and I had joked and agonized over our mutual struggles. We'd been brought low by chemo, radiation, and surgery, then built back up. A year later, scans found that the beast had stirred back to life inside both of us. We had eerily similar recurrences, almost in the same place. Back we went into the throes of chemo and radiation. We'd tilted the odds in our favor, only to see them tilt wildly back the other way. Every few months we'd meet for lunch along some boulevard in New York or Washington to exchange gallows humor and to talk of our fears and our moments of illumination as we buttered our bread. We shot each other texts exulting over clean scans or just asking, "How you doing?"

"At least I know what will kill me now," Martin said with a smile at one such lunch.

Because of all that, Martin was like a brother to me now, a fellow combatant and celebrant.

As we walked up Fifth Avenue, I asked him how he was doing. We had both chased away all detectable cancer clusters but were careful with our language. "I am treated," Martin said. "That's pretty much all I say. That I am treated." All theoretical survivors must settle on their own formulations. That was Martin's.

"I like to say that I am in a clearing," I said. "Not in the clear, but just in a wide clearing with the forest too far away to see. I may be out of the woods, but I never know for how long."

Martin stopped at a swank sidewalk café in front of the Bergdorf Goodman bridal shop, and said, "Quick glass of champagne?" We secured a table and ordered drinks from a waiter in a black bow tie. I went for the tastiest of Negronis. Martin asked if the walk had changed me, and I threw up my arms. "I'm not quite sure what a religious experience looks like for an aging modern urbanite with a taste for Negronis," I told him. "But I'm pretty sure I had one."

Martin raised his glass with a smile. When I told him of my rapture at seeing the New York skyline the morning before and mentioned the Fitzgerald quote about the Queensboro Bridge, Martin recalled how Mark Twain was similarly overcome when he spied Damascus from the mountaintop on his wanderings in the Middle East in 1867.

"I've felt like I've been glowing for days," I told him.

I mentioned my brother Kevin, and how he'd had his own illuminations and epiphanies, despite the much darker prognosis. We talked about trees, and how cancer had opened our eyes to the power of trees, as it had to so much else. And that while we would never wish the curse on anyone, we would wish on everyone the way cancer had cleansed our eyes and deepened our gratitude and altered our perception of time.

As we left the café and approached the park past the Pulitzer Fountain and Grand Army Plaza, Martin took command of our route and led us down a looping path through a tunnel. When we came out the other end, Martin paused and did a sort of "Ta-da!" with his arms and we stepped into sunlight and an eruption of blossoming and leafing trees around the Pond with the elegant Plaza Hotel looming high above to our left.

The entire park was an utter riot of spring and humans responding to that spring. Kids on swings. Strollers out everywhere with their dogs. Lovers in rowboats on the lake by the arched bridge. Saxophone players playing soulful solos. We walked past a young Paul McCartney on a bench with a guitar who sang, quite well, about a blackbird singing in the dead of night. About sunken eyes that learn to see. And when the guitarist sang the last line of the chorus, Martin laughed and repeated it under his breath, as though it were addressed to us. "You were only waiting for this moment to be free."

We were heading up the grand promenade, Olmsted's Mall with the statues of all the writers, all of them dead and many now long forgotten, and when we went down the steps to the tiled arcade, a woman stood leaning against a high column in a bright teal wedding dress that spilled all around her. She looked to be made of cotton candy. A man beneath the vaulted ceiling sat on a stool and played a warbling tune with a long bow on a stand-up Chinese violin. Its notes reverberated around us as we walked.

We humans, when we care to, so naturally create spontaneous beauty for each other.

Ahead rose the Bethesda Fountain and the Angel of the Waters, that winged bronze beauty that floats above a wide fountain pool and holds in one hand a lily, and with her other hand blesses the healing powers of the water that spills from around her feet. Olmsted and Vaux, the park's brilliant architects, pushed ahead on this fountain even in the depths of the Civil War. The angel was put there beside the park's first lake to commemorate and celebrate perhaps the most vital moment in New York's history: the provisioning of fresh water to the city. Workers applied the mortar to her base and surrounding pool on the same day in December 1863 as other workers in Washington lowered that mighty feathered head onto the Statue of Freedom atop the Capitol. A statue to freedom and a statue to water, and in between a walk that had celebrated both.

Throughout his ordeals, and still now as a treated one, Martin would come often to stand at that magnificent pool and bow his head to the Angel of the Waters. He came on the worst of days when he feared he might not make it, and on a spring day like this when new life burst all around us. As we stood there, Martin repeated the prayer he recites every time he visits, a common prayer from the Talmud called the Shehecheyanu. He said it first in Hebrew, and then in his preferred version in English: "Thank you, God, for giving me life, for sustaining me, and for making it possible that we might arrive at this Time."

There wasn't much we could add. We had both arrived at this time. Everyone in the park and the whole of the city was immersed in that time, that blossoming day, the lifting of grief from the city. Gratitude, we both knew, is a deep physical state of thankfulness for one's very being amid the wonder of it all. On that afternoon, it was infectious.

Martin's wife, Gail, arrived with their dog on a leash and the three of us walked to the foot of Bow Bridge, that most elegant of spans, set there to arch over a narrow point in the Lake in 1862. We all hugged and said goodbye and I zigzagged among the families and couples capturing themselves in photos on the bridge and walked into the Ramble.

Here, on the north bank of the Lake, the park's designers had created their masterpiece, a large woodland of hills, ravines, and waterfalls interwoven with twisting paths designed to disorient the walker. A bit of the Adirondacks dropped into the heart of the city. Until then, the world's few parks were prim, aristocratic places, often private and neatly trimmed. Nature made orderly. Olmsted put a man-made slice of public wildness into the heart of a growing city. When the Ramble opened in the summer of 1859, right on the cusp of all the horror to come, tens of thousands of people poured into it daily to escape the city's clamor and stink. Children were "gamboling about in great numbers," gushed the *New York Herald* that July, "joyous and happy as the birds which were singing around them."

My ramble had brought me to Olmsted's "wild garden" just as I envisioned when I walked out my front door, and I took its circuitous paths, running and dawdling in turn. In this city known for its rigid grid of avenues and streets, these were the most contorted of trails I had walked the whole way from Washington. There was no straight path, but one path still led to another, and by whatever route you chose you found your way forward and out the other side, as all of us do wherever we travel.

I didn't tarry much. The sun was tilting low, and I knew that Shailagh was coming down the other way, from our little apartment up north, and I was eager to see her. I dodged the lovers on blankets—so many lovers—and the long leashes of people out running with their dogs, such an abundance that I wondered if a single soul remained indoors.

I walked beneath cherry trees that rimmed the Reservoir, their limbs groaning under the thickest of pink flowers, a degree of ostentation that surely made some Creator proud. I emerged bent over onto the open grass: no Penelope weaving, no ring of warring suitors or bedraggled dog that whimpered when he saw his long-gone master. Past the pink flowers I saw my wife coming the other way, loose-limbed, too, on that spring morning, beautiful, smiling, herself a destination.

CHAPTER 25

THE POST-AMBLE

I t had to happen. It was Saturday, the morning after my arrival. As Shailagh slipped behind the wheel, I tossed my pack in the back of the car and crumpled into the passenger seat like one of those gargoyles peering from a cathedral. To any stationary pair of eyes at the roadside, I was again the silhouette of a spirit, the tracings of a man speeding by. We were heading south fast, changing lanes as needed to avoid the lumbering car or truck. For nearly a month I had avoided this world, had slipped over it or under it or skirted alongside it, but I was now a part of it again, doing in reverse in four hours what had taken twenty-six days in the opposite direction. A single hour of driving devoured more than four days of walking. I was heading home.

I sat without talking much, forehead pressed against the glass, and tried to catch sight of the landmarks and to point them out as we went. The Edgeboro Landfill where I caught my first faint glimpse of Manhattan. The strip of woods along Cranbury Brook where I paddled beneath the roaring turnpike. But it was hard to reorient my compass amid the road signs and across twelve lanes of traffic. It was hard to identify the clues fast enough. Everything was a jumble when coming at it from that angle and at that speed. Everything shot past in a blur, and there was no looking back. When we sped over the big waterways, the Raritan, the Delaware, the

Susquehanna, my retinas widened to take in the expanse of light and the memory of having crossed them by foot or small boat, but soon the woods converged, and they were gone.

"Now don't go all gloomy on me," Shailagh said as we pulled into the garage of our house on Capitol Hill.

It is a bare fact that all journeys end. You walk in the back door and imagine the return home of the mighty Arab explorer Ibn Battuta or Marco Polo or Lewis and Clark, the millions of wanderers and seekers and pilgrims who crossed the front threshold, went somewhere far, and returned to put their hat back on its peg. There is the joy of the remembered comforts. The smell of the place, the sunlight falling just so in the front hallway. Your chosen coffee is where it should be. Your bed could not be more welcome. The dog, curled on the floor, is so glad to see you. There is the satisfaction of having completed something magnificent, of having stepped outside of time, however briefly.

But there is also a wistful current of regret that it is over. You rue the loss of simple purpose, the lack of miles to be covered when you wake.

"How was it?" a neighbor shouts from her garden across the street. "Did you have fun?"

I opened my closet door and looked suspiciously at the shirts on hangers, the trousers stacked one atop the other after a month when four or five things were all I needed. I thought often while walking how deeply attached the long-ago traveler once was to her horse, bedroll, saddlebags. A sturdy pair of boots being the ultimate belonging. I had developed a similar bond bordering on kinship for everything that went with me: jacket, hat, shirts, socks, buff to shield the neck. Each had served its purpose well.

For days I kept plucking what I needed from my pack, which remained there on a chair in our bedroom, still stuffed. I will confess to having fallen in love with that pack, and with my shoes, those faithful ones with the hole in the toe. I took the silver tetradrachm from my pocket and put it back in its little box on my dresser. We cup in our hands the tiny things, the durable things that will outlive us, our children, and their children's children.

And yet the glow remained. The glow when I turned to see the rain falling outside the tavern in Reisterstown, or when the snow came at me suddenly when cutting through fields in far southern Pennsylvania. The glow of the hymns of the afterlife the kids sang to me in Farmersville. The glow of the multihued opening to the sky in the Quaker meetinghouse. The glow that seized me on the bridge when I caught sight of Manhattan from a distance. I had sought to explain this glow, but perhaps its origins were far simpler than I thought. Perhaps it was simply the glow of gratitude, a lasting reflection of the thanks the places themselves had offered as I went. My cancer ordeal taught me, and the walk then reinforced, that gratitude is not a thought or an emotion but a physical state that sweeps over you and inhabits you, akin to the welcome warmth of a day or the surprise at being drenched by rain.

———◆———

Friends asked what I had learned, and I tried to explain. If you go out your front door with an eye for all that baffles, amazes, enchants, and keep at it day after day, giving in to the landscape and letting the rhythm of your steps guide you, it's astonishing what can ensue. Within days you understand why the holy books have whole sections built around the stories, the one-off encounters, of men and women out walking. Very particular things—a sermon by a man out getting his trash can; the hand-forged hinges on an old barn; how the maples flower, then leaf—acquire very particular meanings. They tell stories that weave together into a riddle that is long and flowing and difficult to explain, should you feel the compulsion to explain. You bring meaning with you when you go looking for meaning, and the more of it you bring, the more you get in return.

What you find is often fragmentary and slippery. Our histories—personal, tribal, national—are mosaics of broken pieces and shards of tile and stone. They contain within them, perhaps in equal measure, order and disorder, reason and randomness. Some sections are bright and shimmery, others grimy, unsettling, hard to decipher. Shame and love can mingle. The love you feel for your country can deepen along with the knowledge of the shameful things we've done. There is ugliness, but also beauty in the ugliness. What we remember of an era may reflect more than anything our desire to give it the best gloss.

You see these great disparities when out walking our national landscape. You see what has collapsed, gone to seed, been buried, torn down, plowed under. And you see what human hands have polished, preserved, put atop a pedestal high on a granite horse.

The microhistories you stroll through say a lot about the greater whole. The forgotten cemeteries for the Black dead, where the earth is gobbling up even the few stone markers, along with the memory of their achievements and struggles. The constant reminders—along the canals, beside rock walls that line the fields, under the bridges—of entire generations of lives given over to silent labor. Digging, hauling, blasting, leveling, assembling plank by plank, spike by spike. Labor, by our measure now, beyond all imagining.

You see how one Pennsylvania town rode out to greet the Confederate troops and helped supply them, while another just a few hours' walk away diminished its fortunes for a decade by torching the bridge to keep those same troops from crossing the Susquehanna. You see how we hold up and honor the unworthy while neglecting and forgetting the ones whose moral clarity made us squirm. You see how, for centuries now, a small but solid chunk of the country has built astonishingly orderly and prosperous lives while shunning the cars and gadgetry and waste that the rest of us hold so dear. You see the many experiments, most of them dead and forgotten, others ongoing. And you ask yourself, who is doing it right?

In the clamorous debate over American greatness, we too easily forget the primary source of our strength. It was not the principles the pilgrims brought with them. It wasn't the courage or the derring-do of the early waves of settlers. It wasn't the writings of Adam Smith or James Madison or the framings of the framers. It was the land itself, that glorious expanse of rivers, forests, mountains, and fields little spoiled by the people who already inhabited them. The walk allowed me to honor a tiny slice of that inheritance. It gave me the time to pause at those great rivers. We have done that land few favors, but we know, whatever we do, it will outlive us and persist.

I never expected to convince myself or anyone else of anything. You must go out to see for yourself. Early travelers who took the same paths concluded that young America was too uncouth, too fond of drink or guns or chewing tobacco, too riven by cruelty and a chaotic egalitarianism to survive. How can a unified thing, they asked, ever be woven from so many colors, cultures, languages, classes, religions? How could that Pluribus be made into an Unum? Others came away awed by the irrepressible energy of the young republic, confident it was bound for greatness. The same questions posed in 1830, or again in 1860 as the nation teetered, feel relevant once more.

I found a buoyancy and curiosity and zest among the bulk of the people I met, but thousands more shot past me on the roads and highways that I know nothing about. I am reluctant to extrapolate from my particulars to argue that we are a happy or troubled land, though I suspect we are both in unequal measure.

———◆———

A night or two after I got back, I took my Airedale, Benny, out for a walk. We went out through the same gate I always go through when walking. We went to the end of the block, crossed the street, and walked back along the other side.

On the corner, months before, a crew of men with huge saws had felled a tall magnolia. The family that lived in that house had moved away. Two boxes of unwanted belongings sat on the sidewalk. The family had an old black Lab with a graying nose that was friendly despite its bark. But I had never gotten their name and couldn't clearly recall how long they had lived there. Coming back down the block I saw a neighbor outside who I've known for decades. She lost her husband two years ago and lived alone now. I had no idea what she endured in her solitude. I passed a young sweetgum tree, freshly planted, and tried to recall the tree it had replaced.

I had gone out and walked a decent slice of the country through much of a spring and had come away greatly enriched, only to find that the single block I lived on contained depths and mysteries I would never plumb. People have lived lives in my own house that I know nothing about. I could devote a lifetime of study to my lone block and then perhaps, just maybe, do it partial justice. What the land had looked like before the plows and shovels came. The story of each house's origin. What if you sat in the front garden for days on end just watching the neighbors come and go? Or invited each to dinner, week after week?

My one solid conclusion was we should approach our own certitudes with caution. The more you look, the more you think and study, the more you open other doors and the more you understand how little you know. "If you should ask me about the ways of God," St. Augustine wrote, "I would tell you that the first is humility, the second is humility, and the third is humility. Not that there are no other precepts to give, but if humility does not precede all that we do, our efforts are fruitless."

Distill it for me, friends would suggest when they asked the simplest, most pointed questions. "Did you enjoy yourself? Did you have a good time?"

"I did enjoy myself," I would say. "Other than marrying Shailagh and having kids, that funny walk was one of the best things I've ever done."

———◆———

A few weeks after I returned, I drove back up through a portion of the route I'd walked. I wanted to check on a few things and drop in on a few people. I managed to find the Herders' house near the bridge that was too narrow for a pedestrian to cross. I knocked at the door. A wide-eyed John Herder appeared, wearing the same pair of patched khakis as on the morning I ran into him and his wife out walking beside Cattail Creek. He was astonished to see me and to hear that I had gone to the Hoovers' farm on Crooked Lane, more than a hundred miles to the northeast, and had passed along their regards. I told John the Hoovers were doing fine, even if Alta Hoover was due for hip surgery soon.

"David passes along his regards as well," I said.

"So glad to hear that," John said. He soaked up every detail and told me to drop by next time I passed through.

I went up to York and had dinner with Mayor Helfrich and the other friends there who had been so kind as to show me around. In a month I made more friends than I usually would in years. The next morning, I met with Paul Nevin and went out by boat on the Susquehanna with him and others, well above where the petroglyphs are. I drove as far as Lancaster County, where I met Neal Weaver and his wife and seven children in a neat farmhouse with a swing set shaded by a huge tree in the yard.

We sat in a simple kitchen as the children played in the other room. I told Neal how struck I'd been the afternoon I met him by how the kids had sung of their yearning for the afterlife as the sun poured through the window behind them.

He laughed. "They sing those songs, and they agree with the thoughts," he said. "But they very much enjoy being teenagers, too.

Even for myself, it's a challenge. I have so much to look forward to right here that the idea of longing for heaven isn't exactly in the forefront of my thoughts."

He was told to look beyond but quite liked the here and now. Not conforming to the world didn't mean you couldn't embrace its better parts.

We went outside to watch his children play in the yard. "Humanity at its core hasn't changed really since the Roman Empire, or whatever empire you choose," Neal said. "We're facing the same challenges they faced. And in response you try to be cheerful. You try to be a good neighbor. You try to be loving."

As I drove on the freeway from the Susquehanna over to meet with Neal Weaver, the map told me that the road I walked that early April through that stretch of Lancaster County was just over there, past that cluster of gas stations and motels, right on the other side of that plowed ridge, beyond that subdivision, that billboard, somewhere through that cluster of trees. It was all right over there. The butcher shop, the softball diamonds, the risers where the teenagers sang, the farmhouses with their clotheslines, the huge leather book, the arched trusses inside the covered bridge, the crooked lane, the river that ran like dark ale, the abandoned cloister. They were all strung along a road over that way, on the right.

And yet, it felt fantastical. I wasn't entirely sure the road I walked was even there anymore. And even if it were there as the map said, and even if I went to walk it again on another day, another season, maybe in a different pair of shoes, it wouldn't be the same road. I had found a proper seam at the start of that one spring and had slipped into it. The road I walked was there on that one day. Other roads and other seams await. But that road is no longer there.

ACKNOWLEDGMENTS

The idea to walk out my front door and head to New York began as a jest, became a puzzle, then a quandary, and finally a prolonged stretch of obsessive study and map-gazing well before the actual stroll. Only then did it become a book project. Along the way arose scads of people who offered encouragement, inspiration, advice, contacts, priceless mentions of rare and exotic things, and, yes, water to quench a wanderer's thirst.

This book is in many ways an extended thanks to them. We are all solo agents—born alone, die alone, and so on—but the richness of the passage in between depends wholly on the people met along the way. I owe so many of them singular thanks.

My wife, Shailagh, was a steadfast supporter and cheerleader along with our daughters, Lillian and Frances. All three, in spirit, accompanied me the whole way. Many friends never once rolled their eyes but instead egged me on, among them John Le Coq, Gardiner Harris, Joel McCleary, John Miller, Peter Fritsch, Jack Dougherty, Jon Ward, Andrew Nelson, George Durazzo, Linda Douglass, and Michael Siegel.

As a virus rattled the world and dashed my walk plans in early 2020, Ruth Noble Groom and Robin Johnson gave Shailagh and me refuge on their farm along the Eastern Shore of Maryland. Their company, and the seasonal splendor of that place, opened my eyes to myriad wonders and made the walk, after a year's delay, so much more vibrant.

As I built out the walk itself and sought wise ones to meet along the way, I began to tug on an essential part of the fabric of the universe, by which I mean the thread that connects friends with friends of friends.

In this realm I must thank the great York, Pennsylvania, contingent: Jamie Kinsley, Michael Helfrich, Jim McClure, and Samantha Dorm, who helped me dive deep into their town. Heading east from there came a long line of luminaries, among them Paul Nevin, Leroy Hopkins, Tom Baldrige, Robin Sarratt, and Tom Ryan, who all opened magical doors. In Lancaster County I can never repay the spontaneous generosity and gratitude shown by Neal Weaver and those stellar kids at the Farmersville Mennonite School, who sang for me. I owe much to Amos Hoover for his time and resources, and to the Fry family for letting me into their house. Ed Baldrige, brother of Tom, offered much wise counsel and fishing advice. Charlie and Mary Walsh on the outskirts of Philly gave me my first home-cooked meal and well-timed laundry services. Their web of friends and contacts—among them Brian McGuire, the inestimable Signe Wilkinson, and the wise George Schaeffer—brought multiple wonders in the days ahead. In Doylestown, Katia McGuirk went leagues out of her way to house us in Henry Mercer's incomparable tile studio. Outside Princeton, New Jersey, Susan Hockaday and Mait Jones provided the perfect respite of food, sleep, and meaty conversation.

Strangers rose to the occasion to provide invaluable moments. Travis Manger emerged along a path to tell the true story of Washington's Crossing. The Hunterdon Hiking Club brought cookies wrapped in origami. In Cranbury, New Jersey, a big salute to all the folks at the town Historical Society but above all to Peggy Brennan and her son, Tim, for the brilliant loan of a kayak. My guides through the various rings of the Edgeboro

Landfill, Robert Leslie and Brian Murray, were like two Virgils in one, humorous and wise. Heather Fenyk showed me wonders along the Raritan River, while Stu Conway hauled me across to Staten Island. The young Aaron Blau introduced me to the Taimanov Variation of the Sicilian Defense on a bright Friday afternoon in Washington Square Park.

As I went, every morning before I set out, I wrote an account of the previous day and sent it to several hundred readers by email—"friends, families, and curious ones," I called them. Those daily dispatches were in turn passed to a larger and larger audience and became the raw material for this book. I owe abundant thanks to all those who replied with such enthusiasm to those daily missives and tossed me other nuggets and ideas. You were, in every sense, my first readers.

A few close friends—Dante Chinni, Aaron Zitner, John Miller, Paul "Woody" Woodhull, Michael Ryan, and Martin Indyk—came to share a few miles with me along the way. Their accompaniment made those miles all the richer. Phil Kuntz and Mike Allen went still further and brought boats to help me cross rivers, for which I thank them heartily, as I do my last river pilot, Kevin Murray, who swept me across the Hudson.

As with the walk, singular forces conspired to make this book possible. Bridget Matzie appeared from nowhere as I strolled toward Valley Forge; in an instant she became my agent and an unwavering source of support. I knew we were in league from our first chat. Alexander Littlefield, then of Houghton Mifflin and later of HarperCollins but now of Little, Brown, grasped the magic of the whole project, leaped to back it, and became the ideal editor, sharp-eyed and committed. Without his faith this book would not exist. Alex then turned over his stewardship as editor to Jessica Vestuto, who brought a valued and fresh set of eyes. My wise doctor, Ileana Esparraguera, made me stronger and helped me ward off the evils of cancer and deer ticks. "Just keep walking," she said, and I did.

I owe a deep debt of gratitude to the artist George Hamilton, who I met on a lark and who then jumped at my suggestion that he illustrate each chapter. He did so with charm, patience, and good humor. Our mutual pal Jeff McGuiness offered every imaginable service, including his flair for photography. Both were invaluable muses.

I couldn't have gotten by without a contingent of astute first readers, including Frederick Kempe, Jeff McGuiness, Helene Cooper, Bryan Gruley, Alex Angell, Michael Pollak, Peggy Dowd, Jon Ward, Peter Fritsch, and my wife, Shailagh. Their edits and gentle nudges made the early drafts so much stronger. Andrew Sanger saved me some embarrassment with his fine fact check.

A fanfare of thanks to my mother, Gretchen King, who has been there all along, whispering sweet *be-carefuls* in my ear for many a decade. Her high standards have boosted my own.

And finally, I must thank my older brother, Kevin, who taught so much to so many of us, even when we didn't quite know it. He was a great fan of this saunter and watched it with a smile from afar. Kevin is gone now, but I see his knowing grin all the same.

A NOTE ON READING, AND WALKING

The literature of walking is, in a sense, as old as literature itself but not as old as walking. Many walkers wrote, and many were written about. Nearly all the prophets in every faith were inveterate walkers. Many performed miracles or had illuminations while out walking. There is no need to list those books.

As fine a start to any walker's reading list would be Rebecca Solnit's fine history of walking and the literature of walking, *Wanderlust,* which delves deep into the Western history of wandering and its influence on art and the human mind. There are many great works written by walkers. Basho's *Narrow Road to the Interior* still inspires, as does Thoreau's essay "Walking," of course, which remains as lively a romp as ever.

More recently, there is abundant enchantment in Patrick Leigh Fermor's trilogy on his 1933 walk from Holland to Constantinople, which begins with the incomparable *A Time of Gifts.* Though hers wasn't a walking book, Rebecca West's *Black Lamb and Grey Falcon* remains a model of the closely observed travelogue. Bruce Chatwin's *In Patagonia* and W. G. Sebald's *Rings of Saturn* showed how other paths could be taken with enduring flair.

Many works help set the ground for my walk and deepened my understanding of landscape and the human imprint as I went. My hodgepodge of a list would include Robert Macfarlane's *The Old*

Ways, Ellen Churchill Semple's *American History and Its Geographic Conditions,* William Cronon's *Changes in the Land,* David Hackett Fischer's *Albion's Seed,* and Douglas Waitley's *Roads of Destiny.*

More than anything, though, I spent weeks roaming through the online archives of the Library of Congress and amassed a vast archive of old maps and largely forgotten early American travelogues. I filled my laptop with PDFs of long out-of-print editions of the notes and scribblings of those who had traveled the early United States to make sense of the place or to entertain readers far away. Works like Dr. Hamilton's *Itinerarium* from 1744 or Anne Newport Royall's *Sketches of History, Life, and Manners in the United States* from 1826 or Isabella Bird's *The Englishwoman in America* from 1856.

Some of these writers came to make a point—often to dissuade their countrymen from falling for America's allure—but most arrived with the earnest desire simply to examine the place in all its baffling detail. When I pored over those books, I was struck by their almost innocent open-mindedness. I thought, "What if a modern naif were to wander out from his door and look at an overrun patch of our country in much the same way? What if you could turn the overly familiar into the unfamiliar, and look at it as if for the first time?" Those books helped open a passage through which I walked.

ILLUSTRATIONS